Lesley – with happy
of times past – and my
very best wishes –
+ love, Janet
Sept. 9. 2002

Rhythm and Timing of Movement
in Performance

of related interest

The Social Symbolism of Grief and Mourning
Roger Grainger
ISBN 185302 480 5

Bulgarian Folk Customs
Mercia MacDermott
ISBN 185302 485 6 hb
ISBN 185302 486 4 pb

Rhythm and Timing
of Movement in Performance
Drama, Dance and Ceremony

Janet Goodridge

Jessica Kingsley Publishers
London and Philadelphia

First published in the United Kingdom in 1999 by
Jessica Kingsley Publishers Ltd
116 Pentonville Road
London N1 9JB, England
and
325 Chestnut Street
Philadelphia, PA 19106, USA.

www.jkp.com

Copyright © 1999 Janet Goodridge

Library of Congress Cataloging in Publication Data
A CIP catalog record for this book is available from the Library of Congress

British Library Cataloguing in Publication Data
Goodridge, Janet
Rhythm and timing of movement in performance : drama, dance and ceremony
1.Movement, Aesthetics of 2.Rhythm 3.Tempo (Music)
4.Theater 5.Dance
I.Title
792.8

ISBN 1-85302-548-8

Printed and Bound in Great Britain by
Athenaeum Press, Gateshead, Tyne and Wear

Contents

List of Figures

Acknowledgements

Thanks are due to the following people: Father David Steindl-Rast for permission to reprint lines from a poem (Chapter 3); Ann Hutchinson Guest (Director) and Jane Dulieu (Associate Director) The Language of Dance Centre, London – for access to archives and permission to include notation from the collection; staff of Museum of Mankind Library, London – for access to material (Chapter 4); David Vaughan (Curator, Cunningham Archives) – for access to archives; Charles Woodford – for access to Doris Humphrey material; staff of New York Public Library Dance Collections – for access to material (Chapter 5); the late Rudolf Laban and Lisa Ullmann (former Director, Laban Centre) – for learning opportunities as student and later as Senior Lecturer at the Laban Centre, and for access to Laban archives and permission to include material (Chapter 6); Julia Franks (therapist and former Rave events promoter) – for an interview and comments on a draft of the rave dance section; Linda Shanson – for comments on an early draft of Kathak dance observations; Edie and the late Victor Turner – for discussion and hospitality during a research study visit (Chapter 8); Gerda Geddes – for her teaching, discussion and comments on a draft of the chapter; staff and class members at Henderson Court and Kingsgate Community Centre, London – for their co-operation and class participation; Chungliang Al Huang (President/Founder Living Tao Foundation) – for his teaching, permission to include two examples of his calligraphy from the Living Tao Foundation calligraphy set, quotations from Huang (1982, 1987) and for reading a draft of the chapter; Shirley Freriks for comments on a draft of the chapter, William Bascom, for discussion of environmental matters, and all other Tai Ji friends (Chapter 9); Joann Kealiinohomuku (Director, Cross Cultural Dance Resources (CCDR), Flagstaff) – for access to CCDR archives, for her introduction to the Yaqui Easter and for research journeys, and for comments on a draft of the chapter; Lisa Otey and Kathleen Williamson – for hospitality during study visits; Alison Grady – for information about the Roman Catholic church; staff of the University of Arizona Museum Library Collections, Tucson – for access to archives (Chapter 10); Allison Jablonko – for her willingness to allow access to film and research material, and for hospitality during a research visit and for comments on a draft of the chapter; Michael O'Hanlon – for discussion and comments during research and on a draft of the chapter (Chapter 11); David Horn (Curator, Guards'

Museum) – for interviews, access to archives, comments on a draft of the chapter and for permission to use photographs and other material (Chapter 12); Martha Davis – for two interviews and study material (Conclusion).

As work on writing this book proceeded, several other people read chapters and made suggestions. My thanks to David Blewitt, Mary Firth, Rosemary Howard, Ruth Serner, Phyllis Taylor and in the USA to Pat Brooks and Nancy Zendora. I am very grateful to Jenny Pearson and to James Roose-Evans for encouragement and for comments on final drafts of the text. Special thanks to Wendy Robertson and staff at Type-it-Right.

Permission to use photographs and other illustrative copyright material was received from Studio 3 Arts, photograph p.54; The Royal Academy of Dancing, notation p.89; Millicent Hodson, illustration p.94; Dana Reitz, drawing p.91; Berg Publishers, chart p.75; Siobhan Davies Dance Company, photograph p.149; Judith Greenbaum, drawings p.35, 36, 178; Roy Rappaport, photographs p.241, 246, 248; Kumari Liyanage (Sri Lanka High Commission, London) Sinhalese script p.175; Victoria and Albert Museum, prints p.31, 52, 59, 84, 165, 204. Thanks are also due to Kiki Gale (Director) East London Dance (ELD) for permission to use photographs from the ELD collection.

In addition, the author has received permission to include quotations in the text as follows: excerpt from 'The March Past' from *Collected Poems* by Philip Larkin. Copyright © 1988, 1989 by the Estate of Philip Larkin. Reprinted by permission of Farrar, Straus and Giroux Inc. and of Faber and Faber Ltd; extract from *Slowness* by Milan Kundera, translation copyright Linda Asher, HarperCollins Publishers Inc.; quotation from *On Acting* by Laurence Olivier, Weidenfeld and Nicolson, The Orion Publishing Group; lines from *Yaqui Deer Songs/Maso Bwikam: A Native American Poetry* by Larry Evers and Felipe S. Molin. Copyright © 1987 by The Arizona Board of Regents. Reprinted by permission of the University of Arizona Press; extract from the book *The Seven Spiritual Laws of Success.* Copyright © 1994 Deepak Chopra. Reprinted by permission of Amber-Allen Publishing, Inc. P.O. Box 6657, San Rafael, CA 944903. All rights reserved; quotation from Words and Music by Ira Gershwin/George Gershwin. Copyright © 1926 Warner Music Corp. (renewed). All rights reserved. Reproduced by permission of IMP Ltd.; lines from 'The Second Coming' by W.B. Yeats: reprinted with the permission of A.P. Watt Ltd. on behalf of Michael Yeats and of Scribner, a Division of Simon & Schuster, from *The Collected Works of W.B. Yeats,* Volume 1: The Poems, Revised and edited by Richard J. Finneran. Copyright © 1924 by Macmillan Publishing Company, renewed 1952 by Bertha Georgie Yeats; illustrative diagram 'Takada drumming' by Lazekpo and Pantaleoni, African Music (1972) 4/4. Reproduced by permission of Andrew Tracey, Editor; Diagram of Santa Clara Pueblo from Music and Dance of the Tewa Pueblos by

Getrtude Kurath. Copyright © 1970. Reproduced by permission of the Museum of New Mexico Press.

The material in some chapters was originally explored in 'Rhythm and timing in human movement with reference to performance events: drama, dance and ceremony' (1988) Ph.D. dissertation, Department of Anthropology, University College, London. I record a debt of gratitude to the late John Blacking whose comments and enthusiasm as chief examiner and subsequently were most supportive, and to other inspirational teachers and friends, too numerous to mention individually, to whom I owe much.

Introduction

Rhythm will, I believe, soon be proved to be the ultimate building block in not only personality but also communication and health ... the rhythm of a people may yet prove to be the most binding of all forces that hold human beings together. (Hall 1983, pp.170, 224)

An essential dimension of our work lies in the rhythms of our interactions. (Knox 1992, p.2)

Everyone has rhythm in him until it is blocked. (Brook 1993, p.18)

I think theatre has a lot to do with putting the audience in contact with the gods, whatever that means. That's where theatre comes from. (Lepage in Delgado and Heritage (eds) 1996, p.143)

Theatre, drama, dance, ceremony, ritual – although distinct, these are related performance genres which involve related modes of action. I have found that studying them as such, aided by an anthropological approach, enriches the perception of each. This is my basis for sharing some ideas about the use and observation of time and rhythm in human movement in performance events.

Ideas about time elements have captivated and intrigued me during thirty years of on-going study in the arts, education and anthropology, and in work as a movement practitioner. The application of these ideas in the practical situation of theatre-rehearsal, studio class or anthropological field-work has not only been enlivening, but frequently also a rescue resource. For instance, I have applied them as a teacher in dance class planning, or when employed as movement director in developing a sequence or scene. When faced with challenges such as these, or as an anthropologist observing and trying to analyse the structure of a ceremony, I have drawn from an understanding of time elements in movement. This is just one strategy found to unlock the seeming mystery of 'what makes it work'; which is not to deny the existence and usefulness of others, developed from considering different approaches to movement, which can also enrich practitioners' work.

A performance event, be it a performed work of drama, a dance, a ceremony or ritual, is a totality in which participants use a combination of energy, space and dynamics with time elements, in particular environments. These elements do not exist in isolation or as separate entities. A performer's use of space with all aspects of movement creates the impression, and establishes or changes the mood of audience or congregation. However, when trying to improve work practice it is possible to observe and concentrate on elements separately, to good and useful effect. I have found too that appreciation of a performance as a whole can be heightened by focusing on the time elements. Their significance in a particular context may be considered, rather than seen simply as decorative features in a performance. I hope this book will stimulate an interest in all these matters.

The viewpoint here adopted is primarily that of a spectator rather than a performer. But as examples demonstrate, it has been enhanced by my own and others' experience of teaching, performing, choreographing, directing and observing performance. The examples are introduced to illustrate the use of rhythm and timing in different contexts, and from different viewpoints, in order to bring life to ideas and theories.

Imagination is required when reading about movement. There are some photographs and a limited miscellany of other visual clues, but these can only provide hints along the way – even the exciting immediacy of a photograph can only represent a moment within an on-going flow of events.

> Think, when we talk of horses, that you see them
> Printing their proud hoofs i' the receiving earth;
> For 'tis your thoughts that now must deck our kings,
> Carry them here and there; jumping o'er times,
> Turning the accomplishment of many years
> Into an hour-glass. (Shakespeare, *King Henry V*)

Why a book on time and rhythm in performance events? I have found that, despite the richness of the subject and the importance frequently ascribed to the phenomena of rhythm and timing in the arts, the topic as a whole has been neglected. Critics make tantalising references in relation to theatre performance, tantalising because the subject has not been thoroughly pursued. Take for example this comment from critic Veronica Harwell:

> Noh is the hardest of Japanese performance forms to crack – Japanese friends mostly find them slow to the point of hypnosis. That's not unapt, because the unreal time and permanent slight tension induce a meditative state. There are echoes of the trances of shamanism here behind the cool Buddhism. The slightest denouement – for famous example, a spiderwoman ejecting a sudden web – jolts. (*The Guardian*, 13 July 1994)

Or a remark on comedy: 'The two men agreed that timing was all important in a performance' (Victor Lewis-Smith, reviewing Ken Dodd's interview with Jeremy Isaacs, *Evening Standard*, 14 March 1995). In contexts as diverse as the rock and rave youth dance of popular culture, or the various forms of meditation and Chinese-derived movement practice, the incidence and effect of rhythm and the importance of timing are not contested. There have been some serious studies in various academic disciplines such as by the eminent anthropologist Edmund Hall (1983) and see Davis (1982), but the challenge of addressing and clarifying the subject has still not been fully taken up in performance studies. In fact, not since the American dance writer John Martin (1939) observed when commenting on the 'vexed subject' of rhythm: 'Indeed as soon as rhythm is mentioned, we are likely to find ourselves enveloped in as dense a fog of mysticism and vagueness as that which beclouds the subject of form itself'. In this book I seek to begin to address this lack, to clear the fog and to provide a compilation of ideas on the subject taken from a number of sources. I bring together existing scattered information, refer to pioneering work on various aspects of the subject and include some original unpublished research material.

As a broad generalisation, I have found in teaching movement that there are usually a few class participants whose sense of rhythm (as it is frequently described) may appear dormant, but that the majority do respond to and enjoy emphasis on the development of time elements in movement work. It appeals equally to young and old alike. Furthermore, although I am not a therapist, I am convinced that there is considerable healing potential in the sensitive, informed use of movement rhythm. Indeed, the work of movement therapists attests to this. For example, Siegel and Blau (1978) write about respiratory patterns in relation to movement rhythm – 'breathing together'; Fraenkel (1983) and Schmais (1985) have looked at synchrony among other aspects of rhythm as curative factors in movement therapy. When they discuss communication and empathy in therapy, Cox and Theilgaard ascribe importance to 'the domain of rhythm' and state: 'We have now reached the border of another landscape ... it has something to do with rhythm and beat, which make their presence felt in both theatre and therapy' (1994, p.136). An experienced practitioner, Cynthia Knox, writing about movement maintains 'awareness of our own rhythms, our movement style, our repertoire and range is crucial'. She suggests further that one of the reasons some therapists are more successful than others may well be that 'they have a wider range of rhythmic modulation ... they are aware of timing, attuned to the need for constraint and relaxation' (1992, p.172).

There are many instances where the use of particular time elements in movement benefits those suffering from forms of physical or mental impairment. From time immemorial, mothers have known that a rocking rhythm soothes babies or disturbed children, and I well remember Veronica Sherborne's use of this in her movement work with people of all ages who had learning difficulties (see References (films) 1982). More recently, in the field of autism, Donna Williams, who has written autobiographically on the subject, has found that she

Davening

uses rhythmically based movement, such as a repetitive rocking motion, in her attempts to get the left and right hemispheres of the brain to function in an integrated way, and to induce calm in herself when feeling stressed. Williams suggests that others can help autistic people by using the time element of pace more sensitively, by moving, speaking and using the contact of touch, more slowly (Williams 1996, pp.124–125, 205).

The most memorable learning can frequently be found in recognising one's mistakes. As an inexperienced young teacher I once inadvertently misused a repetitive movement pattern (albeit reinforced by a drum) which after some considerable duration caused one student to sink to the ground feeling disturbed. This was an experience I have never forgotten and one which certainly alerted me to the power and potential effect of rhythm. At that time I was ignorant of evidence about the suggested influence of rhythm, such as in trance states, in Tsongan girls' initiation rites for instance with 'fast rhythmic drumming at basic brain wave frequencies [and] energetic dancing which causes a flow of adrenalin and a drop in blood sugar content' – Southern Mozambique, Africa (Johnston 1974, pp.60–61).

Rhythm and timing of human movement, from the conception of the fetus to the final stillness of death, are universal in human physical experience. This is often instinctive, unconscious, as for example in the timing of the pulse, breath, peristalsis or the functional action of limbs. These processes are taken for granted almost, unless we suffer impairment or injury. Whether instinctive or planned and consciously used, there is much to investigate about time elements and the significance of their use in different societies, cultures and contexts.

Speech, sound and music are frequently used to generate, determine or accompany rhythm in movement, especially in dance, as in the drum use above. Many of the principles, formulations and ideas about rhythm and time in music overlap with those about time elements in movement.[1] However, my intention in this book is to focus principally on the use of time elements in bodily movement and other visual aspects of the performance environment, whether or not some form of sound is also present.

What does it mean to speak with the body? In Portuguese, one says that the skilled *sambista* is able, and obliged to *'dizer no pé'* – speak with the feet ... in the Rio carnival: there is eloquence in the white shoes, in the silver high heels scraping the asphalt ... [in the shanty-towns] the base feet stamping down on a

---

1   Indeed music has been influential in my own interest in the subject, which as a child was stimulated not only by the clear patterns and 'nature rhythms' of Revived Greek dance, but also by my mother's 'music and movement' teaching at the piano. As invaluable training in rhythm, I am particularly grateful for extensive practical experience of early polyphonic choral music, at both school and university. Interest in jazz and African, Indian and South American music were important later influences.

concrete floor. The dance [samba] is a complex dialogue ... the feet keep up a rapid patter, while the hips beat out a heavy staccato and the shoulders roll a slow drawl ... a story of racial contact, conflict and resistance. (Browning 1991, p.1)

This book is written for anyone who is interested in movement, in communication through movement. Fields of work to which it may be applied include the expressive arts, teaching, directing, performing, arts' therapies, inter-personal communication and anthropology. It is designed to provide support for drama, dance and movement practitioners who want to take their work and their thinking about it further. I hope the contents may be useful as a springboard to develop movement imagination and creativity, to broaden ideas of what it is possible to experience through the medium of movement, to include in movement practice, and to notice in performance. Teachers or those who work with people in other ways may wish to introduce or pay more attention to movement in sessions. Thinking about rhythm and timing and a full range of time elements could be a useful start.

No book can replace the experience of courses and practical work, and this is certainly not intended as a 'tips for teachers' manual, but it is designed to encourage interested readers to think further about time elements in performance context. Part I may perhaps be useful as an introductory reader on the subject: it directs attention to a range of ideas and theories about rhythm, timing and time elements in performance, with quotations and examples from many sources. The chapters in Part II indicate ways in which we may apply ideas and theories in performance observation and practice; factors and elements of movement rhythm and timing are described and classified. Suggestions are made for the development of skills in movement observation, with particular examples from Twyla Tharp's choreography, Indian Kathak dance and rock and rave events. One chapter focuses on an application of ideas about rhythm and timing in a personal experience and sharing of Tai Ji movement practice. In Part III, contrasting approaches and descriptions of rhythm and timing in action are presented: in Yaqui Indian Easter ceremonies, in traditional Maring life (Papua New Guinea) and in a well-known British event – Trooping the Colour.

A cross-cultural, interdisciplinary perspective, and an attempt to consider the arts in the context of society as a whole, are evident in some chapters. I think this approach developed initially from an interest in classical Greek drama, medieval drama, early European pageants, masques and other integrated arts' performance forms. Aided by the study of anthropology with its non-ethnocentric viewpoint, the approach has been further developed through knowledge of societies where it is not customary to separate or define the arts in the western European manner. All this has led me to consider my own specialisms in a new way and to experience expanding horizons.

However, some disclaimers are necessary here. Since the topic covers such a wide field of study, certain limitations in the contents are acknowledged. My examination of contributions to studies by other writers is selective, and much has been omitted. Moreover, although I make some reference to aspects of the use of time elements in the history of drama and dance, I do not adopt a historical perspective overall. The space–time concepts of physics are not discussed. Many contexts have the potential for examination of time elements in performance. This volume provides only a sampling.

Terms used in the field of study perhaps need a few words of explanation.

Anthropology: broadly stands for studying peoples of the world. *Social anthropology:* the comparative study of different societies; how human society is structured and how it functions; social, economic, political and ritual organisation. *Ethnography:* the essential part of anthropology which provides direct information about a society with the collection of data through observation, direct enquiry (and with varying degrees of participation in the life of the people concerned). The approach is investigative and descriptive rather than critical or judgmental. *Cultural anthropology:* includes the study of material culture and evidence of 'artistic expression' with other aspects of anthropology.

Theatre anthropology: inter-cultural research into techniques of performers, and performance principles and traditions (Eugenio Barba is in the vanguard of this research). *Anthropology of performance:* a somewhat broader field of study than theatre anthropology, more closely linked with social and cultural anthropology.

Performance: in daily usage to 'perform' means to carry out, to do something, to execute an action or a task. Social scientist Goffman applies the term in a restricted sense to everyday behaviour, but defines 'performance' in conventional theatre terms as 'that arrangement which transforms an individual into a stage performer, the latter, in turn, being an object that can be looked at for engaging behaviour, by persons in the audience role' (1974, p.2). We may perhaps consider the concept of performance more simply as some form of enactment, or we may describe it broadly as a public communication process, an intentional interaction in a designated location. As Goffman suggests, it requires one or more persons in the role of performer and an audience; but there are different kinds of performer–audience relationships, purposes and expectations world-wide – whether in theatre, ceremony or ritual. Performers or executants of any event bring particular focus and energy to the task, and the presence and participation of the audience or congregation affects the whole. Through the performers' powers of expression and with other aspects of presentation such as music or visual effects, the aims are to evoke intensification of experience and perhaps to alter moods or attitudes among the spectators. Or more succinctly, from Bauman's definition, performance is 'a heightened mode of communication framed in a special way' (1992, p.41).

Performance events: this umbrella term is used to include not only conventional western drama and dance but also festivals, ceremonies, rituals, masquerades, carnivals, processions and other public spectacles. (Visual artists also use 'performance' to describe their 'live art' events.) *Drama, dance:* there are problems in applying and using these terms cross-culturally, since they do not necessarily translate into the experience or languages of all societies. Many do not have separate words for 'the arts'. However, in this book I hope contextual usage of the terms will be self-explanatory.

Ceremony, ritual: these are terms which invariably shade into one another in usage. Apart from its use in referring to repetitive, everyday habits, 'ritual' is usually understood as prescribed formal behaviour, frequently associated with a mythic past or with a specifically religious or spiritual meaning. For instance, ritual may be enacted to communicate with a spirit world or directed 'to secure the blessing of some mystical power' (Wilson 1957, p.9). Other anthropologists eliminate the religious element in their definitions of ritual but conclude with Leach that 'it serves to communicate information about a culture's most cherished values' (Leach 1954, pp.25–38). In the enactment of one event 'ceremony' might be the formal, prescribed order, the outward form of procedure, while 'ritual' might constitute the central core of meaning. Turner, stressing an important function of ritual, believes 'Ceremony indicates, *ritual* transforms' (1982, p.80). This transformation can be of many kinds – for example it may concern movement from one season to another, or from one stage in an individual's life cycle to the next. Or, as Roose-Evans emphasises, ritual essentially involves a process which effects a change (1994, p.10).

The ceremony or ritual event consists of a planned orchestration of symbolic action with restricted, specific objectives and social functions. Certain aspects of the process are like that of theatre performance, including a particular location, the presence of specialists, the need for preparation, separation of the activity from everyday life and time, and specific use of conventions, language, gesture and so on. In the context of a ritual, presence at the event involves full sharing, participation and concentrated attention – bearing witness. A strong degree of audience involvement validates and reinforces a sense of community. Enactment may be considered essential for a group's collective identity or survival, and thought of as causally effective, whether or not any results actually occur. Roose-Evans and others urge us to think seriously about the human need for ritual and to consider how we might set about regenerating ritual forms and devising ceremonies, as indeed some people are doing today (Roose-Evans 1994). Time elements are a key factor here, which I hope will become clear as the study proceeds.

However we may choose to define or explain them, the activities of theatre, drama, dance, ceremony and ritual are related and not always separate, which is seen especially in the work of some performers and theatre traditions. For instance, American modern dance doyen Martha Graham's dancing was close to ritual, and ceremony is certainly evident in Japanese traditional theatre.

Apart from an apparent human need for all these activities, perhaps, as commonly thought, they also share roots in the distant past. I prefer to avoid an evolutionary perspective, but it is generally thought that early Greek tragedy has inherited something of the seriousness and structure of ancient rites, as Graham discovered.

Despite these academic and solemn thoughts, it has occurred to me that rhythm and timing in performance may seem a frivolous topic for these frequently troubled and disturbing times.

> Turning and turning in the widening gyre
> The falcon cannot hear the falconer;
> Things fall apart; the centre cannot hold;
> Mere anarchy is loosed upon the world. (Yeats, 'The Second Coming')

Yeats' words sometimes appear all too relevant today. But if we feel as if the forces of division and disintegration are rife, perhaps rhythm may be summoned to our aid to nourish integration with its enlivening presence and unifying potential.

PART I

Ideas and Theories

1

Rhythm in Human Movement

Rhythm is that which asserts, it is the form of movement, it is vital.

(François Delsarte, in Shawn 1954, p.55)

'Fascinating rhythm, You've got me on the go!' In his lyrics Ira Gershwin complains of a 'darn persistent' rhythm that 'pit-a-pats' through the brain. It is a common experience: a reaction to a tune which has a captivating sequence of beats and varied accents. Rhythm here consists in an arrangement of beats and accents, with tempo, into a pattern.

To identify and have a mutual understanding of what is meant by 'rhythm' in music and words is relatively straightforward. But the concern of this study is how to recognise and identify rhythm in human movement – a different, more complex affair. Whether in everyday life or in the context of drama, dance, ceremony, ritual, performance or movement session, we may readily agree with Delsarte that it is vital, but how may the bodily use of time elements that create rhythm be described?

When we are working to develop skills in the observation of rhythm, and awareness of the possibilities of its use, a helpful beginning is to identify what is meant by the term and to note how it is used. However, this can be confusing, since in the performance context we meet a diversity of perception, opinion and understanding of rhythm on the part of both performers and spectators. 'Sense' of rhythm varies with each individual: performers differ in the way they assimilate or learn the rhythm and time content of a work, and spectators' perceptions are influenced by past experience, which may also have included practical performance experience.

In everyday life, what do we see when we look at people moving? Let us take an example: I was sitting in a London café recently, with a view of three busy pavements. Looking out for use of time elements and for the location of rhythm in the body, in the time it took to write the description, I noted: a skipping child with swinging plaits, pulled along by a striding woman; a group of four dawdling window shoppers with uneven, casually placed steps; a couple walking and talking, gesticulating emphatically; another couple, arms linked, walking smoothly in step with each other, with marked continuity of flow – size and pace of steps matching; people's heads moving up or down, as landmarks were located or maps consulted; some sharply turning side to side with eye-focus changing as people crossed the street, one man's head involuntarily moving up and down in time as he plodded along. There were many variations in arm swings, or in the way arms were sometimes kept still, usually when anchored through carrying bags, briefcases and other objects, or in pockets.

All this movement must have been mostly instinctive and without conscious intent. We take for granted many primary influences on our movement – such as the force of gravity, for instance. Perhaps I did see consciously adopted rhythm when, finally, a young woman, apparently in a hurry, walked quickly by with a strong, repetitive, driving beat, and with matching arm swings which assisted her forward motion.

Figure 1.1 Energy in action: varied patterns, randomicity and some shared timing from NewVic dancers as they improvise in a street environment.
Source: Hugo Glendinning

Figure 1.2 Work rhythms.
Source: *Georg Agricola,* De Re Metallica *(1557)*

I have described simple patterns of movement. To return to the Gershwin song, as in music, from both the performer's and the viewer's standpoint, rhythm in human movement may indeed essentially be described as consisting of the arrangement of components into a sequential pattern or series of patterns. A sense of this is communicated bodily to a baby carried on its mother's back when she dances – as is customary in some places. Physically produced patterns of rhythm are evident in everyday actions, in repetitive working actions, such as sawing or hammering – actions which a rhythmic motion can help to energise and which are sometimes transferred into folk dance context, and further 'rhythmicised'.[1]

Such patterns are derived from a performer's intention and from the use of energy – nervous and muscular power – and from varied ways of handling energy

---

[1]   This is vividly illustrated in composer Giorgio Battistelli's *Experimentum Mundi.* Derived from the repetitive action-rhythms of various artisans and crafts workers' occupations, the piece has been described as a scenic concerto. In the 1995 UK International Festival of contemporary music. (Almeida Theatre, London) the performance consisted of Italian workers demonstrating their trades in a co-ordinated ensemble, complete with the necessary tools and materials: stone mason, pasta maker, coopers, carpenters, pavers, masons, smiths, knife-grinders, and show makers (with additional percussion and spoken text from Diderot's *Encyclopédie ou Dictionnaire Raisonné des Sciences, des Arts et des Métiers* (1751–1776).

in space through time duration. An experienced performer knows how to activate the potential range of energy output we all possess. Whether male or female, both draw on inner *animus* (vigorous) and *anima* (delicate) energies for performance presence and according to performance need. For the Balinese performer these contrasting energies are known as *keras* and *manis*; in India they are *tandava* and *lasya*. Indeed there are many terms used for various aspects of energy in performance cross-culturally. Again in Bali, for instance, there is not only recognition of the energy use acquired through long training – *cesta kara*, but also of another form of energy – the performer's less predictable, inspirational power during performance, known as *taksu* (Barba and Savarese 1991, pp.74–94). In ritual, or in some traditional forms of performance the energy may be seen as divinely inspired, or related to spiritual powers. In an account of the various Mexican Concheros dance groups for example, anthropologist Susanna Rostas tells us that the pre-Columbian deities (with whom the Mexica – an 'Indianity'-promoting group – wish to commune during the dance) are conceived as different forms of energy, and that some dancers talk about the dance in terms of energies (1998, pp.98–9).

In my example, energy and rhythm were evident in the patterning of accents and changing tensions in people's bodily movement, in muscular action, in repetition; in gestures and in transference of weight in steps of various kinds. This weight transference led to other rhythmic movement, such as the swing of arms as people walked and the swinging plaits of the child. Rhythm was also evident in the interplay of tempi, dynamics, pauses and duration.

Returning to usage of the term, when people say 'rhythm' they may be referring to the use of any one of its constituent elements such as beat, accents or tempo. Or they may be sharing my frequent use of it as an umbrella term which encompasses all those elements, and more. Alternatively, *a* rhythm may describe one particular pattern of movement.

Physiological, biophysical or 'natural' features of rhythm

Some physiological features of rhythm can be observed easily with the naked eye; others, referred to as innate or inner rhythms, are less accessible or readily discernible. These require the use of technological equipment for their observation. For instance, it was easy for me to see the outward bodily action of the child on the pavement, transferring her weight from one foot to the other. I could recognise the characteristic 'dotted' skipping pattern which is reliant on our two-legged body structure', ♩♪ ♩♪ or — – — – right, right, left, left.

Figure 1.3 Rhythm of sea and shore.
Source: Margaret Lapping

But I could not observe her pulse rate, breathing pattern or the movements of her
internal organs which were occurring instinctively and involuntarily.[2]

All human rhythms are rooted in co-ordinated physiological processes. We are
affected too, by the rhythms of the natural environment. These include seasonal,
lunar and circadian rhythms of the day/night cycle which relate to the cyclical

---

[2] Although we may not be able to observe 'inner' rhythms in other people, perhaps we can visualise or
develop a sense of some of our own. This may sometimes be evident in theatre performance. For
instance, in a programme of solo works in celebration of his fiftieth birthday, Mikhail Baryshnikov
premiered a piece, inspired and accompanied by sounds derived from the rhythm of his own heart
beats – with the aid of M.I.T. technology. And dance artist Deborah Hay has been exploring her sense
of inner rhythms in a deeper way for many years. 'I dance by directing my consciousness to the
movement of every cell in my body simultaneously so that I can feel all parts of me from the inside…'
(Hay 1977–1978, p.21). Thus some performance artists develop and use particular inner awareness,
perhaps better described as imagination – since 'a single cell in the body is doing about six trillion
things per second' (Chopra 1996, p.7). A complexity of rhythms inhabits us – and renders external
everyday and most performance rhythms extremely simple in comparison.

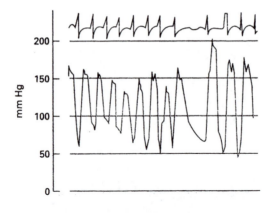

Figure 1.4 Body rhythm – the heart: electrocardiograph readings showing arrhythmia – atrial fibrillation – and pressure recording below showing varying pressure.

nature of ecological processes too, all dominated by our primary energy source, the sun.[3] And as Chopra writes:

> Your body is not separate from the body of the universe, because at quantum mechanical levels there are no well-defined edges. You are like a wiggle, a wave, a fluctuation, a convolution, a whirlpool, a localized disturbance in the larger quantum field. The larger quantum field – the universe – is your extended body. (1996, p.69)

Ideas about environmental rhythms may seem far removed from rhythm in movement performance, but our inner biological clocks are 'in sync' with them through the process of 'exosomatic timing' – that is, the phasing of an inner bodily activity with outer events (Hall 1983, p.18). We take staying in phase for granted – it is out of our conscious control. We are likely to notice it only when the biorhythms which regulate body functions are disturbed or disoriented – to which anyone who has suffered from the effects of jet lag will testify. Gay Gaer Luce's *Body Time: The Natural Rhythms of the Body* (1972) and Martha Davis' (ed.)

---

3   Astrologer Margaret Lapping writes: 'We are each born into three rhythms of light and dark which stay with us from the moment we are born until the day we die. The most obvious of these is the change from night to day. Then there is the cycle of the Moon, from the dark of the new Moon to the brightness of the Full Moon; a cycle which we experience through the lunar month of twenty-eight days. Finally there is the summer/winter change. After the summer solstice, the sun gradually loses strength, and, as the days grow shorter, the growing darkness brings us eventually to the longest night at the winter solstice. There is one night in the year when these three rhythms coincide and we touch the deepest darkness of the year. This is at midnight on the night of the New Moon that falls before the winter solstice. The actual date will vary each year, for instance in 1996 the date is 10th December; in 1997 it is 30th November. (The summer-winter cycle only applies at high latitudes. In tropical climes the rhythm is different.)' (1997, unpublished manuscript).

Interaction Rhythms (1985) are informative introductions to the subject. Davis presents a range of approaches. Luce in particular stresses the need for awareness and understanding of our own 'rhythmic structure' and for 'feeling our rhythmic nature' (Luce 1973, p.10). She writes, 'Invisible rhythms underlie most of what we assume to be constant in ourselves and the world about us. Life is in continual flux and the change is not chaotic' (Luce 1973, p.16).

In physiological studies 'rhythm', 'cycle' and 'periodicity' in particular are investigated in studies of breathing, pulse rate, brain waves, neuromuscular co-ordination, muscular exertion and menstruation. Physiological processes have been observed and measured in various contexts in relation to health, bodily skill, efficiency, ageing and perception, and in everyday behaviour, communication and interaction. This results in quantitative analysis, based on various kinds of measurement and frequently making use of time-lapse filming in order to undertake detailed observation and analysis. In one such study, Condon (1978) established that each of six different brain wave frequencies is linked to specific aspects of self-synchrony. In the performance arts context, an example of a quantitative, physiological approach to rhythm may be found in some studies of dance technique (Ryman and Rannie 1978). However, as already mentioned, our internal rhythms are generally less noticeable, except during strenuous exertion, or unless things go wrong. Changes in rhythmic patterns of movement occur in illness – most evident in illnesses such as Parkinson's disease, or in the after effects of a stroke.

Research from the University of Minnesota provides a striking example of an aspect of the significance of biological rhythms. Director of the University of Minnesota Medical School's Chronobiology research, Franz Halberg, studied circadian rhythms in relation to internal bodily functions. He suggested in the early 1980s that biological rhythms should be used more fully in medical diagnosis (reported in *The Observer*, 20 September, 1981). These include rhythms of brain impulses (on average, several per second), heart beats (about one per second), the sleep-wake cycle, the menstrual cycle, pregnancy patterns, body temperature fluctuations, blood cell counts, adrenal gland activity, enzyme levels and hormonal function. For example, Halberg suggested that abnormal rhythms in certain hormone levels can be a clear indicator that the patient is a potential breast cancer victim years before the disease develops.

There has been criticism of the standard medical belief that there is a constant 'normal' temperature, blood pressure and heart rate. These vary in a predictable way over the 24-hour cycle, and the effectiveness of drugs can vary enormously depending on the time of day they are taken, as shown in Halberg's findings. In the same report, William Hrusbesky, Assistant Professor of Medicine at the University of Minnesota Medical School, remarked: 'We want to change substantially the practice of medicine. It would mean reorganising hospital schedules and bringing patients in at unusual hours. But doing and timing are such complementary elements that we cannot afford to go on ignoring them.'

Gunther Hildebrandt of the Institute for Ergophysiology at the University of Marburg has stated: 'It has been found that the rhythmics of the human organism function utterly harmonically – that is, the frequencies of pulse, breathing, blood, circulation etc., as well as their combined activities. We can observe that these rhythms are strictly co-ordinated.' Haase points out that interrupting these rhythms actually causes illness – 'particularly in cancer cases we observe a total irregularity of all rhythms … rhythmic chaos' (quoted in Berendt 1988, p.119).

When she was considering biophysical processes in relation to dance, anthropologist Kealiinohomoku explained how dance or dance-like behaviour appears to excite neurotransmitters in the brain:

> Neurotransmitters release peptides that affect performers' emotions, precipitate a variety of physiological changes, and create innumerable side-effects through a complex of interactions. A feedback loop goes from perception to behaviour to chemical responses to emotions, back to reinforced or transformed behaviour and enhanced apperceptions. (1981, p.1).

This idea differs from the linear, central brain-controlled behaviour which formerly was thought to control our 'biological' or 'internal' clocks and resulting physical movement.

Cultural and social factors

One problem of relating physiological or biophysical research to human movement expression is that of distinguishing between biological rhythms and the influence of social or cultural conditioning factors. Despite her emphasis on the significance of 'natural' features, Luce stressed that our sense of time is culturally conditioned. When explaining social behaviour, anthropologists have generally placed their emphasis on cultural and societal influences, certainly in Britain. In the USA too, Birdwhistell maintained: 'While body motion behaviour is based in the physiological structure, the communicative aspects of this behaviour are patterned by social and cultural experience' (Birdwhistell 1970, p.173). More directly in relation to biological rhythms and experience of time, British anthropologist Blacking suggested that although they may influence feelings and even performance, 'they do not necessarily determine *experience* of time' (1977a, p.16).

In relation to ritual, some anthropologists (pre-eminently, Turner) have found that they could not isolate the use of symbols in ritual from biophysical or psycho-biological processes. Turner, who in this context also included reference to rhythm, asserted that ritual movement 'draws on biological, climatic and ecological rhythms, as well as social rhythms' (Turner 1982, p.81). Indeed, the biological constant underlies all human enactment and life patterns, including all the variations in social or cultural systems that occur cross-culturally. Ways in which societies differ in their use of rhythm and time serve to highlight its significance. Along with all the other variations between peoples, not only are there distinct cultural differences in this usage, but rhythm affects human interaction in various ways (for instance, see Condon 1982). Anthropologist Edward Hall, the pre-eminent authority in this field, contrasts what he calls the American-European attitude to the use of time with a range of other attitudes. For example, in a broad generalisation, he contrasts what he has observed as the characteristically slower tempo of normal transactions among the American Indians in the western part of the USA, with whom he lived for a number of years, to the faster 'whites' and 'blacks'. He writes: 'The power of the rhythmic message within the group is as strong as anything I know. It is one of the basic components in the process of identification, a hidden force that, like gravity, holds groups together' (Hall 1983, p.184–185).

In performance events, cultural diversity in rhythm is evident in a number of performance features – in the style of performing, use of preferred tempi, style of dance steps and patterns, and use of gesture in acting. We can be in danger of

Figure 1.5 Everyday timing in the past: strolling, pausing as an orchestra plays, and the rhythm of stylised greetings. A Perspective of the Grand Walk in Vauxhall Gardens (1765).
Source: Courtesy of Victoria and Albert Museum

making oversimplified stereotypical generalisations if we carry this idea too far. However, as an example, a 'Japanese' style of performance and performing in Ninagawa's production of *A Midsummer Night's Dream* was unmistakable, and the use made of rhythm and timing was certainly a contributory factor (Mermaid Theatre, London 1996).

This performance style combined recognisable elements from traditional Japanese theatre (Kabuki, Noh) with an everyday, Japanese 'folk' style of movement and behaviour. The former was seen in Titania's performance – in her sweeping gestures, distinctive head movements and use of accented performance attack. The 'folk' style was seen in the performances of Bottom and his crew of 'rustics' (also known as 'the mechanicals'). For instance, they adopted patterns of bustling steps and the rhythms of everyday actions from Japanese kitchens and rural life. These styles were combined with the overall energy, distinctive technical mastery, visual effects, use of orchestral music and experimental theatre techniques – a mix of styles and theatrical ingredients for which Ninagawa is famous. There was effective use of time elements, reminiscent of experimental theatre techniques, seen, for instance, in an extended, exaggerated slow motion sequence of studied shock and amazement when the mechanicals reacted to Bottom's appearance as an ass. Thus this production provided an example of overall directional style and stylistic use of rhythm and time elements. Seeing this variety and individuality coming through perhaps helps to overcome the mistake of making one-dimensional stereotypical observations.

Social influences on our use of rhythm may include the stratum of society from which the individual comes, the family group, and any distinctive group to which the individual might belong – like a teenage gang. Bottom's crew had clearly adopted a group style of movement behaviour and shared rhythm. In a play, the changing situations which occur throughout its course affect a character's rhythm. Other influences to consider are: location (for instance, urban or rural), historical period, age of the character, intention and mood changes within the role, as well as an actor's individual personality and personal idiosyncrasies. With some actors, these last personal rhythm characteristics may be clearly evident in every role undertaken. As Hall says, 'Rhythmic patterns may turn out to be one of the most important personality traits that differentiates one individual from the next' (1983, p.180). Other actors may be more successful in relinquishing their own patterns and in adopting a new movement-rhythm personality for each role.

Inter-personal communication

The patterns of rhythm which provoked the most audience laughter during Ninagawa's *A Midsummer Night's Dream* production occurred during the interaction and inter-personal exchanges of the rustics. There has been a considerable amount of research into inter-personal communication, both verbal

Figure 1.6 Developing synchronicity. This is sometimes encouraged through hearing a shared beat or by moving with physical contact. Here it is evident with use of eyes and with reliance on a leader who is carefully focusing on the way ahead. Dance workshop session, East London Dance.
Source: Phil Polglaze

and non-verbal, with the use of micro-analysis of movement in filmed segments – much of which concerns aspects of biophysical rhythm. This is not the place for a full survey, but some examples are needed since communication is a key feature in performance events. These references make a useful contribution to our quest for identifiable characteristics of rhythm in human movement.

I have already referred briefly to a physical sense of rhythm between mother and baby, the most obvious, basic inter-personal communication rhythm there is, both before and after birth. As one important contribution to studies of this subject I cite the work of Judith Kestenberg (1977). For instance, she noted early preferred 'tension-flow' rhythm in babies, of gratification, frustration, excitation, relaxation, random activity and play. Kestenberg made use of, and expanded Laban-derived procedure and terminology. The time elements she noted were frequency of repetition, degree of intensity, rate of increase of flow characteristics ('free' or 'bound'). Kestenberg usefully differentiates between the rhythms of 'tension flow' and 'shape flow'. Fluctuation in tension flow arises from muscular action, and 'The rhythm of shape flow consists of alternation between growing and shrinking of body shape' (1977, pp.86–90). A related study of mother and baby from Beatrice Beebe demonstrated that rhythmic variations in a mother's arm movements influence the level of engagement with her baby (Beebe 1982).

Interactional synchrony was first described in 1966 by Condon and Ogston, who originally suggested that it is established by sound cues. Stern and others have suggested it occurs when people perceive and relate to a shared underlying pulse (Stern 1973). Through intensive film analysis, Condon discovered ways in which human behaviour 'is ordered and rhythmical, at many levels, and with respect to both speech and body motion and to personal and interactional behaviour'. (1968, p.2). Kendon and Ferber studied how people greet one another. They referred to rhythm, synchrony, duration and timing of gaze.

> Synchronizing one's movements with another but yet not meeting the other's eyes or in some other way signalling a request for contact in an explicit fashion is commonly followed by explicit contact between P and the person whose movements P picks up … By simply picking up the rhythm of another person's movements one can establish a connection with him. (Kendon and Ferber 1971, p.122).

When I asked an engineer who is concerned with environmental matters how he would define rhythm, he immediately replied 'It's vibration! I see it as energetic vibration.' Indeed, vibration or oscillation is the fundamental idea of rhythm in the whole physical world. 'Just feel the vibes, man!' Neuroscientists are familiar with the fact that neural circuits tend to oscillate rhythmically. It has now been shown that 'these oscillations are not restricted to the cerebral context but occur at various levels in the nervous system' (Capra 1996, pp.284–285). Byers found that the interpersonal and speech/movement synchrony is a product of biological oscillators which impose temporal order on communication behaviour, in temporal units of 10 c/sec. and 5 c/sec. His ultimate goal was to discern 'the underlying grammar of the rhythmic interplay and to relate this directly to interpersonal relatedness' (1972, p.90). He considered that movement was organised on a biological basis although culturally patterned. Byers' results support Lashley's 1951 prediction that the neurophysiological problem of how the brain manages serial ordering would be resolved by the discovery of underlying ordering rhythms.

Chapple measured frequency and duration of actions in interaction and emphasised the importance of biological rhythm in his early human communication research:

> Consider the enormous range of biological rhythms in the human body, fast and slow, transmuted and integrated by the complex interdependence of the somatic, autonomic, and endocrine nervous systems. The resultants of this synthesis of movement and sound act directly on us, spatially and temporally differentiating our interactional patterns. (1982, p.50).

Chapple described how the rhythms which consist of 'biological (relaxation) oscillators' synchronise at varying levels of complexity (a hierarchical organisation of biological oscillators) from RNA and DNA metabolism and cell division to the cycles directly observable in the whole organism. Chapple and Condon's film presentation of their findings at a research conference demonstrated self and interactional synchrony occurring in fractions of a second (reported in Davis (1982)).

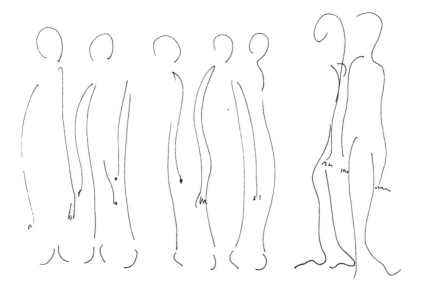

Figure 1.7 A sense of entrainment and balance. Regular, synchronised patterns of rhythm may develop from people standing and softly swaying, slowly moving with gradual shifts of weight – until others enter perhaps to join in or with a change of plan.
Source: Judith Greenbaum

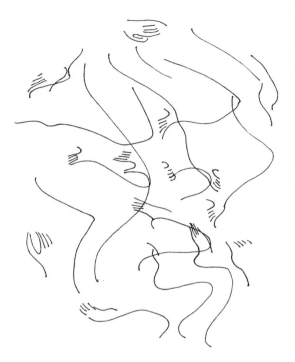

Figure 1.8 At first sight a lively, uneven, irregular rhythm of hands and lines of action. But most hands seem to be moving towards a common centre and with a shared upward impetus: perhaps a growing sense of synchrony is implied.
Source: *Judith Greenbaum*

An influential pioneer in the field, Birdwhistell, coined the term 'kinesics' for 'the science of body behavioural communication' (see Birdwhistell 1952, 1970). His interest was in the multi-channel, cross-referencing patterns of interpersonal communication, and he stressed its complexity. The time elements he included for observation were mainly tempo and use of a recognisable, sometimes shared, 'beat'.

Drawing on evidence from these pioneers and others, we become more aware of the tendency towards synchrony in compatible human relationships and in nature – such as are seen in flocks of birds, or schools of fish. Some descriptions of synchrony refer to it as 'entrainment' or 'mutual phase locking'. Following evidence from science, Berendt's definition of entrainment (or sharing a rhythm) is to 'vibrate in harmony' (1988, p.117). Thus here we may be reminded of my engineer friend's definition of rhythm as vibration. An extreme example of synchrony in ritual may be found in the trance-worship of some Pentecostal religious sects, where observers have remarked upon the shared, synchronised breathing of participants (Kane 1974; La Barre 1969).

A tendency towards synchrony which develops in the performance context may be particularly noticeable when a comedian 'warms up' an audience. If it is achieved successfully this grows into a shared tempo and sense of timing in the delivery and response to jokes. It can be seen, too, in both speech and movement, in a successful double act. In a tribute programme for the actor Ronnie Barker, Ronnie Corbett, his long-standing partner in *The Two Ronnies* BBC TV comedy series, remarked that he considered a key reason for the great success of their

Figure 1.9 Rhythmic interaction: traditional English dance in processional form travels through the streets, calling at houses, clubs, pubs en route – from 9 am on Easter Saturday. In iron-clad clogs, the Britannia Coconut dancers of Bacup, Lancashire perform two dances alternately. They are accompanied by a silver band and a man with a whip – the 'Whipper In' – to whip winter away and make room for the dance. Garlands are used in one dance; in the other, with an intricate pattern of steps and leaps the men knock the wooden cotton-bobbin 'nuts' which are attached to hands, waist and thighs.
Source: Doc Rowe

acting partnership was their shared timing (*Ronnie Barker: A Life in Comedy*, BBC TV, 1 January 1996). (See Chapter 2 for further reference to performance timing.) Productive company rehearsals are the result of a shared, driving forward tempo, according to James Levine, conductor and artistic director of the Metropolitan Opera, New York: 'They have to have a kind of interactive, forward stride – otherwise they don't function' (interview, *Naked Classics: The Boss*, Channel 4 TV, 19 January 1997). Members of a dance ensemble may well experience a form of entrainment when they work together to 'pick up' a unison movement from the choreographer. It occurs in a movement class when students have really 'tuned in' and are working together, perhaps from the basis of a shared beat. This kind of work generates group energy and can provide a powerful experience of group synchrony. George Leonard found examples of entrainment in the relation between preachers and congregations, and in harmonious husband and wife relationships – as well as in those of mother and child of the kind described by Kestenberg and Beebe (Leonard 1981).

During preparations for a revival of Arnold Wesker's army-based *Chips with Everything* (Royal National Theatre, 1997) actors who had experienced military training, and some of the others who had been rehearsing, remarked to interviewing journalists on the satisfaction they felt in the correct performance of synchronised, precisely timed drill. McNeil describes his experience of this in a study of the topic: 'conscious only of keeping in step so as to make the next move correctly and in time somehow felt good ... a strange sense of personal enlargement ... becoming bigger than life, thanks to participation in collective ritual'. McNeil labels this process 'muscular bonding' and suggests that it involves 'a characteristic altering of consciousness that sets in as the rhythm of muscular movement takes hold' (1995, pp.2–8). We can see this 'human penchant for moving together in time' in parades, demonstrations, exercise classes. It is well known that such action overcomes fatigue, and, more ominously, well-drilled troops are more efficient in battle. The spectacle of massed Nazi salutes in documentary films of the 1930s still retains a terrifying power.

Canetti refers to this phenomenon in his ground-breaking study and categorisation of crowds. He suggests that shared rhythmic action was important in primeval times and that survival was achieved through group unity, seen at its most powerful when members are 'performing in exactly the same way and with the same purpose', a dense, egalitarian consensus. Within this scenario the 'communal excitement' of a *rhythmic* or *throbbing* crowd' develops, which Canetti sees exemplified in the *Maori haka*, originally a war dance (1962, pp.30–34).[4]

---

4   During an otherwise shared event, lack of synchrony may be significant. For instance, anthropologist Monica Wilson noted 'little common movement, each [person] dances alone as if fighting a single combat' in her vivid account of the dancing, wailing and drumming during East African Nyakyasa burial rites' (1957, p.23).

In relation to the performer-audience connection, Jean-Marie Pradier remarks: 'perceiving the movement of others induces a response in our own body – in a religious ceremony, political demonstration or performance' (Pradier 1989, in Barba and Savarese 1991, p.215). Giving or sharing a performance is an exercise in inter-personal communication. Actors communicate with fellow actors on stage, with the audience; dancers interact with others in a dance ensemble. The leader of a ceremony communicates with the participants. The use of movement-rhythm and timing, perceived as the interlinked set of features and inseparable components described, is evident and significant in all these processes of communication, on stage or off, and whether with gods, spirits, fellow humans – or indeed, with animals.

In conclusion, we can see that in performance, or in a performance event, there are in process a number of influences and different features in the bodily use of time elements that create rhythm, or 'a rhythm'. These include the visible, physiological patterns which we can observe with our eyes, the less discernible biophysical features, the performers' inner rhythms, the influence of natural environmental rhythms, and other rhythms of the historical era and environment; cultural conditioning, social influences and personal characteristics as well as those of a performer's or director's adopted styles. The total pattern emerges as a correlation of parts, a complicated, many-layered mesh of relations between components. It emerges not only from each individual performer's use of rhythm, but also from the rhythms of interaction and of group activity. A complex web indeed.

2

Patterns in Time

Metricity, Flow, Timing and Other Aspects of Rhythm in Performance

Figure 2.1 The exciting possibilities of rhythmic intricacy which are sometimes beyond a performer's control: Naomi Lapezon rehearsing Robert Cohan's Sky.
Source: Douglas Jeffery

A performance is a flow, which has a rising and falling curve. To reach a moment of deep meaning, we need a chain of moments which start on a simple, natural level, lead us towards intensity, then carry us away again. (Brook 1993, p.83)

Performances gather their energies almost as if time and rhythm were concrete, pliable things. (Schechner 1985, p.11)

Metricity, flow and structure

Dictionary definitions of rhythm generally emphasise metre or metricity. A metric pattern is primarily one in which there is a discernible regular pulse or beat underpinning the structure and which can be measured and counted. As Alice's ambiguous statement informed the Mad Hatter, 'I know I have to beat time when I learn music'; and *we* know this means she had to keep to a regular, even pattern. If movement is described as 'rhythmic', 'rhythmicised' or 'rhythmical' this usually implies actions which are clearly metrically based, 'in time', or perhaps performed with 'a swing'. For example, anthropologist Monica Wilson describes the dance-movement of women during East African Nyakyusa burial rites who were 'swinging their hips in a kind of rhythmical walk' (1957, p.24). On the other hand, 'rhythmicality' is sometimes used in contexts further removed from metricity, for example: 'The dance begins slowly, concerned with that incredible concentration of physical rhythmicality that Cunningham's dancers possess' (Clarke 1987).

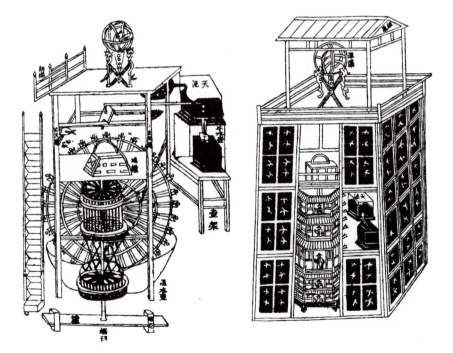

Figure 2.2 Keeping time: East and West, expertly crafted clocks (and watches) are familiar symbols of status and achievement. A famous Chinese astronomical water-clock tower, 11.3m high (37ft), designed by Su Sung, completed in 1094. Inside and outside views show a clock-driven bronze armillary for observation of the stars on the top floor and a celestial globe which rotated daily on the first floor. On the ground floor – a water wheel escapement which drove all the wheels in the tower. Figures with bells appeared from doors in the five-storied pagoda at the front of the edifice, to sound the times of day. Source: Ancient Chinese woodcut

The basis of metricity is a form of clock time on which we have come to rely more and more and may wear on the person as a constant reminder – mechanical, electrical, digital, electronic, computerised – an increasingly artificial time environment. In one sense, clocks have to do with lack of freedom, but they bring freedom, too – keeping appointments at agreed, sychronised times liberates other time. Clocks are not a new phenomenon – ticking and chiming, they have dominated from clock towers in Europe since the fourteenth century in most cities, even marking every quarter of an hour. Night watchmen called the hours. Before this there were elaborate time-reckoning methods used by astronomers as well as water-clocks, sand-clocks, sundials. Etymologically, 'metre' is from the Greek *metra* – uterus. It is interesting to note that this etymological root conveys something much more natural about measurement – the female inner clock. In Sanskrit too, *matri* = mother, *matra* = measure (Berendt 1988, pp.99–101).[1]

There are different concepts of rhythm in different countries and performance traditions; a study of ideas and practice in one single country can provide a full research topic. An anthropology of time and rhythm seminar in the Folklore and Ethnomusicology departments at Indiana University, Bloomington (Spring 1981) scheduled 24 sessions on African dimensions of time alone! A full examination of cross-cultural differences cannot be undertaken here, but it can at least be noted that a definition of rhythm which emphasises metre is not necessarily appropriate in non-western contexts. Moreover, it is too limiting in relation to performance arts in contemporary forms, or where improvisation is included, in which non-metricity may well be the basis of action. Even though metric patterning may occur, it may not be a prime organising factor. For instance, choreographer Merce Cunningham's dance-time structure is based on duration, on setting actions, body rhythms and phrases in given lengths of time. We learn this, and that for him rhythm is principally lodged in physical action rather than in metrically based pattern when he exclaims: 'What is rhythm? You're going to say that rhythm is simply giving metric beat? Rhythm is what anybody does in terms of physical action, it's what anybody does in time' (1980, p.10). See also p.121.

Among various definitions of performance energy in Bali, one includes the term *baya* (wind); in Japan it is defined as *ki-hai* (spirit, breath) (Barba and Savarese 1991, p.81). Definitions such as these help us to understand the process, the way in which a flow of energy animates the performer's actions. In the last chapter there was reference to the play or fluctuation of energy as a basis of rhythm, and some definitions emphasise that 'flow' is its essential characteristic. The word 'rhythm' is derived from the Greek '*rhuthos*' cf. *rheo* to flow: 'Rhythm literally means "a particular way of flowing"' (Barba and Savarese 1991, p.211).

---

1 Without clocks, the natural processes of the body, human needs, activities and environment govern the passage of time.

Movement rhythm in performance then, may also be described as a patterned energy-flow of action, marked in the body by varied stress and directional change; also marked by changes in level of intensity, speed and duration (including duration of both action and stillness). Csikszentmihalyi has drawn attention to the phenomenon of what he calls 'flow' in human events, and his reading of the term may also be applied in performance. He describes as flow the 'holistic sensation' which is present when we act with total involvement. This sensation is characterised by 'a unified flowing from one moment to the next' (1975, pp.35–36). At a primary level, the flow or flux of matter through a living organism is the rhythmic basis of its life.

As Schechner's comment at the beginning of this chapter implies, in a

Figure 2.3 Visual rhythm: horizontal lines of flowing energy.
Source: Liane Payne

performance this rhythmically patterned flow of action has an accumulative effect as the event proceeds. Elements of rhythm and time are used to generate varying levels of performance intensity – performers' energies are gathered, used and shaped to provide and promote the flow of action.

On one hand, it could be asserted that, taken in its broadest sense, rhythm is the general flow of action; on the other, that it confines and specifically shapes the flow. Turning briefly to the Greek classics, Plato (c.340 BC) who held that the conscious 'feeling' for rhythm (and harmony) distinguished man from animal, emphasised this shaping function of rhythm when he defined rhythm as an ordering of movement (*kineseos taxis*) distinct from the 'non-rhythm' of kinetic chaos or kinetic continuum (*Laws* 665A). It seems too that Plato was alert to the effects of rhythm. An example which he gave was that the order of rhythm of lullabies 'dominates fright and calms mental sense' (*Laws*, Book 11).

Aristoxenus (c.370 B.C.) made a useful distinction when he identified the difference (referred to in Chapter 1) between 'rhythm' in general and 'a rhythm' which stands alone, with a recognisable 'before' and 'after'. He also emphasised the significance of moments of cessation in the endless flow: alternation of movement and rest as central in the ordering of rhythm. Indeed, alternation is an essential feature of rhythm, as we move between fast/slow tempi for instance, and ever-changing degrees of tension and relaxation.

If rhythm can be thought of as inherent in the flow of action and also as confining, shaping, organising the flux, we are concerned here with both process and product. That is, with both the moment-by-moment interplay of elements derived from rhythm and timing factors, and also with individual rhythms and with the way they build into the total form of the play, dance, ceremony or ritual. (The same build-up occurs in a movement class – in its time-frame and environment.) Two structural levels may be identified here. Time elements and rhythm in the micro-structure may be observed in the performers' use of gestures, motifs, phrases; in the macro-structure from the durational level of phrases through to a complete work, and also in the wider context, for example in a series of performances, festivals (or movement classes).

Timing

Timing: 'the act of determining or regulating the order of occurrence of an action or event, to achieve desired results' (*Oxford Advanced Learner's Dictionary of Current*

Figure 2.4 Working together: concentration while sharing the timing of a jump during a dance workshop, East London Dance.
Source: *Phil Polglaze*

English 1986); 'the regulation of the speed with which something is performed so as to produce the most effective results' (*Webster's New Twentieth Century Dictionary* 1979).

Thus in relation to rhythm in performance, 'timing' essentially refers to those aspects of rhythm (in the general sense) which relate to the placement of an action or an event in time duration, to 'moments when' in the performance span, and to aspects of tempo. The contextual significance of incidents, actions, stillness and pausing, can to a greater or lesser extent be underlined by timing, sometimes referred to as 'rhythm'. A former attempt by the writer to direct drama teachers' attention to the topic: '[We must consider] the rhythm of preparation, action and recovery, of attention, intention, decision, of anticipation and the event, of meeting and parting' (1970, p.21).

In David Hare's *Amy's View* (1997), young actor Toby seems to be referring to timing when he visited the experienced Esme in her dressing room after a matinée, and asks what she thinks of his performance in a shared scene. He comments: 'I think I'm beginning to get the hang of that last scene. The rhythm. You always bang on about rhythm. And I thought this afternoon … well, actually the rhythm wasn't too bad.' However, although 'rhythm' and 'timing' may share the same time elements and refer to the same performance features, I have more recently found it useful to think about timing separately for the purposes of study and practical work. I am not alone in this – Hutchinson Guest deals with timing as a separate topic in *Dance Notation* (1984, pp.20–21) and James Kennedy describes Ashton's view of Fonteyn as 'a dancer whose sense of rhythm and timing it was his delight to educate' (*The Guardian*, 24 August 1988).

Agnes, as 'a stickler on points of manners' in Albee's *A Delicate Balance*, refers to timing as one of the graces essential in her mission to maintain, or 'hold' the family. Indeed, timing is usually well understood in an everyday, social sense or context. Skill in its use brings success, not only in social relations and etiquette, but also in diplomacy, negotiation, chemistry, cooking, military discipline, and in surmounting obstacles; as well as in animal training, athletics and games of all kinds. In a simple game: the child's 'grandmother's footsteps' requires a sharp sense of timing from all concerned. We are safe to approach and try to reach Grandmother with stealthy steps while her back is turned, but must *freeze* when she suddenly wheels round. If she spots any movement, she will commandingly condemn us as 'out' and having lost the chance to replace her.

A sense of timing is present in all skilled performance – in contexts as far apart as an operating theatre or a game. Golfer Jack Nicklaus has commented:

Feeling the weight of the clubhead against the tension of the shaft helps me to swing rhythmically. As the back swing progresses I like to feel that clubhead's weight pulling my hands and arms back up. Starting down I like to feel the weight of the clubhead lagging back – resisting, as my thrusting legs and hips pull my arms and hands down. When I can 'wait' for these feelings, I am giving myself enough elapsed time to make all the various moves in rhythmical sequence. (quoted in Lowe 1977, p.177)

Or a fine example from photography – opera and theatre director Peter Sellars, writing of Guy Gravett's opera production photographs in his obituary:

In life, as in photography, he saw beyond surfaces, saw into people and their motivations, was alert to relationships, and was alive to the necessity of change, the presence of the new ... it shows so powerfully in his work – timing was everything and his skill carried not just the split second it took to press the shutter, but the deeper question of what was the moment before, and what might be to come. (*Opera*, August 1996, p.902)

The 'split-second' timing referred to here reminds me of the hero's action in tales of initiation, who, as Eliade tells us, may have to pass between two millstones in constant motion or between rocks that can clash together at any moment (1991, p.83). Steven Paxton, master of dance improvisation, explains a similar, extra-rapid reaction in the timing of the practised improviser: 'This quickness is faster than habitual movement/thought and is based on acceptance of the imminent forces, letting the body respond to the reality it senses and trusting it to deal with the situation intuitively' (quoted in Steinman 1986, p.98).

For a performer, movement director or teacher, paying attention to timing may include choosing the moment, regulating the rate, ascertaining the time taken, or the number of times an action occurs – or should occur. By such means the detail of an event registers effectively with an audience – or in a movement session, with a class.

Timing in the use of pauses may be particularly expressive. When dance critic Edward Denby was writing about some frightening episodes in a dramatic section of a dance work, he referred to their effect: 'the episodes become frightening because their exact timing projects them so forcefully. Note for instance the scaring effect of the waits between where nothing at all happens' (1965, p.102). One may observe a number of features in relation to timing: the moment when entrances and exits of performers occur, when a performance – or any aspect of a performance – begins or ends, or is interrupted; and how the sequences and events are ordered and arranged. Preparation, anticipation and aftermath as well as moments within the event itself are part of the overall timing of the event. There are references to the subject cross-culturally; for example, Foerstel studied group interaction when she lived with the Manus (Admiralty Islands, Pacific Ocean) and noticed what happened when individuals who had a 'poor sense of timing' were in a leadership position:

Most of the Manus seemed to be sensitive to the timing of events; they knew when an event should occur and how long it should last. Due to the type of intensity which characterized the Manus' life, they can tolerate only certain units of time, and then seem to drop into complete exhaustion. A dull individual, with a poor sense of timing, usually created friction … [in] a position of leadership … a drift situation … different aspects of the event he is leading begin slowing down, until nothing seems to be functioning properly … relaxation that leads to disruption eventually builds up tension, and a new leader springs up who stimulates the group into new activity. (1977, p.11)

Thus, timing may be significant in establishing leadership in performance events and in the actual process of leading by anticipating (even fractionally) the action. Systems of cueing in performances of all kinds and in a wide range of contexts can be considered as part of timing.

The subject may be studied in terms of the overall balance and cohesion of the durational structure, or in terms of the effective use of change and contrast in tempi within it. Matters concerning performers' ensemble, their work together in dancing, enacting, reacting one with another – all relate to use of timing; and as noted in the last chapter, to synchronicity or entrainment.

Figure 2.5 A moment in comedy: movement when words fail. At the end of his tether – an unexpected sudden, strong action, exaggerated beyond everyday decorum. The power of rhythmic attack is glimpsed in this shot of Richard McCabe as Ford in The Merry Wives of Windsor *(Royal National Theatre, Director Terry Hands, 1995).*
Source: Douglas Jeffery

In theatre work, an entrance is deemed to be well timed if it occurs on cue, that is, at the planned moment of action or dialogue. Also, as noted in relation to synchrony in Chapter 1, successful comedy and appropriate audience response are determined chiefly by use of timing. American comedian Jack Benny was well known for his impeccable exploitation of this. He could wait, without moving, for as long as 30 seconds before delivering a further line – to an inevitable roar of audience laughter and applause (*Make 'Em Laugh!*, BBC Radio, 23 September 1997).[2] John Gielgud has referred to the significance of timing in comedy, such as in George Robey's and Charlie Chaplin's performances. For instance, Robey 'paused as he surveyed the audience and had them roaring with laughter before he uttered a word – these geniuses and their successors can use the pause and illuminate a silence with an individual magic beyond words' (*The Daily Telegraph*, 24 January 1981). Thus, audience applause can be manipulated by timing. For example, Anne Salmond describes climactic moments of a popular Maori orator's speech. Salmond asserts that he captured his audience through the timing of his gestures, when he turned and changed direction, as well as through the tempo of his walking with use of acceleration (1974, p.56). To take a banal, commonplace example, we know that advertising companies make use of timing to induce response to TV commercials. In any context, the build-up of rhythm to a climax is structured through use of timing.

In relation to synchrony: 'good' timing occurs when people unconsciously or intentionally synchronise their action or stop together, or take turns to move in a complementary manner. Spontaneity, surprises and interruptions can be well timed, too, for apt, comic or other effect.

In ceremony, effective timing occurs when everything happens according to plan; when, for instance, as described in Chapter 12, the Queen arrives at the appointed place on Horse Guards Parade during the Trooping the Colour ceremony. Until 1986 the Queen was on horseback and arrived, bringing her horse to a halt precisely as Big Ben struck eleven o'clock. (Now she follows the same time-schedule in a horse drawn carriage.)

Timing can of course be 'bad' as well as 'good'. We do not know if the criticism was appropriate or what the performer's intention may have been, but Irving Wardle, for instance, criticised a Spike Milligan show for that reason: '[an item about] Japanese zip-fasteners, allowing up to four suicides a day, and a teeth-brushing version of 'The Flight of the Bumble Bee' which would have convulsed the house if they had been less perfunctory and better timed' (*The*

---

2   The performer's sense of timing is not necessarily related to a sense of clock-time. For instance, although comedian Jimmy Tarbuck's timing was considered 'brilliant', apparently he had no idea of how long he'd been on stage during his act – 'time itself meant nothing to him'. And we learn from the wife of that superb master of timing, Tommy Cooper, that her husband was always late (comments from *Heroes of Comedy*, a Channel 4 TV compilation).

Times, 4 December 1982). Bad timing would be evident in classical ballet for example if the ballet hero and heroine 'muff' the lift and the dancer finds herself flat on the floor. A personal example of bad timing in performance context took place many years ago when (enthusiastically attending a drama course) I was acting the part of a nun. When I left the stage on the way to execution, the words 'Into Thy hands I commend my spirit' were spoken after the sound of the executioner's axe had resounded through the auditorium! Perhaps interesting as a ghostly or surrealistic effect, but this was not the director's intention here. Thus bad timing may occur through inaccuracy or through lack of developed sense of timing or sensitivity to a situation. An 'untimely' remark or action is one that is mis-timed, usually ahead of when it should be. An untimely death frequently refers to that of a young person – which we consider has happened all too soon.

Other aspects of timing and rhythm in performance: the role of rhythm in drama, dance and ceremony

Various kinds of performance events, performance genres and styles may be distinguished partly through their differing use of time elements and rhythm. There is a conspicuous example of this in traditional Noh drama in Japanese theatre. The movement in Noh is accompanied by instruments in such precision as to match the action and gestures throughout. Each of three drums in the ensemble has a repertoire of approximately 200 patterns which are played in a specific order determined by the genre (see Malm 1960).

Differences in the use of time elements and rhythm may reveal how genres occasionally mix in one event. For instance, towards the end of the contemporary play Yasmina Reza's *Art* in the 1996 London production, there was a sequence concerned with re-hanging a painting. The painting had been the centre of controversy in the play. The two characters who had been mainly concerned with this were demonstrating and sealing the new found renewal of their friendship through the action of re-hanging the painting. The tempo and timing altered: a marked change of mood – something different was happening. This was the first and only time in the play that the actors moved in unison. The two actors synchronised their movements as they walked gravely towards the painting, lifted it, and adopted a slow walk towards the wall. A mood of solemnity prevailed, a marked contrast to all that had gone before. Together they hung the picture. Together they stepped back with timed steps in unison, to view the result. A symmetrical use of gestures and movement in the space also contributed to the effect – which was surely that of a ceremony. Or we might term it a ritual, since the sequence was charged with significance and meaning. It symbolised the burying of a quarrel, at least for the time being.

For both performer and spectator, rhythm (to include timing) contributes to the intensification of experience contained in the performance event, be it dance,

Figure 2.6 Tradition and traces of ceremony in dance. Where paths meet and cross, spectators have gathered in a town centre in Yorkshire to watch the Handsworth traditional longsword dancers. A basic step retains the beat (marked by a musician's tapping toe) while the dancers' tracks and varied patterns of held swords generate a sequential design of spatial rhythm.
Source: Doc Rowe

drama, ceremony – or mixed genres. Incidentally, rhythm works in this way in games too. Appropriate, that is to say culturally and contextually correct, use of rhythm and timing may be said to bring power to the event. Misuse is likely to weaken focus and concentration and to reduce impact. As Dean has pointed out in relation to drama, 'two special features are common to all rhythms – vitality and power of attraction' (1966, p.234). These features are particularly evident in dance rhythms, not least in Spanish Flamenco, where performance is heightened by characteristic acceleration at times, and the sense of a dancer's conflict – with the rhythm of inner demons, perhaps: 'Cortes talks much as he dances – faster and faster. His fingers leap, his arms spin as he describes Flamenco as "a fight. A fight against oneself. It's erotic, angry, yet spiritual and mystical"' (Joanna Coles' interview, *The Guardian,* 22 March 1996). A performer's use of and sensitivity to rhythm are crucial in the production of effective, highly charged, strongly registering work in drama or dance.

In drama, elements of rhythm and timing (obviously together with other aspects of dynamics and performers' use of space) distinguish character, generate mood, and convey inter-relationships. With reference to the characters in a play and their expression of moods and feelings, Plato reminds us how actors utilise rhythm to convey the emotional life of the characters they are playing: 'Rhythm is [generated from] an emotion released in ordered movements' (from *Timon*).

The concept of characterisation through rhythm is of course far from being a new idea in drama (or in drama-based dance). Again in ancient Greece, Aristotle writes about it: 'Rhythm alone, without harmony, is the means of the dancer's imitations; for even he, by the rhythms of his attitudes, may represent men's character as well as what they do and suffer' (*De Poetica*). As Irmgard Bartenieff emphasised, we form judgements about character and mood by association with the rhythm of the body tensions they reflect (Bartenieff and Lewis 1980). And Byers refers to time elements in relation to animal characterisation:

> If a stage actor wants to 'imitate' a crow, an elephant or a terrier, he cannot look very much like these animals but he can get applause from his audience if he actually reproduces the temporal characteristics of the movements of the animal he is imitating. (1972, p.42)

Rhythm is used to create the excitement of anticipation or suspense in drama, both before an event and at times during it, and also to create the theatrical effect of surprise. When I asked a theatre practitioner if she could remember an example of this, she immediately referred to a sequence in a Japanese Kabuki play when the male actor was performing as Spider Woman:

> He was moving terribly slowly – creepy crawly – and you were beginning to wonder if he was going anywhere. It was totally against our western culture's idea of pace of movement. A pause, and then – ZAP from his finger ends, and out shot these envenomed ribbons of poison – right out into the air – and they moved FAST as he waited, poised for further action – this made it theatrical after the slow beginning, which had been a kind of fluid, meditative process. (personal communication, Stuart 1995)

With notable exceptions, it has to be said that we are more likely to see full, expressive use of movement rhythm in drama from companies outside England. A conspicuous feature of traditional Japanese theatre is the inclusion of what we might term 'dance-movement', as witnessed in the Spider Woman's behaviour. The blend of what in the west we might recognise as 'dance' and 'drama' in the sequence, again demonstrates the limitations of using these terms cross-culturally. The example reminds us of the enormous variety that there is in the use of rhythm and timing and their constituent time elements, in performance throughout the world. Not only is movement rhythm included in Japanese theatre, it is an expressively significant component in the event. Moreover it is imbued with a particular concentration which is promoted by use of time elements.

I think this concentration partly stems from the use of a reduced scale or condensation of action in some aspects of Japanese performance which is interesting in relation to use of rhythm. For instance, there is a tradition that a dancer's movements must be restricted to the spatial area of one tatami floor mat (size: 1.91 x 0.95 metres).[3] Perhaps this relates to the Japanese myth of the origin of dance, first performed on the top of a drum to tempt the sun goddess out of a cave. Concentration of movement has greater impact. The concept is illustrated in the Izumo shrine ceremonial Kagura dances. One priest, followed by a single maiden, dances on one mat (see Gunji 1970). An extreme form: in the dance type *Kamigata-mai* the ideal is to dance without actually moving. The purpose is to show intense strength or power.

Figure 2.7 Japanese actors in a scene. A man threatens a woman in front of a verandah; an artist's portrayal which displays the presence of rhythm and timing during interaction, enhanced here by an intensity and directed energy in the gestures.
Source: Kuniaki. Courtesy of the Victoria and Albert Museum.

---

3   This is the size of mats in Kyoto. Sizes vary regionally: in Tokyo 1.76 x 0.88m, in Nagoya 1.82 x 0.91m. A Japanese friend told me that when learning the Tea Ceremony, as an assistant serving guests she was instructed not to stray beyond the limits of the tatami mat spread in front of them, and to traverse it fully with a precise and identically placed eight steps.

In the examples of traditional Japanese performance styles I have seen, I have found that every part of each single movement is imbued with a degree of significance which is generally totally unknown in the west. An overall subtlety in the use of energy in rhythm, in timing and in the use of time elements may be observed, which is seldom seen in western theatre. Techniques of performance are relevant here. There are a number of concepts about these elements in Japanese theatre training. For example, *Okisa* in Japanese performance means amplitude or breadth of expression. But this is not achieved with obvious large movements in the western manner. It is achieved by techniques such as making a preparatory movement in an opposite direction to the main gesture, and producing a slight pause before it. *Jo-ha-kyu* is another concept which contributes to the rhythm of a traditional Japanese performance. It describes three stages of an action phrase. Broadly, *jo* refers to energy held in check at the beginning, *ha* to a form of release or breaking free, and *kyu* to the ending, a powerful, sudden stop. This may be identified as an intense form of what musicians might call '*rubato*' timing when some energy is held back between one movement or pose and the next (see also Gunji 1970, pp.71–73). Moreover, Zeami refers to retention of energy and specific sense of timing at endings:

> He [the actor] must be careful not to lose his intensity even down to the deepest recesses of his heart at such times as the moment after the end of his dance, song, dialogue, gesture, etc. The feeling of concentrated intensity in the depths of the actor's heart is sensed by the audience and thus the silent pauses are made interesting. (quoted in Nakamura 1971, p.51)

As the Spider Woman actor's movement demonstrated, single gestures can contain a wealth of meaning or importance. The pauses before and after his 'zap' were perhaps examples of *mie* in Kabuki acting: the high point of the art. This is the still movement which occurs at a climax: 'when the actor must impose himself upon his audience with the maximum power of his resources' (Kramer 1978, p.25). Although this demonstrates an economical use of gesture, there is elaboration in traditional Japanese performance movement rhythm too. Mood changes can be marked by use of intricate rhythmic patterning. The placement of accents in the rhythmic pattern is often detailed. Carl Wolz, who has made a considerable study of the genre, comments: 'it is considered uninteresting to dance on the beat. An aesthetic judgment is made of a performer on the manner in which he times and weaves a dance phrase in and around the rhythm of the accompaniment' (1977, p.57). In general, features of rhythm, timing and time elements in movement, accompanied and emphasised by sound, help to generate the concentration, intensity, timeless calm and power inherent in traditional Japanese theatre performance.

Figure 2.8 The reduced acting area intensifies the action in the actors' bodies, with strong projection and focus both down and outward; accents in hands and faces. The timing here shared between experienced performers – without eye contact – contrasts with the young practitioners' demonstration of synchronicity in Fig. 1.6. The simultaneity of the actions and symmetric spatial rhythm of the grouping contrasts with the unresolved discord and disturbance of the situation. A tense moment captured from a performance piece, Through the Net, *produced by Studio 3 Arts with writer Julie Garton. Jonathan Zito was stabbed to death by Christopher Clunis, a diagnosed schizophrenic, at Finsbury Park underground station December 1992. This piece was a dramatic exploration of the tragic event and of the Ritchie Report. It provided a focus for health authorities' training to provoke inter-agency discussion on mental health issues.*
Source: Simon Ashmore Fish

To return to western theatre, there is a further point to make in relation to reduced scale in performance, when the actor's general movement around the stage is limited. Frances de la Tour, as Stephanie Abrahams in the London production of Kempinski's *Duet for One* (1980), spent almost the entire play in a wheelchair.

However, the detail and variety of her use of rhythm and the full range of timing elements which she employed were striking. For instance, contrasting tempi, moments of stillness, varied and emphatic use of head turns, hand action-patterns, sharply and variously angled arm gestures were clearly evident. All this and more in her use of rhythm certainly helped to draw and hold audience attention – and it contributed to the judged success of the performance. A more recent example was Dame Maggie Smith's acclaimed London stage performance as the unfortunate vicar's wife in Bennett's *Bed Among the Lentils* (1996). Although she did move around the stage a little, the actor's face was the most mobile and expressive part of her body. The free, non-metric rhythm and phrasing in the small movements of her facial features were an object lesson in an actor's use of what Laban termed 'shadow movements'. The humour, pathos – and ultimately tragedy – of the piece seemed to be etched by the detailed play of rhythm across those ravaged features.

An actor's use of movement rhythm and its potential is even evident at the end of a performance. Olivier directs attention to its importance in an established western actor's acknowledgement of applause in a traditional manner:

Eyes take in the gallery, hold for a moment.
Eyes take in the upper circle, hold for another moment.
Eyes to the dress circle, longer hold, more money here.
Eyes to the stalls, even longer.
Then to the left and to the right, for the boxes. Treat the boxes as if there was Royalty seated in them.
Then slowly let the head come completely down, chin almost on chest. Play the modesty …
Wait for a moment, then play the modesty, again. Arms outstretched to the company on either side …
Wait for another beat and then move forward.
Hand on heart, then final bow …
By this time they should be on their feet. If not you've got something wrong. (1986, pp.94–95).

The text is of course the basis from which the movement rhythm and timing in drama context is derived. We can see this clearly exemplified in the plays of Samuel Beckett, for whom not only was the passing of time a frequent theme, but also who gives actors clear indications of the use of the movement-rhythm and timing he requires as an integral part of the text. In his short plays there is a link with the idea of intensity brought about by reduction, together with the precise rhythmic patterning demonstrated in the reference to traditional Japanese theatre. As Alvarez remarks of the moving mouth of one character (which is all we see of her) in *Not I*: 'It is the theatrical equivalent to one of Francis Bacon's appalled images: a whole world of anguish squeezed into the tight white circle of a mouth gabbling violently on the fine edge of hysteria, as if to pause would be to expose itself to pressures which would tear it apart' (1974, p.134). The text of Beckett's 35 seconds long *Breath* includes precise reference to timing and to 'strictly synchronised light and breath [sounds]'. In his longer plays Beckett makes full use of varied duration, timing changes, accent patterns, interruption and the protracted delays for which he is famous. He exhibits total awareness of the way use of rhythm can help produce mood changes, as from farce to pathos. The text of *Not I* is interspersed with dots to indicate duration of pauses or stillness. Michael Davie reported that Beckett told actor Billie Whitelaw during a rehearsal that she had paused for two dots instead of three (Davie 1976). Stressing the importance of timing in Beckett's plays Ms. Whitelaw, speaking of her rehearsal work for *Rock-a-bye* stated: 'I'm beating time the whole time. Also, even if at first the script is not fully understood I know that if I get the rhythm and music of it right it works' (Whitelaw 1982). Thus, particular use of rhythm may characterise the work of a writer: 'every writer has his own rhythm, as distinctive as his handwriting' (Frye 1957, p.268).[4]

Thinking chiefly about text, philosopher Susanne Langer recognised the central significance of rhythm in drama: 'Rhythm is the commanding form of the play ... it is precisely the rhythm of dramatic action that makes drama a "poetry of the theatre" and not an imitation (in the usual, not the Aristotelian sense) or make-believe of practical life' (1953, pp.355–356). Contrasts in rhythm bring a play to life. For instance in Shakespeare's *Twelfth Night* some contrasts stem from: Orsino's dreamy gloom, Viola's bright presence, and Sir Toby's mocking, rumbustious challenge to the established order – represented by the sober restraint of Malvolio at his first appearance. And as Russian director Vakhtangov stated: 'To perceive the rhythm of a drama is to find the key to its presentation' (1947, pp.121–122).[5]

It is a commonly held view that rhythm is the basis of dance, and in west European theatre performance it is certainly in dance that the most conscious, intentional, planned and detailed use of bodily rhythm may be found. Choreographer Agnes de Mille comments:

> The true [dance] artist will develop a sense of rhythm complex and subtle, not just the mechanical reflex to a downbeat, but a sense of shape and dynamism in musical phrase and dynamism in gesture, and an inner pulse that lies beneath all these and that is the true life beat. The last is essential; without it all the rest is useless. The artist deliberately plays on all these dynamics, swinging between

4   See George (1980) on aspects of rhythm in scripted drama.
5   Exaggerated rhythmicised movement in drama is sometimes seen in expressionist-style productions, in experimental work, or may be used for comic effect – as we have seen in examples of Dennis Potter's plays for television when apparently serious business men are moved to burst into a song and dance routine.

them, on-beat, off-beat, between-beat, delaying, dragging, precipitating, syncopating. (1962, p.82)

In dance, rhythm is usually heightened and exerts power as a motivating force which generates action and form. The rhythm of any musical accompaniment may well be an influential or determining factor. An obvious example of this is in classical ballet, for instance in the choreography designed for traditional versions of *Swan Lake*, with music by Tchaikovsky.

Rhythm has an energising, infectious quality in dance, for spectators as well as for performers. 'It's not the difficulty of a dance that makes the audience happy, it's rhythm' says American dance critic Edward Denby (1960, p.22). This has been exemplified in the work of many artists – the arresting, contrasting work of

Figure 2.9 'Rhythm has an energising, infectious quality in dance': Lynn Seymour in Ashton's Four Brahms Waltzes *in the manner of Isadora Duncan. The dancer is in firm contact with the earth, Isadora-style, while retaining forward impetus and a sense of upward aspiration. A feeling of flinging exuberance and full use of personal space is temporarily restrained as her arms enfold – energy in the hands – ready to open wide to the sky. The dancer's hair swings back in rhythmic abandon while the mood and sense of rhythmic flow is fully expressed in her face.*
Source: Douglas Jeffery

American choreographers Paul Taylor and Trisha Brown springs to mind, and is now an element in the popularity of contemporary American choreographer Mark Morris. Known for his choice of music (from Purcell, Vivaldi and Handel to Brahms and Lou Harrison) he not only responds to the inspiring rhythms of the music, but also brings out a full rhythmic range in the movement of his dancers. For instance, in *L'Allegro, il Penseroso ed il Moderato*, their steps and gestures seem to spring out of the music as the spatial rhythms of interweaving groups and lines joyously fill the densely populated stage with deceptive ease, or create patterns of 'divinest melancholy'. Perhaps influenced by early experience of performing in a Balkan folk ensemble, Morris adapts folk dance step patterns in his choreography and with dancers' individuality strongly present, a sense of community rhythm is generated. This elicits an empathetic response in the audience as the rhythm is shared and enjoyed by all. Through rhythm, energy is channelled and shaped to create dance presence: 'The actor or dancer is she who knows how to carve time concretely: she carves time in rhythm, dilating or contracting her actions' (Barba and Savarese 1991, p.211). In performance, perhaps as in sport, the rhythmic flow of action takes over, and a state of being out of everyday or clock time may

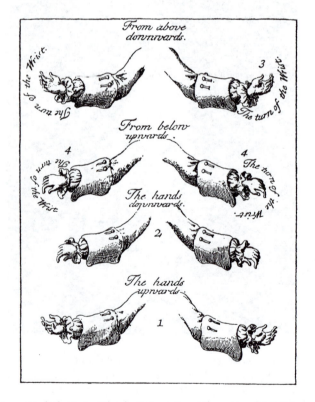

Figure 2.10 Movement-rhythm in period style: timing action at the wrists – 'First Representation of the Arms showing the Movement of the Wrists' – Dancing Master Pierre Rameau's guidance for the minuet dancer.

Source: *From* The Dancing Master *(1725)*

be achieved. (Also see further reference to flow and sense of 'timelessness' in the next chapter.)

As mentioned in the last chapter, the use of time and rhythm contribute to what I referred to as a distinctive signature or style in performance work. In dance this may be evident to a greater or lesser extent in a choreographer's work, in the individuality of a dancer's performance, or in a specific dance style or technique. For instance, a number of western contemporary dance techniques can be distinguished by their contrasting uses of rhythm and timing: for example, the use of muscular 'contract-release' rhythm in Graham-based work, or the distinctive use of breath rhythm in Humphrey-based work (further described in Chapter 5). Again as suggested in the last chapter, rhythm may reaffirm cultural style in national performance usage, and it can indicate social or historical milieu. We see this readily displayed in the 'folk' or 'historical' dances of any nation.

In ceremony, time elements, rhythm and timing are particularly significant components of the whole event. They obviously determine what has been referred to as its macro-structure in time. This includes duration of the event and of its various phases, order and pattern of the phases. We can turn to anthropologists in order to gain some insight into the use of rhythm and time

Figure 2.11 A ceremonial Chinese procession in Canton, c.1900.
Source: Courtesy of Victoria and Albert Museum

elements in ceremony. For instance, Chapple and Coon were known in the early 1940s for their suggestion that ceremonial events are structured by natural and biological rhythms. Others, such as Reyman, followed up this work several decades later. In his observation of south-western Pueblo ceremonies, Reyman noted a relation between the time elements of duration, repetition and tempo. For instance, one repetitive performance he saw increased and decreased in tempo until the last two rounds when it became noticeably more upbeat and intense (1978, p.83). Leach identified 'slow, measured behaviour' with the important first stage in a ritual, a formality which goes with 'sacred time', further discussed in the next chapter (1961, p.136).

Use of timing is seen clearly in Britain, on formal secular ceremonial occasions, particularly those which involve royalty or political leaders. For instance, the rate of the Queen's progress along a line of presentees is carefully controlled, and surely both sacred and secular ceremony depends fundamentally upon temporal elements. Some further examples: Gell has demonstrated the significance of duration in ceremony in his study of the Umeda (New Guinea) annual cycle (1992). Verger in his study of trance states in Yoruba (Africa) Orisha writes 'The musical speed of the rhythms are appeals and praises to the God but have also ... a powerful and at times almost irresistible effect on the mind and spirit of initiated worshippers' (1963, p.14).

Hughes, writing of the nature of rhythm in healing ceremonies, states it is not regarded as a purely auxiliary element 'but one essential to the ceremony, one which could not be dispensed with'. Furthermore, he found that tempo was a particularly significant factor (1948, pp.118, 173). A Macumba priestess in Brazil comments that rhythm and timing is even more important than the meaning of the words in religious ceremonies: 'Our gods respond to rhythm above all else. When the rhythm changes, their behaviour shifts accordingly' (quoted in Branley 1977, p.47).

In some cultures, certain rhythms may be associated with particular deities, as Charles Gore observed in Ogun deity shrine rituals of Benin City, Nigeria. For instance, at an initiation into Ogun 'two initiates were instructed to dance to the rhythms of the deity at the beginning and end of every day ... in order, in the words of the Ohen [priest] "to catch the steps"'. The purpose here was to provide practice in the ritual conventions of the possession dance which create 'a special relationship with the deity'. Oguname (water) was represented by 'fluid and slow movement', Oguneron (fire) by 'heated and more erratic movements'. Gore explains further that the Ohen's ability to perform is of fundamental importance: 'It is during the Ohen's performance of the dances that the deity assets itself and this is assessed by the onlookers. They will evaluate these skills critically' (1998, pp.76–77).

Figure 2.12 A Shakers' service, out of doors, c.1845. From an illustration of the time in Lossing (1848). Artist unknown.

The use of time elements has long been recognised as significant in religious practices, in some of the more outwardly expressive Christian church services, and in various forms of meditation, both eastern and western. In Jewish Hasidic worship, movement rhythm is used to induce concentration and greater devotion: 'They insist that bodily movement and gesticulation during prayer arouses one's emotions and maintains one's state of concentration throughout the period of worship' (Riddle 1907, pp.218–219).

Many examples could be added. Instead, here is one extended example which provides a striking instance of movement and dance rhythm and timing within ceremony – essential features in the meetings of the 'United Society of Believers in Christ's Second Appearing', a Christian millennial movement, better known as 'the Shakers'.[6] The patterns and gestures of the dances which the Shakers

6   The sect was founded in the eighteenth century in Manchester, England, then emigrated to New England from whence the movement expanded to the American West. It declined in popularity after the mid-nineteenth century, but a very small community related to the sect still exists in the USA. It was a religious movement which incorporated a new, rigorous way of life and, as Andrews, the foremost authority on the subject, states, it represented 'a form of protest against the world's wrongs and a search for a more perfect form of social organisation' (1963, p.v). The Shakers are now especially renowned for their fine design and craftmanship seen in furniture and other household items.

performed during their meetings developed from their religious ideas, and as symbolic representation of their beliefs.

Observers' descriptions of meetings bear witness to the fact that rhythm and timing were key features. As David Benedict (1824) recounts, there was effective build-up of tempo and use of rapid steps to express and generate fervour 'as if overwhelmed with ecstasy and joy.' For instance, in a meeting which Benedict attended, about 50 men and women 'moved with a quick step around the hall'. This 'figure' or pattern of movement represented 'marching the heavenly road'. In one of their dance-songs we find reference to the joyous 'flow' of their sense of union:

> We love to dance, we love to sing,
> We love to taste the living spring,
> We love to feel our union flow,
> While round, and round, and round we go! (*Millennial Praises* 1813)

Recurrent features of rhythm included: use of repetition; unison, synchronised movement such as occurred in stepping to the beat; jumping and turning; the vibratory, shaking action which gave the Shakers their name; and movements reminiscent of the whirling dancing Dervishes. Individual patterns of rhythm also featured in the meetings, as well as the use of metric patterns and a shared pulse which would have usually been taken from the beat of any accompanying songs.

William Plumer observed repetitive jumping up and down 'about four inches' off the ground and he gives us an example of whirling – two women whirling 'for the space of fifteen minutes ... nearly as fast as the rim of a spinning wheel in quick motion'. He continues with one of many descriptions of the characteristic shaking movement which in this case occurred after an 'impressive' talk by an elder: 'The motion proceeded from the head to the hands, and the whole body, with such power as if limb would rend from limb. The house trembled as if there were an earthquake' (1782, pp.305–306).

Unison action would have matched the particular rhythmic pattern of the songs and there were times when the 'spirit seized all members' together (Haskett 1828, pp.189-191). But it is interesting to note that individuality was also stressed. 'In the best part of their worship every one acts for himself and almost every one different from the other' (Rathbun 1782, pp.7–8). All the movement – whether unison or individual – with personal patterns of rhythm – was performed 'as the spirit moved'. This, which apparently brought about an amazing degree of rhythmic variety, especially in the early days of the movement, is clear in an extract from *The Testimony of Christ's Second Coming* (1810, p.xxv). After sitting quietly in silent meditation, members would be taken 'with a mighty trembling, under which they would express the indignation of God against all sin...singing and shouting...and walking the floor, under the influence of spiritual signs, shoving each other about – or swiftly passing and repassing each other, like clouds agitated by a mighty wind' (quoted in Andrews 1963, p.6). That there could be a wide variety of individual movement rhythm in Shaker meetings is evident from the Rathbun's account. While some people were singing, speaking or making other sounds,

> others will be drumming on the floor with their feet, as though a pair of drum-sticks were beating a ruff on a drum-head; others will be agonizing, as though in great pain; others will be jumping up and down; others fluttering over somebody and talking to them; others will be shooing and hissing evil spirits out of the house, till the different tunes, groaning, jumping, dancing, drumming, laughing, talking and fluttering, shooing and hissing, makes a perfect bedlam; this they call the worship of God. (1782, p.12)

Phases of movement such as this in meetings were not brief interludes – lasting 'about an hour' according to Plumer (1782).

The inclusion of both the metricity of 'measured dance' and free movement rhythm in the meetings is interesting: 'At length, what was a measured dance becomes a wild, discordant frenzy…whirling round and round' (Greeley 1838). One may conjecture that this would have contributed to the enjoyment and power of the proceedings, and invigorated participants, enabling them to extend their meetings for a considerable time.

Celebration of their life together was evident in the Shakers' gatherings, during which periods of dance were often followed by what we might call 'group hugs'. As Plumer writes, this was a time when, with men and women in separate groups (given their beliefs about the need for separation of the sexes), they 'embraced and saluted each other'. An example of an accumulative group rhythm, this built into two, three and four people coming together 'until a dozen men were in that position, embracing and saluting' (1782, pp.305–306).

The form of the Shakers' meetings varied over time and the movement apparently became more organised as it progressed. For instance, as a later development Andrews provides references to 'straight rows' of dancers and to a 'square order shuffle' which was again increased to performance in 'the skipping manner'. Ring dances were inaugurated around 1822 and patterned marching processions took place and were enjoyed both indoors and outside through the countryside (Andrews 1963, pp.141, 142). Andrews describes one ring dance in particular which was performed in concentric circles. These circles symbolised the various manifestations of Christ's teaching through time – from the inner circle which represented Christ's own era, progressing through to the outermost circle which represented the millennial movement – the true message of the spirit and manifestation of the prophetic word of God – embodied in the Shakers themselves.[7]

In this chapter various relatively isolated examples have been included to illustrate a series of ideas about rhythm and timing, ranging from the discussion of metricity, flow and timing to other suggestions concerning rhythm in drama, dance and ceremony. However, my final example from the Shakers draws attention to a full context for movement rhythm and timing. Elements of movement do not exist in isolation, and although I am encouraging some dissection of performance in this book, rhythm and timing elements are best considered in the context of a whole, set within performance frame and conventions – which is the subject of the next chapter.

---

[7]   Indeed, in all the movement they performed, the Shakers believed they were led by the power of the spirit of God, and that movement was a totally acceptable form of worship. In later years, perhaps as a response to criticism, they made references to precedents for this in the Bible (Andrews 1963, p.140). They believed that dance was a God-given gift both to dancers and to the church and that 'the faculty of dancing, as well as that of singing, was undoubtedly created for the honor and glory of the Creator' (Wells and Green 1823, pp.84–85).

3

*Time Elements
and Performance Conventions*

A public celebration is a rope bridge of knotted symbols strung across an abyss. We make our crossings hoping the chasm will echo our festive sounds for a moment, as the bridge begins to sway from the rhythms of our dance. (Grimes 1982, p.282)

A calendar expresses the rhythm of the collective activities, while at the same time its function is to ensure their regularity. (Durkheim 1915, p.10)

One striking aspect of performance is its polyrhythmic nature. That is, in a performance event we can distinguish different time patterns occurring both sequentially and simultaneously, and inter-relating in various ways. These time patterns, which contribute to the overall rhythm of the event, include not only patterns of the performance or ceremony itself, but also the patterns of preparation, backstage activity, audience or congregation arrival and departure. Included too is any post-performance activity such as time taken by the director to give company notes, stage crew striking the set – or altar boy snuffing out the candles.

The polyrhythmic structure and time boundaries of performance are influenced by performance conventions. Mutually understood by performers and audience in any given context, these conventions become established over time and are peculiar to a particular culture or society. Whether we are thinking of the Sudanese Nuer, whose 'daily timepiece is the cattle clock, the round of pastoral tasks' (Evans-Pritchard 1940, p.101) or the city business executive with a 9 to 5 job, performance conventions are to some extent influenced by everyday life and affected by customary patterns of work and leisure.

Thus from the comforting recurrence of English village church festivals to large-scale annual ceremonies in all parts of the world, performance time is set within the larger time-frame of the life of the people concerned. It also relates to perception and sense of time; how we think of the processes that occur in time;

how we perceive our lives in terms of seasons or rituals and celebrations; how we decide when events should occur. In the west, we are encouraged from childhood to remember birthdays, and, as Canetti points out, there seems to be 'an irresistible attraction in the idea of linking one's name with a regularly recurring date'. He goes on to write of time's significance in the life of people and rulers, essential in any form of political organisation, fundamental in the order:

> The regulation of time is the primary attribute of all government...The prestige of the Chinese legendary rulers derives in great part from the effective regulation of time which is ascribed to them ... Kings embodied the whole period of their reign ... They were time. (1962, pp.397–399)

Rhythm is the essence of time, in the sense that intervals of time define the sequence of events. 'Time is a relation between events, with respect to which they are distinguished as simultaneous or successive, and as becoming, enduring or passing away, as changing or permanent' (Munro 1970, p.106).

In order to consider some aspects of time in relation to performance events and the performance time-frame, let us imagine we have arrived in a country hitherto unknown to us. Our intention is to attend a performance event. How may some knowledge of time elements in relation to performance frame conventions aid us?

Figure 3.1 Time imagined as a double-headed serpent: ancient Mexican symbol of time. Other visual representations of time or life's journey are found elsewhere, such as in the form of a tree, spiral or labyrinth.
Source: Liane Payne

Figure 3.2 A view of time and the cosmos – the rhythm of the turning heavenly spheres, planets: Atlas holding up the world.
Source: German woodcut (1559).

Time: sacred/profane, subjective sense/objective measurement, performance/everyday

It would be useful to know what the nature of the event is likely to be. Should we prepare for a solemn occasion or are we to expect a casual, everyday atmosphere? Anthropologists make a useful distinction between different experiences of time as 'sacred' or 'profane' which might help here. If the event we are hoping to attend is a ceremony or ritual, perhaps it will involve us in experience of 'sacred' time.

'Profane' everyday time is perceived as going forward, and sacred, 'mythic' or ritual time which may relate to a society's mythic past, is perceived as going back. This time is recovered and re-lived during rituals and festivals. In initiation rituals, young boys may re-enact birth in the form of entry into manhood, during which they gain knowledge about the origins of their society. Throughout this ritual process they will be shut away from profane, everyday time (Leach 1961). 'Sacred' time implies more than the ritual content or theme of the event; it describes an experience of time which is qualitatively different from that of daily life, and may relate beyond the everyday world to the whole cosmos. Among the Algonquin and Sioux American Indians, for example, a link between seasonal rituals and the cosmos is evident in the structure of their sacred lodges. As Eliade comments, these represent the universe – symbolising the year as a journey round the world, through the four cardinal directions as signified by the four doors and windows (1959, pp.73–74).

Knowledge of the distinction between 'sacred' and 'profane' time may even determine something as mundane as what to wear when we attend an event. For instance, when I attended the Yaqui Easter ceremonies (described in Chapter 10) I found I was experiencing for the most part 'sacred' time and learnt to make an appropriate choice of clothing in relation to the ceremonies of the day. On the Good Friday not only was bright coloured clothing to be avoided, but also the wearing of jewellery or a hat during the Stations of the Cross procession, when traditionally the Yaqui women are bare-headed and wear their long hair unbraided. For the 'Gloria' celebrations on the next day, it was recommended that best clothes and bright colours be worn, but I considered the day was still partially in 'sacred' time. I felt we moved into 'profane' time when evil had been ritually defeated and the performers had re-joined their families after their arduous days of ceremonies.

Thus there may be movement between both 'sacred' and 'profane' time during one event. Indeed, in relation to performance in general, it is useful to think in terms of these two senses of time as on a continuum. Even some theatre work or parts of a performance may be experienced as being towards the more 'sacred' end, others as closer to 'profane' or everyday time. Although, as I have indicated, performance time conventions in general may be influenced by everyday life, they serve fundamentally to set the even apart from it. Perhaps this is seen at its most extreme in a solemn ceremony, hence the saying 'to stand on ceremony' which essentially means to keep one's distance and to avoid the ease, familiarity and timing of everyday behaviour.

Furthermore, if we have identified the 'time nature' of the event we are proposing to attend as primarily 'sacred', we may need to be prepared further for what philosophers call a metaphysical time experience, an experience of 'timelessness'. This is clearly described by theologians and also with reference to traditions of meditation practice in which mundane, ordinary awareness and sense of time are transcended.[1] As Capra explains, mystics tell of experiencing 'an infinite, timeless and yet dynamic present' (1991, p.197). Or, as Hui-neng states

---

1   For instance, in the practice of Indian Yoga, through *pranayama* – the rhythmicisation of breathing and gradual slowing down of the respiratory system – 'there is no adept … who, during these exercises, has not experienced quite another quality of time' (Eliade 1991, p.86). Also, Indian myths and philosophy refer to the rhythms of 'Cosmic Great Time' (see Eliade 1991, pp.57–91; Aurobindo 1948).

'The absolute tranquillity is the present moment. Though it is at this moment there is no limit to this moment, and herein is eternal delight' (Hui-neng quoted in Watts 1957, p.220). These two senses of time may exist simultaneously. Anthropologist Drid Williams writes of the Carmelite nuns' experience: 'It is as if the Carmelite has two "maps": one which locates her in ordinary space–time, and another consisting of an "interior territory" of a spiritual and psychological nature in which she is located at the same time' (1975, p.113). As a continuing reminder of spiritual life-time, prayers are customarily said at precise intervals through the day and night in places of religion worldwide, from the Christian monastery to the Islamic mosque.

A sense of timelessness or endless flow of time may also be experienced during memorable theatre performances, and encountered in what is sometimes referred to as the psychological experience of time in therapeutic contexts. For example, therapist Maggie Scarf writes of a psychological sensation of time when she describes how one of her patients spoke of a 'molasses-like feeling of being stuck in endless time' (Scarf 1980, p.347). 'Time travels in divers paces with divers persons' says Rosalind in Shakespeare's *As You Like It* (Act III, sc. 2) and, in contrast to the last example, a common estimation of time in emergency experiences is that it speeds up, as in 'my whole life flashed before my eyes'. For the young, time can seem endless, but as we grow older, or when we concentrate on a job which interests us, time seems 'all too short'. 'The time just flew – I don't know where the time went!' Philip Larkin expressed an experience of an impressive, brief event seeming longer than its actual duration in his poem *The March Past*:

The march interrupted the light afternoon
… And all was focused, larger than we reckoned,
Into a consequence of thirty seconds.

This illusory, subjective sense of time – how time 'feels' to us – is distinguished by philosophers from the 'objective' measured clock-time of engineers.

A further distinction may be made between the experience of time in the theatre and in daily life. As anthropologist Turner asserts, 'no one could fail to recognise … when "dramatic time" has replaced routinised social living' (1982, p.9). Though criticised for some aspects of her dance theory (see Alter (1987), Bartenieff *et al.* (1970), Cohen (1982)), philosopher Susanne Langer's description of the experience of time during performance events which she considered (from the spectator's viewpoint) is useful here. She first developed this concept in relation to music and applied it to dance:

The realm in which tonal entities move is a realm of pure *duration*. Like its elements, however, this duration is not an actual phenomenon. It is not a period – ten minutes or a half hour, some fraction of a day – but is something radically different from the time in which our public and practical life proceeds ... an altogether different structure from practical or scientific time. (1953, p.109)

Turner has referred to physical biological changes which occur when we inhabit performance time. The state which deep absorption in the performance of ritual can generate in us has been deemed 'ergotropic' and identified by neurobiologists as exhibiting 'arousal, heightened activity and emotional response ... [with] increased heart rate, blood pressure, sweat secretion, pupillary dilation and the inhibition of gastrointestinal motor and secretary function' (Lex 1979, p.136).

Performance planning, timings, calendars

To return to our imagined trip and intention to see a performance: coming from a culture in which precise dates, diaries and set appointment times are the order of the day, we will want to know when the event is due to begin. 'We will start when we are ready, when the time is right.' This is one answer which may be given in some places. It is interesting to note here that the ancient Greeks had two gods of time, *Chronos* – the god of absolute, eternal time (hence our words such as 'chronometer') and *Kairos* – the god of favourable time – the 'right' time. The starting time of the performance we are hoping to attend may be determined by when a clock strikes the hour, or when the sun rises, or when everything is in place and 'it feels right'. It may be a time dictated by *Chronos*, or as indicated by *Kairos*. Some peoples determine starting times and even the days of performance events with more of our kind of mechanical-clock dominated precision than others. Chapter 2 included reference to the way in which clocks have ruled us from church towers and town squares for centuries, but, as Brother David Steindl-Rast poetically remarks:

> Time was not always
> Ticking. Time was not
> Discovered, but invented
> To hobble the timeless dance.[2]

We might think that an obvious place to find out at least on which day a performance is due to take place would be some form of local calendar. Through their study of calendrical systems anthropologists can help us to advance our understanding of how time elements affect or determine the framing of performance cross-culturally. They have indicated how these systems both derive from society and dictate to society.

To put these ideas in performance-event context, the traditional Hopi calendrical system provides an example. When I visited the Hopi, I learnt that

---

2   From a poem published in *Tui Shou*, Living Tao Foundation, Issue 2 February 1997.

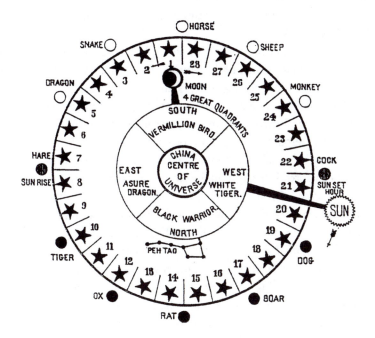

Figure 3.3 An ancient oriental calendar-clock. Three hands travel round the dial to represent the movement of sun, moon and seasons (indicated by Ursa Major or Peh Tao).

their year is structured in two halves, separated by the solstices and by the residence of the *Kachinas* – the masked spirit figures. The traditional Hopi belief is that these live with them for one half of the year and for the other half they return to their mountain home. Ceremonies and dates are scheduled to match. Hall also remarked on this characteristic when he lived with the Hopi. For instance, one day he asked when an event had taken place. Perhaps in the manner we use our Christmas period he was told 'it was just before *Wowochim*' (Hall 1983, p.38). He eventually discovered that meant it occurred in November.

Thus a local calendar may not provide us with a clear, straightforward answer. Some calendrical systems seem immensely complicated to those of us who are outside the system. Most combine several dating systems in one, such as civil and religious dates, and days favoured for certain activities, all with an interlocking pattern of performance events to match. Gell describes the Buddhist Thai calendrical schemes which indicate favourable and unfavourable days for personal and group activity. These are based on the four-phase lunar cycle, the planetary seven-day week, a cycle of twelve animals which applies to years and days, as well as esoteric cycles which are to do with times for feeding spirits, and 'the orientation of a giant subterranean dragon which turns on its axis as the year proceeds' (1992, p.76).

Let us imagine that our proposed visit takes place in Central India, in order to attend some of the village rituals of the Muria Gands. If so, we would discover that in addition to several other dating systems, they have a calendar of ritual events which is different for each village. This is so that gods of village clans and their devotees can travel and participate in each ceremony in turn (Gell 1992, p.89).

Timing of a ceremony may be pre-ordained on a regular basis (perhaps seasonally), it may be socially determined, or decided by other means. A series of related events can spread throughout a year. For instance, during the time Hugh Richardson witnessed the annual ceremonies in Lhasa, the capital of Tibet, the whole year was the performance time-frame for the annual series of events. There were just about 60 days devoted to both secular and Buddhist ceremonies during the year.[3] If our imagined visit is to a traditional group of Maring in New Guinea, we would have to wait until the pigs and crops have grown before we could experience the most exciting ceremony of the year (see Chapter 11).

The British climate affects or determines the timing of seasonal events, and this is the case elsewhere too. Jonathan Reyman, in his study of annual and circadian rhythms in south western Pueblo ceremonies, discovered that shifts in the use of the plaza depended on the time of year, corresponding to the earth's passage round the sun. Predictably, the greatest ceremonial efforts and community involvement were at the crucial agricultural times of seed preparation and germination – when rain was needed.

Sunrise, sunset and the lunar calendar determine the timing of ceremonies in many places. The Wahgi of Papua New Guinea calculate their calendar 'from shifts in the point at which the sun rises and relate these to wetter and drier times, and to such processes as the swelling and ripening of pandanus nuts and fruit' (O'Hanlon 1993, p.14). These items are important in the Wahgi system of gift exchange which (with associated ceremonies) is a central feature of their life. We need to look no further than an English parish church for an example of the influence of the moon on the timing of ceremonies; the Christian Easter date is governed by the moon:

EASTER-DAY (on which the rest depend) is always the *First Sunday* after the Full Moon which happens upon, or next after the *Twenty-First Day of March*; and if the Full Moon happens upon a *Sunday*, *Easter-Day* is the Sunday after. (*The Book of Common Prayer* of the Church of England)

3   Richardson lived in Lhasa before the Chinese communists took over in 1959, and his observations refer to this period.

The traditional Chinese calendar is based on the cycles of both sun and moon and also takes the movement of stars as well as other categories into account, all thought to influence human existence. For instance, of the many festivals determined by the calendar, the Chinese New Year with its traditional ceremonies and celebrations occurs at the time of the full moon on the 15th day of their first (lunar) month (usually some time in February in the western calendar). When Richardson observed the annual ceremonies in Lhasa, Tibet, he noted the influence of the positions of the sun and phases of the moon on timing: 'Every important event took place in the first half of a lunar month, and in the morning, while the sun was in the ascendant' (1993, p.11).

One of the most exciting beginnings of a performance event I have witnessed was in the early morning of 6 January, 1993, in Jemez Pueblo, New Mexico. I was one of a handful of people, mostly local, who had gathered to witness the start of the ceremonies. We were standing around on the edge of the village, wrapped in striped blankets against the cold. It was a day in celebration of *Les Trois Reyes* – the three kings – a blend of native Indian and Christian tradition. A group of several men, playing drums as they came, assembled nearby. We were all facing east, away from the Pueblo, towards the glow in the sky – waiting for the sunrise. The drumming continued. The day dawned – this was the cue. Thick smoke from a preliminary ritual fire appeared on a distant high ridge. With a growing sense of wonder and excitement, I began to see an outline of masked figures moving on the skyline, intermittently visible through the smoke. I could distinguish the strong outline of a buffalo head-dress, and later those of deer, ram and antelope. Sometimes out of sight, these figures made their way down the hillside and eventually arrived where we were standing, then continued with the drummers into the centre of the Pueblo. The ceremonies had begun.

Duration, punctuation, tempi and attitudes to use of time

As the previous comments demonstrate, starting time, duration of the event, ending time, tempo and the degree of precision of any of these in any culture are determined by local or cultural convention. In her study of rhythm in dramatic text Burns states: 'The audience knows that the play is going to last two or three hours, or in the Japanese or Indian theatre many more. Within these confines the dramatist has first to project the time-rules that will govern the events and make them coherent' (1972, p.94). Tolerance or acceptance of duration varies culturally and socially. For example, Indian audiences are happy with performances that last all night; just as young people in the west throng rave events throughout a night.

Punctuation of the event is one feature of timing to notice, especially significant structurally when the performance is long. Schechner emphasises the structural importance of this in describing a trance dance he witnessed in a Sri Lankan village, the 30-hour-long *Thovil* ceremony: 'What holds the *Thovil* together is a series of punctuations – ritual chants, further decoration of the performance oval, expected dances and farces – that keep up the people's interest' (1977, p.48). Comprehension of a prolonged time sequence can be difficult if one is not of the culture concerned. For instance an Indian *tala* – rhythmic sequence – can be 108 beats long, but an Indian dancer (or musician) would be aware where *sam* – the first beat of the sequence – falls.

The timing of beginnings and endings of events is treated differently in various performance contexts and places. Before the dramatic 'swish!' of the theatre curtains opening, all theatre-goers share that anticipatory pleasure as they gaze towards it – perhaps wondering what is going on behind it. McPhee described the delayed entrance between the curtains which was typical of performances he attended in Bali:

> If there are curtains, the only hint of the actor behind them is his voice, or the twitching folds gathered in his hands which move in time to the music. This is the dance of the curtains, a prologue to a prologue, for when the curtains finally part, the dancer remains framed in the entrance, to continue the preliminary dance that delineates his character … These entrance dances, perhaps the most beautiful of all in their delay and abstract elegance, take a long time to perform. (1948, p.188)

Cultural custom and context largely determine duration and tempo of performance. Again in Bali, Schechner writes of how the 'power' of a trance dance affects the structure of the event: 'How long the theatrical gestures will be performed; how many repetitions of cycles of movement; what permutations or new combinations occur – these things are unknown, and depend on the "power" of the trance' (1977, p.43). If a long duration or slow tempo is an unfamiliar performance mode, perception and enjoyment of the whole can be lost. As an audience member, expectation of rhythm is naturally affected by the customs of one's own culture. This is particularly evident in an individual's response to tempo. For example a western visitor comments that he overcame his usual, native-based expectations of a play's tempo when watching Japanese Noh drama, which he found very slow at first –

> It is so slow that you almost push forward. You want to make it faster. Your muscles push to get the actors going. Instead as it goes on they become even slower, and by the very fact that it becomes slower and slower, before you know it you are completely caught up; whereas if it goes in the way you first wanted it to go, you would remain on the outside as an onlooker. (quoted in Strasberg 1965, pp.244–245)

Wolz describes how in Japanese Bugaku style also, the prevalence of slow tempi provides an alien experience for a western audience: 'Though there are different tempi in Bugaku, even the fastest would be considered adagio by Western standards … movements are extended in time to give the viewer an opportunity to

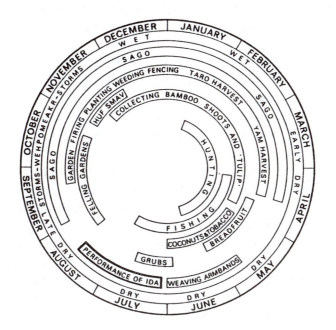

Figure 3.4 The annual cycle of the Umeda, Papua New Guinea. The temporal focus of the year: the performance of the ida ritual July–August, with the appearance of a series of masked and painted dancers, aimed at increasing the supply of sago, with regeneration of the human population as the underlying theme (see Gell 1992, pp.37–49).
Source: Alfred Gell

enjoy every subtle gesture. Economy of means and leisurely contemplation are important aspects of all Japanese art' (1971, pp.32–33).

Tolerance, expectation or acceptance of the length of a performance has been found to vary cross-culturally. Peter Brook has spoken of variation in the attention span of an audience which he experienced while presenting The Mahabharata. He compared the relatively short attention span tolerance in Los Angeles with Tokyo where the audiences 'didn't move' for the nine hours of the show (Delgado and Heritage (eds) 1996, p.51). Tolerance also varies from past to present. Kenneth Branagh's four-hour film Hamlet was threatened by cuts which distributors demanded 'to satisfy the shrinking attention span of modern audiences' (Richard Brooks, The Observer, 13 October 1996).

Moreover, people's attitudes to everyday time varies, both individually and cross-culturally. Edward Hall wrote of his early confusing experience with contrasting attitudes to time which he encountered simultaneously in Arizona: from Hopi native Americans, and from Navajo native Americans, from 'white' men, tourists from eastern USA, office people operating within bureaucratic and banking times, as well as the overall USA time system. He considered 'the culture gap today is as broad and deep as it ever was' (1983, p.29). In his writing, Hall demonstrates the unique character of patterns and perception in a culture's time frame.

If time is considered to be a scant resource, it affects the way lives are lived and events planned. The central Indian Muria have this concept of time which is derived from their agricultural way of life, based on the process of rice growth in different seasons. They have a phrase *pabe mayor* – 'I have not got time.' The Umeda of New Guinea, who have no sharply differentiated seasons and subsist on the year-round agricultural production of sago, have no such attitude or expression in their language (Gell 1992, p.88). Attitudes such as these can affect performance events. In a typical West European or North American city where the 'short of time' syndrome prevails, it is rare to find theatre performances that last longer than two and a half hours. In London recently I heard people remark that they 'hadn't got the time' to attend a day-long performance of a linked series of plays by Robert Lepage. The writer Norman Lebrecht, commenting on this tendency, observes how, in the USA an advertisement for a Mozart CD *For the Morning Commute* asks: '"Want music that speeds you on your way? Let Mozart make your day! Mozart … is the ideal composer for the 20th century commuter. He was always in a hurry to finish the many commissions that came his way"' (How Dumb Can You Get?, *The Daily Telegraph*, 26 February 1997).

Hall suggests that our attitudes to time can also relate to whether or not we prefer to do more than one thing at once. He observed that in Northern Europe we tend to prefer to do one thing at a time, a 'monochronic' mode, whereas in the Mediterranean region people are happy with a 'polychronic' mode – several things going on at once. In the latter context, appointments are frequently broken, there is no sense of being 'on time', and interaction characteristically occurs with several people at once (Hall 1983, pp.45–46).

How may this relate to performance context? In earlier centuries, multiple staging ('polychronic mode') was an accepted norm in Europe, but in western theatre today, the convention is for a single focus of attention (true to Hall's characterisation of our preferred attitude as 'monochronic') and a multi-focus presentation can bemuse or even disturb members of the audience. Theatre directors may be criticised for 'split focus' (when more than one thing is happening simultaneously on stage), although of course considered acceptable in crowd scenes or in more experimental theatre productions. However, Zimmermann's radical 1965 opera *Die Soldaten* attracted some adverse criticism for this characteristic. Opera critic David Blewitt reported the 'shattering impact' of the work which, however, greatly impressed him. In his review of the first British performance, Blewitt describes the staging requirements:

Zimmermann wanted to surround the audience with twelve stages, each with its own orchestra and projection screen so that, as in Artaud's Theatre of Cruelty, 'the

Figure 3.5 Time and Fortune: a view of the changing rhythm of life. Astrology and the turning Wheel of Fortune were common themes of medieval Europe – here Mars is in the ascendant, with the Sun and Venus to follow.
Source: German woodcut (c.1490)

spectator, placed in the middle of the action, is engulfed and physically affected by it'. The composer, though compelled to settle for three screens in a traditional theatre, still requires different actions on both stage and screen to play simultaneously. (*The Stage*, 19 December 1996)

There is generally a single focus of attention at any one time during a ritual. In the context of ceremony, a clear example of fully accepted split-focus occurred during the ceremonies in Lhasa, Tibet, to which reference was made earlier. Richardson recounts that on the 30th day of the second month – 'The Golden Procession of the Assembly of Worship' – while four monks marched and performed a series of slow prostrations to the Dalai Lama, other dances were taking place and 'a joker, holding a whip and bucket and leading a cow, prances round the arena teasing the people in reach. The cow is the [legendary] *Döjowé Ba* which produces wish-fulfilling milk. He pretends to milk it into the bucket from which he scatters liquid over the crowd' (1993, p.80).

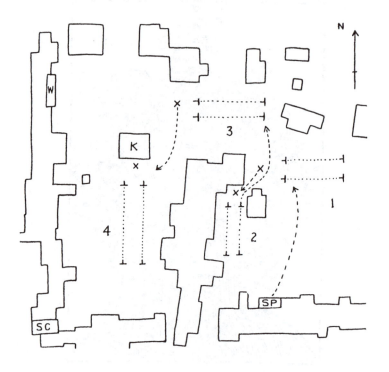

K = ceremonial kiva; W, SC, SP = dance houses of the different moieties in the society;
X = instrumentalists

Figure 3.6 Spatial rhythm of travelling performance: Rio Grande Pueblo Indians' day-long ceremonial dances take place on the plazas between the house blocks. At Santa Clara Pueblo, groups of singers and dancers move between four different plazas, with spectators clustered round each area and on house tops (see Kurath 1986, p.175).
Source: Gertrude Kurath

Sequential order, performance space and adaptations

A mode of sequential ordering can be characteristic of culture or context. For example, traditional British performance is related to a notion of events set out in a linear, logical fashion through time (in accordance with 'monochronic mode'), with an expected beginning and ending, and development of intensity at some points to reach a climax. Audiences have in general expected a cause and effect pattern of action with associated increase and decrease of tension and tempo. In this culture in general there is concern with the order in which things happen. The English language is notable for the number of words which imply ordering: before, after, during, then, next, earlier, later than. These link ideas of time, space and action in a particular manner. Although challenged in some contemporary work, Aristotle's 'beginning, middle, end' model for play structure has been the accepted tradition in western Europe. In anthropology, Eliade (1959) has discussed the difference between a cyclic view of time, based on the notion of eternal return, and a linear view based on the notion of an ending. He points out how this relates to ritual performance. A linear view of time may be seen as countable in a series of lengths or as a row of similar and dissimilar units.

A non-lineal expectation and connection between events through time in life as well as in performance arts can be found in other cultures. For example, anyone visiting the Trobriand Islands (Pacific Ocean) with Dorothy Lee, would have discovered that no lineal temporal connection is made between events. As Lee reports: 'Temporality is meaningless. There are no tenses, no linguistic distinction between past or present. There is no arrangement of activities or events into means and ends, no causal or teleological relationships' (1960, p.141). Lee suggests that Trobriand action is in the form of a pattern rather than a line. The *kula* which is the central gift exchange system of the culture is a pattern of gifts.

Features of the architecture of performance space, including the placing of entrances and exits, are key considerations for the director when planning performance timing. A most exciting presentational performance timing challenge for director and actors was a Scottish *Macbeth* mounted all around Inchcolm Island in the Firth of Forth. The performance began on a boat as we crossed to the island with the three witches appearing in our midst from below decks.[4] Other characters from the play soon came into view – tiny figures already in action on the distant shore and cliff-top. This created a rare opportunity to experience a juxtaposition of rhythms near and far in performance. In the context of the Tibetan ceremonies which Richardson describes, the setting was inside, around or even on the roof of the Potala Palace, which is situated at the top of a hill in the middle of a plain. Courtyards as well as the space below this impressive edifice were used. The architecture framed and to some extent determined the timing of the ceremonies (1993, p.9).

Conventions of stage size, shape and presentation affect performance time and rhythm such as the use of three spatial levels (hell, earth, heaven) on travelling cart stages or multiple staging in medieval European drama, or the long entrance pathway which is incorporated in the stage ground plan of traditional Japanese theatre, for example. In England to this day, the timing of the Abbots Bromley Horn Dance is determined not only by the calendar and time of day but also by the village street and lane plan and the time it takes to traverse this.[5] I have witnessed the start of the event in the early morning with a blessing ceremony in

4   Production under the auspices of Richard de Marco, Edinburgh Festival.
5   The Abbots Bromley Horn Dance is associated with Wakes' Sunday, which annually honours the patron saint of a local church, in this case St Nicholas, on the first Sunday after 4 September, with the dance-procession on the following day (see Figure 3.7).

Figure 3.7 Abbots Bromley Horn Dance, Staffordshire: rhythm and timing through the ages. A moment from possibly England's oldest surviving ceremonial dance, 'owned' by the current family of dancers for over 400 years. It takes place once a year on Wakes' Monday in the form of a 20-mile processional tour of the parish from the church, with various stops for dancing and refreshment en route, including farms and Blithfield Hall, ancestral home of the Bagot family. Six dancers (traditionally with Maid Marion, hobby horse, boy with bow and arrow, a fool and two musicians) carry reindeer antlers (weighing 16–25lb a pair). With a country dance-step rhythm, the patterns include the line weaving in and out, circling, in two lines approaching and retreating, and changing places. Performed by men, but women of the family have occasionally substituted when necessary.
Source: Doc Rowe

the village church, where the horns are kept from one year's event to the next. From there, the group of dancers, with some spectators following, travel round the village, dancing and stopping at various locations and houses en route to perform particular dances and to have refreshments. The performance ends at the local pub in the evening.

Classical drama and dance, and local indigenous performance in non-western cultures inevitably follow particular conventions of staging, duration, timing, audience response and behaviour. These affect the overall time structure which usually has to be modified when examples are transferred for performance in other countries or contexts, with variable results.

There was a striking example of the effect of adaptation to a different context which I recall from viewing a TV film documentary.[6] In Ire Ekiti, Nigeria, a Yoruba Ogun festival was transferred in a dramatised version to a western-style performance space and performed by a company of dancers. Inevitably much of its impact was lost. Of course this loss was only partly caused by inter-related differences in the use of space and time elements. The ritual event was exciting and significant in its own social cultural context. The timing had been due to the diviner's edicts, and the annual occurrence of the event was used as a marker for the remembrance and anticipation of other events important in the life and history of the people. Director Peggy Harper's objective was not simply to uproot the ritual and put it on stage but, while expressing her respect for the original, to create a new work which 'had meaning for modern African audiences'. Harper herself later admitted 'I realised we could never reproduce the intensity of the event' (personal communication, 1978).

In relation to our study of time elements, the following features of the stage adaptation can be noted. The audience was seated in parallel rows facing an open-fronted (non-proscenium) stage, with the customary distance between the front row and the stage. Entrances, exits, movement patterns and the rhythmic flow of the procedure all took place on the stage. Hand-clapping applause marked the end of the show, in conspicuous contrast to the use and significance of hand-clapping as rhythmic marker in the festival ritual. Furthermore, a large number of people took part in the original which was enacted over a wide, fairly rough, terrain outside, and which lasted at least 24 hours. Thus, to judge from the evidence on film, the performance raised questions about a number of changes, including the use of time elements in the context of adaptation.[7]

Spectators and conventions of audience behaviour

There are also conventions which relate to audience presence which affect the rhythm and timing of performance. It is easy to visualise how the number of participants affected the rhythm and timing of the original event in that last

6　BBC TV, *The World About Us*, 30 November 1975.
7　The 1990 European tour of dancers from Papua New Guinea provided another example of some of the problems of adaptation away from an indigenous location. It was interesting to see the dance steps, but the full rhythm and timing structure, timeframe, environment and significance were missed. As reported on television from Gunnersbury Park, London, the rhythms and full costume with impressive feather head-dresses seemed an exotic oddity in that environment. The outdated, inaccurate words of the announcer did not help: 'Melpa people's first taste of the West was when they ate missionaries. Performing at Gunnersbury Park they are art on legs. Audiences be warned – hang on to your heads as well as your hats' (Thames TV, *01 for London*, 31 May 1990; O'Hanlon 1993, pp.56–57).

example. During his attendance at the Lhasa ceremonies in Tibet, Richardson estimated that approximately 20,000 people were present for the Great Prayer Ceremony on the fourth day of the first month of the year. Monks from other monasteries travelled to Lhasa to take part. The ceremonies of course followed their own timing, but the size and movements of the crowd may to some extent have been taken into account (1993, p.22). Schieffelin provides a striking example from a ceremony in Papua New Guinea of spectators' response making a vital contribution. He describes how during the *Gisalo* ceremony, the Kaluli people react to the dancers' nostalgic songs about the lands and rivers of their community. 'Members of the audience are moved so deeply they burst into tears and then, becoming enraged, they leap up and burn the dancers on the shoulder blades with the resin torches used to light the performance.' This retaliative behaviour appears to be essential for an enactment to be deemed 'successful' since, without it 'the ceremony falls apart and is abandoned in the middle of the night' (1998, pp.202–3). Furthermore, the dancers actually pay compensation to those spectators who interacted with them in this way.

Visitors need to learn what is considered to be acceptable spectator behaviour in terms of rhythm and timing. In most traditional western ceremonies and in theatre performances, although spectators have a participatory role, they are expected to be still and as silent as possible except at times of acceptable, anticipated reaction or applause.[8] In other cultures audiences may be more lively, participate more fully or even seem to interrupt the action. For example, Chungliang Al Huang vividly describes the audience for traditional Chinese theatre, where spectators are familiar with the plays which have been handed down for centuries:

> In contrast to the solemn atmosphere of most western theater, Chinese theater is fun and casual. Behind every seat in the audience there is a tea cup. Hawkers keep going round to sell you tea and food. Hot towels are passed around to keep you awake. People eat lunch and crack watermelon seeds, while children run around and drape themselves over the edge of the stage. It's more of a living, give-and-take situation. There's no set time for applause. When actors do well, the audience sings along with the actors and gets all excited. When they don't do well, they boo and throw things on the stage ... In Oriental theater there's no such thing as exact, set timing. (1987, pp.104–105)

Clifford Geertz witnessed performances in Bali, which 'go on often for very extended periods when one does not attend continually but drifts away and back,

---

8   Audience participation/spectator involvement: in France the verb 'to attend', *assister* (be it an event such as a funeral or a play in the theatre), surely implies more than passive presence (also see Brook 1968, p.155–6).

chatters for a while, sleeps for a while, watches rapt for a while, and stops' (1975, p.403). Those performances are being viewed from a different standpoint in relation to time and within a time and space frame which differs from our own.

Thus, as also noted in the last chapter, performance in ceremony, drama and dance is concerned in a wide variety of ways with interaction between performers, and to a greater or lesser extent with interaction between performers and spectators and with their response. As Barba reminds us: 'to create the life of a performance does not mean only to interweave its actions and tensions, but also to direct the spectator's attention, his rhythms, to induce tensions in him' (Barba and Savarese 1996, p.70). Varied audience response is generated from different performance time and rhythm structures. For example, Schechner points out: 'The use of selective inattention encourages a kind of alpha-rhythm performance that evokes deep relaxation rather than tension. Or, as in the episodic pearl-on-a-string pageants of Wilson, a long-wave rhythm stimulates dropping in, dropping out: a different kind of medication' (1977, p.156).

Various conventions prevail for interaction, and condition time usage during performance. Social conventions, such as the degree of licence or informality allowed, with attitudes to accepted/unaccepted behaviour are influential. Reminiscent of other European mummers' plays, village performances in the Polish *dziady* tradition by masked gangs of 'vagabonds' are enacted with a marked informality. These performances take place randomly, at unspecified times during New Year's Eve and the next day, from village to village and door to door in a cross-country, processional pattern. Characters may include shepherds, gypsies, soldiers, horses, a chimney-sweep, a bear and figures of death and a devil. Unrelated actions take place simultaneously as these characters sing, perform scenes, dance, play practical jokes and interact with local inhabitants. This creates a mix of rhythms, a mayhem of play and performance, inside the cottages, outside in the snow and sometimes up trees. The informality dominates and determines rhythm and timing. It seems that almost anything can happen as villagers are teased – items of furniture go outside, hay and animals are brought indoors from barns, girls are tossed in snow drifts, a host's wagon may be put on his roof – and a quantity of vodka is consumed (Young 1974). On stage, rhythm and timing can express or emphasise degrees of informality or formality to bring out the relative exuberance or dignity of the situation.

Western performance conventions and performance structure

To conclude, some final comments about western conventions concerning time in theatre performance. Performance time overall is ordained by rules of procedure established by long usage, which we are unlikely to question in our own culture. In the context of western theatre traditions, we are used to drama and dance performances occurring as directors or theatre administrators dictate. There are

Figure 3.8 Spectators contribute to performance rhythm. A view of a play in action in the theatre of Restoration England.
Source: Grace Golden, courtesy of Victoria and Albert Museum

conventions with regard to the imagined passage of time through a play, and to the degree of freedom characters are allowed to traverse both time and space. Aristotle's rules concerning 'unity of time' (the 24-action boundary) were originally influential in western classical or classically-derived drama. However, freedom in stage use of time developed. Shakespeare is well known for his acceleration and retardation of real time to assist the development of stage action. In contrast, as Burns points out, 'Passage of time in plays of Ibsen, Chekhov and Strindberg was made to seem as plausible as possible' (1972, p.95). In Ibsen, events of the past often activate the present time of the play: for example, Beate's death in *Rosmersholm*. Chekhov's plays give the impression of lingering in the present.

Some contemporary playwrights have established new conventions, sometimes moving closer to the rhythms of everyday life, sometimes adopting a more stylised approach or a non-linear, perhaps dream-like narrative structure (as seen in film). Pinter provides an obvious example with his innovative approach to performance, rhythm and timing in dialogue and detailed stage directions; or

Beckett who, as described in the last chapter, moved further away from everyday life rhythms, even rejecting any pretence of realism in relation to time.

The traditional western European notion of play division in the theatre is into different scenes and acts. In contemporary drama this has often become a two-act or even an uninterrupted single structure without intervals. Some performances, particularly those in post-modern idiom and thereafter, develop intensity through repetition and steady accumulative use of time elements rather than through the old build-up of scenes and acceleration-climax pattern. We have seen this in the theatre work of Laura Dean, Philip Glass and Robert Wilson for example (see p.123). Work of this sort may take many hours, even days to perform – an unusual experience for most western audiences. This kind of prolonged enactment has a close relationship to forms of ritual performance.

Western theatre performances are punctuated by pauses which are expected for audience applause and laughter. Applause may occasionally even greet the entrance of a 'star' or mark an effective exit. A visitor to our culture might find it strange when the action of a play halts while – as sometimes happens – an audience applauds some effective décor. Intervals are provided which afford audience relaxation from concentration, opportunity for social interaction (and theatre revenue from sale of refreshments). Some, perhaps more 'serious', contemporary plays or theatre events are presented without an interval. The traditional interval between scenes and acts of a play, ballet or series of dance items also allows time for performers' rest, scene and costume change. The same is true of a ritual or ceremony.

With conventions inherited from earlier centuries, dance performance in western classical ballet traditionally either follows an act structure or consists of a series of one-act pieces. Audience intervention during the dancing rarely occurs, but star performers or displays of skill may be acknowledged and action delayed by rounds of applause.

At curtain calls, applause is frequently prolonged. Timing of intervals in contemporary dance performance is determined by length of pieces, each with pre-set timing and uninterrupted by applause. Folk-dance performance on stage normally also follows a similar pattern, but audience applause is sometimes elicited by particular displays of skill during the dance action. Less formal folk-dance performance in a local setting may include greater response and audience participation.

There are many ways of considering rhythm and timing in the dynamics of a performance structure. The micro-and macro-structure of one performance can be observed, or a performance may be considered in the wider context of social group, region, nation or world. The notion of structural and contextual levels of an event is the basis of this approach (Ortiz 1969; Cole 1975; Snyder 1978). Many levels are articulated in one dance piece, a point also emphasised by Robert

Dunn – pioneer-teacher of dance composition, Judson Church, New York, in the 1960s – during a conversation, 27 May 1981, New York City.

Levels of structural analysis may be identified sequentially, a development which extends the perspective with each step: (1) sequence (built from motifs, phrases or phases of action); (2) scene/part/section; (3) set of scenes/parts/sections; (4) a dance, a play, a ceremony; (5) wider context. Use of rhythm and time elements may be identified at each step, from the moment-by-moment interplay of rhythm and time elements at the level of micro-structural actions or motifs – through to the highest compositional macro-structural unit of a dance, a play, a ritual event, ceremony or series of such events, or even in a wider context.

As Snyder argues, 'if one begins to perceive the dynamics of structure, a system reveals itself which communicates more than structure' (1978, p.2). The polyrhythmic nature of performance derives from various strands in the performance structure, in the ordering of events. Although an example in Chapter 2 (note 1) indicated that there is not necessarily a connection between performers' sense of timing on stage and their sense of clock time, as examples in the this chapter have shown, performance rhythm and timing is to some extent influenced by people's attitudes to time and by their ways of planning and arranging performances, whether in the theatre or in ceremonies. Contributory factors include the interaction of performers, staging and environmental conditions, audience behaviour and expectations. The miscellany of ideas and examples cited have illustrated how these influences and factors, together with performance conventions, determine outcome. Time elements – evident throughout, at all levels of analysis – are central in the shared experience of performance and one of the bases of cultural, situational and aesthetic identity, meaning and effectiveness.

4

Contributions to the Study of Rhythm from Observers
Movement Notation and Anthropology

This chapter provides a set of selected references to some of the ways in which rhythm and timing has been observed and noted by professional notators[1] and by anthropologists. It is useful to look at their approaches to the subject since a notator's task is to undertake detailed movement observation, and observing people's movement is part of an anthropologist's job too. How do they perceive rhythm and timing?

Figure 4.1 Visual rhythm: a pattern inspired by Australian Aborigines' Dream-Time Journey motifs – a form of movement notation (e.g. concentric circles = water hole, thick semi-circle = resting (print-mark from squatting on the ground. Other lines may indicate various tracks or flowing water).
Source: Liane Payne

1   Dance (or movement) notation: described by Ann Hutchinson Guest, recognised world-wide as an authority on the subject, as 'the process of recording movement on paper' and as 'a means of communication of the language of dance' (Hutchinson Guest 1984).

Movement and dance notation

Notation systems indicate those aspects of movement deemed important in the particular culture, style and context for which a system was created, and in which it is used. There are detailed notational methods designed to record dance movement precisely, and less precise, non-prescriptive methods which are used for descriptive purposes. Ann Hutchinson Guest (1984) has written a comprehensive account of systems which is essential reading for a study of the subject. My aim here is much more restricted: to provide a compilation of selected examples from the range of approaches to rhythm and timing. As there are over 85 systems from which to choose, this is necessarily a limited selection.

Detailed systems usually combine graphic methods, but following Hutchinson Guest's lead, they can be categorised according to the main graphic method used.

Word abbreviations

Many movement students and teachers have used abbreviations of words to describe movement action as a memory aid. This is fine in use with other people if they are familiar with the original material to which the abbreviations refer. Thoinot Arbeau's *Orchésographie* (1588) was an early version, with for example, the R (for *reverencia*) and d (for *double*). Many descriptions of folk dance and also social, West European ballroom dances today include, for instance, S for slow, Q for quick (see Silvester, 1950). In tap dancing, word descriptive systems exist for identification and teaching purposes using terms such as 'shuffle step', 'step ball change'.

Figure 4.2 Dance steps: figures from Arbeau's Orchésographie, which he included to supplement musical notation of the dance tunes, with word description alongside.

Singer records the rhythmic patterns of Macedonian–Bulgarian dances in terms of S/Q ('slows' and 'quicks') (1974, p.386). At the same time she points out the difficulties of perceiving and performing these rhythms due to changes of tempo, inconsistency and accentual variations from one bar to the next. Others such as dancer/ritual deviser Anna Halprin have used words in a variety of impressionistic methods, usually incorporating floor patterns or ground tracks (see Schwartz 1982). Although quick to write, words or letters are too vague to be of much use for detailed rhythm and timing study.

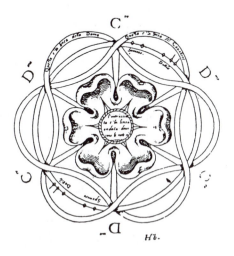

Figure 4.3 Dancers weave in and out as they trace the path of a contrapasso – in the shape of a rose, 'according to the true mathematics after the verses of Ovid'.
Source: Caroso 1600

Track drawings

The single footprint which Crusoe found on his lonely seashore was a mystery. Tracks which provide evidence of where people or animals have been, have always exerted a certain fascination. Track drawings may either give a bird's-eye view of a movement sequence (pattern on the ground) or delineate a choreographer or performer's gestural track. Anthropologists are interested in the tracks indicated on Australian *churinga*, a form of movement notation.[2] (See Lévi-Strauss 1966; Munn 1973). Track drawing systems were prevalent in seventeenth-century Europe, being particularly appropriate for the royal court dances at that time with their stress on the spatial rhythms of elaborate and significant floor patterns. For

---

2   Aborigines' sacred wood or stone slabs – inscribed with lines said to represent ancestors' spirit journeys.

instance, at the triumphant conclusion of *A Masque of Queens*, Jonson's stage directions require the name of the young prince, Charles, to be stepped out as the floor pattern of the dance. In order to provide other indications of the action, the method was usually supplemented by words, symbols or by little drawings such as of tiny horses in the score of Allesandro Carducci's horse ballet *Il Mondo, Balletto a Cavallo* (1661).

The best known and most widely used track system was Feuillet's (thought to be based on Beauchamp). Published in 1700, the method became popular throughout Europe. Feuillet's system included the use of words and small symbols. The decorative track, which expresses something of the grace of an eighteenth-century ballroom, indicates right and left steps with lines penned on either side of a central line, intended to coincide with the bars of the music. Other methods, such as that used by Kellom Tomlinson (c.1720) incorporated music and tracks with detailed engravings of costumed figures in action. Modern ballroom dancers are familiar with Victor Silvester's use of footstep imprints, numbered to indicate timing and sequence on a directionally arrowed track (Silvester 1950). Track notation has been used by early dance anthropologists. Some instances are: Langdon-Davies writing about Catalan dance (1929); Holt recording dances of Celebes (1939); and Mason describing American Indian dances (1944).

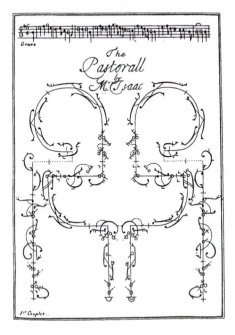

Figure 4.4 An example of a dance notated in Feuillet's popular, decorative system (originally devised by ballet-master Pierre Beauchamp).
Source: Feuillet (c.1700)

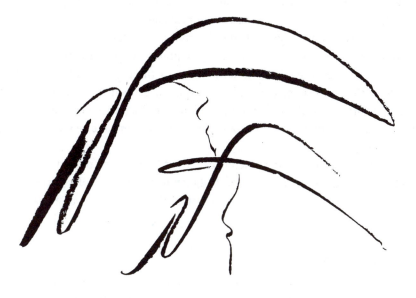

Figure 4.5 A drawing by choreographer Dana Reitz. Repeated Phrase, *from* Quintet Project *(1981). 'When working on a dance piece, one of my main concerns is to find a rhythmic phrase to work from… Drawing… is another way to get at the energy that motivates movement, the direct line of intent and attention, the underlying current of form' (Shwartz 1982).*
Source: Dana Reitz

Contemporary choreographers frequently use gestural track notation in the form of free-style drawings to record ideas, as part of their working process. In relation to rhythm, Dana Reitz, for example, states: '[drawing] is a tool that allows me to see, outside of myself, the direct result of performing a rhythm as I hear it, without trying to copy a completed shape or even to predict one' (Schwartz 1982, p.56). For *Relative Calm* (1981) Lucinda Childs made diagrams of the dancers' spatial pathways in relation to set time intervals (Schwartz 1982, p.49). This form of track drawing provides less detailed information than standard forms of movement notation, but may reveal much about the artist's ideas on rhythm and timing.

With his 'Motation' (1966), landscape architect Lawrence Halprin most interestingly explored the possibility of devising a graphic notation system (with time indications) for tracking kinetic environments whether of street or stage. His system makes use of frames as in film, and 26 basic symbols to indicate features of the landscape: structures, moving objects, direction and angle and other geometric components.[3] Anna Halprin devised a diagrammatic graphic score for the 'Time Sequence Activity' in her community dance work, *Animal Ritual*. Read horizontally from left to right, 11 lines (seeming to represent a flow of energy – performance arteries, as it were) indicate the pathways of performers along which they journey. They travel individually, through three phases of initiation for instance, with specific named ordeals and experiences such as 'burden', 'conflict', 'rivalry', 'courting', 'isolation', 'the hunt'. The lines begin to merge at 'common enemy' and are as one at 'confrontation' before moving on elsewhere (Halprin 1995, p.118).

Track drawing alone is an inadequate method for notation of rhythm in all its aspects. However, it is certainly a useful adjunct to other forms of notation. It can give an immediate impression to the reader of the scale, shape and span of an event.

Pictorial representation

From stick figures to sketches of dancers – again many movement students and teachers have resorted to various representations of figures in action as a memory aid. Most of the fully fledged notational systems place the indications of the moving figure parallel to the music, which is read from left to right horizontally in the usual West European manner. Thus the rhythm and timing aspects of movement are reliant on West European musical form. There are a number of examples. For instance, Zorn's system, published in 1905, incorporated floor patterns with melody and castanets' rhythm alongside a series of stick figures – for the notation of Fanny Elssler's *Cachucha*. The best known example is the well-established Benesh system (1956) which utilises a five-line horizontal stave on which extremities and mid-joints of the body are plotted. The Benesh system was first designed to notate ballet and is widely used, but it has been applied to other styles. For instance, in anthropology, John Blacking included some Benesh notation in his study of Southern African Venda dance.

Gertrude Kurath, respected doyen of dance anthropology (or dance ethnology as it is more commonly known in the USA), developed the Kurath glyph system (1953). This is based on a combination of the Laban system (which is described later) and the use of parts of a stick figure, each part being given a line of the staff. Timing is indicated by horizontal lines across the staff, read from the bottom to the top of the page. Indeed, stick figures are a popular form of notation as a memory aid, and they have been used by many people, such as Bessie and May

---

3   Architects are concerned with the movement of people through their spaces, but some contemporary architects now deal more demonstrably with motion, and use less of the conventional language of static elements. This is evident in projects such as Bernard Schumis' Parc de la Villette or in examples of Zaha Hadid's work.

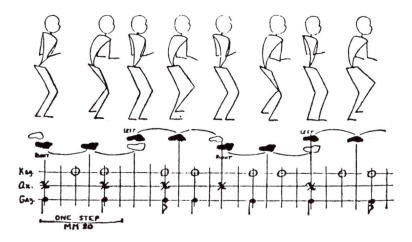

Figure 4.6 Dancers with instruments (gankogui bell, axatse rattle and kaganu drum): stick figures, footprints, and indication of instrumental timing. Extract from a Takada club dance of the Ewe people, Anyakol, Ghana.
Source: Sl Kobla Ladzekpo and Hewitt Pantaleoni

Evans (see Evans B. and M.G. 1937) to record Pueblo dance steps, and Griaule (1938) who used a type of figure notation in describing West African Dogon dances. However, since a pictorial method is essentially a position-orientated method it has severe limitations for indicating rhythm and timing.

Anthropologists are interested in cave paintings of figures in motion – an early form of movement notation (Ucko and Rosenfeld 1967). Dance scholar-artist Millicent Hodson has made a unique contribution to pictorial methods of notation in the reconstruction of a number of early ballets for dance companies which, with Kenneth Archer, she has undertaken since 1987. For example, for Nijinsky's *Le Sacre du Printemps* Hodson collected and studied verbatim accounts, choreographic markings on the musical score, original designs and sketches to execute drawings and paintings of the dancers as she researched and imagined them at different stages of the dance. These she uses as an aid in the reconstruction process (1996) (see Figure 4.7).

Although as Rawson comments '*rhythm* was used as an emotive catchword in post-symbolist art discourse between about 1900 and 1940' (1997, p.103), interesting allusions to the rhythm of a painting or a sculpture have frequently been made, both then and at other times. For the Italian Futurists the essence of modernity was speed, which (with rhythm) they frequently aimed to represent in their art – clearly exemplified in Balla's work (see Millar and Schwarz (eds) 1998). The extent to which a static picture can convey movement rhythms and relationships, and differences between a dancer's perception of rhythm in movement and a graphic artist's perception of rhythm in a painting are subjects which cannot be pursued fully here, but may be considered briefly in relation to various pictorial representation systems of notation. Souriau describes the 'phrasing' of a picture and stylistic differences in this regard:

> the slow, full majestic *phrasing* of a Veronese ... the rugged phrasing of Caravaggio, powerful in its boldness, brutal, even a bit melodramatic; the essential polyphonic and architective phrasing of N. Poussin; or again the pathetic and tormented phrasing of Delacroix. It is entirely reasonable to note a likeness with these characteristics in the music of Palestrina, Monteverdi, Bach or Berlioz. (1961, p.138)

In his discussion of rhythm in pictures, music, mood and feeling, Bayer suggests rhythm is basically an emotional force with alternation of storm and calm, and

Figure 4.7 An example of Millicent Hodson's work – pictorial representation of timing: The witch leaps to make the young men jump. Augurs of Spring, *Act 1, Scene I.*
Source: Millicent Hodson

concludes 'what each and every aesthetic object imposes upon us, in appropriate rhythm, is a unique and singular formula for the flow of our energy' (1961, p.201). Bayer brings dance and pictorial representation together when he asserts that understanding of a work of art lies in understanding its rhythmic construction: 'We understand a work of art correctly, then, as soon as we perceive it correctly in the rhythmic-formal sense, and as soon as we feel its true emotional content through this formal perception' (1961, p.29). Goldberg reflects that

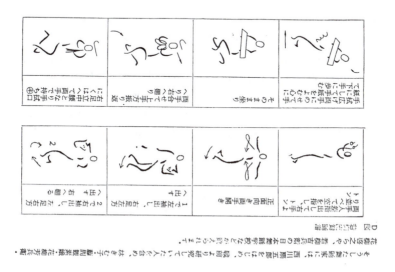

Figure 4.8 From Japan: an example of notation using a pictorial method with accompanying words (one page from the complete system).
Source: Ann Hutchinson Guest collection

Margaret Schreyer's woodcuts used as a form of notation for Lothar Schreyer's Expressionist play *Crucifixion* (1920) vividly evoke its rhythmic style – 'bands of zig-zagged instructions match the exaggerated shrieks and staccato movement of the action' (1982, p.5). It is clear that the concept of spatial rhythm in movement relates closely to the artist's concept of rhythm, and to the choreographer's sense of design, as the comment from Dana Reitz has already indicated (see Figure 4.5).

Music notation

All the systems based on music notation naturally help us to envisage the metric pattern of movement. For example, Woodard based her notation on the dance and music notation system of the Jogjanese court, in order to examine structure in Javanese dance (1976, p.10). However, there is frequently ambiguity about timing in systems based on music notes. For instance, the duration of a note may indicate a dancer's arrival and 'held' position, or gradual movement into a position through the duration of the note.

If we look at some contemporary composers' scores, and those of ethnomusicologists who have had to address the problem of the notation of non-metric rhythm or unfamiliar rhythmic forms, we find an interesting range of features of rhythm, and ways of indicating these (Karkoschka 1966; Ladzekpo and Pantaleoni 1970; Koetting 1970; Cole 1974).

Abstract symbols

Laban's system, briefly mentioned in the last chapter, is perhaps the best known of those which make use of abstract symbols (known as Kinetography in Europe and as Labanotation in the USA). Since Laban's death in 1958 the system has continued to be developed and applied in different dance and other movement contexts. To notate rhythm and timing, the method utilises a vertical stave which is read from the base, with bar-lines to indicate metrical division of time and

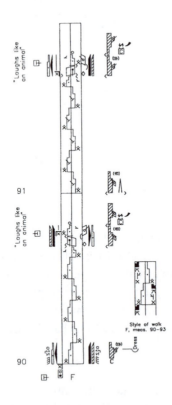

Figure 4.9 An example of Labanotation from The Language of Dance Series No.3: Nijinsky's Faune Restored, *by Ann Hutchinson Guest. Read from the bottom of the staff, these two measures (bars) show the faun's action after he has picked up the dress discarded by the Chief Nymph – he is travelling to and fro and 'laughing like an animal' whilst holding the dress.*

symbols to represent different body parts. Rubato or cadenza-like form is allowed for by the use of *ad lib* signs. Wedge-shaped symbols indicate accents or presence of 'more than average strength' or 'little strength'. Floor patterns with spatial directions can be inscribed alongside the main staff, and are also indicated within the staff by directional signs. The system achieves economy – one symbol representing duration, body part, level and direction. If use of a full score appears too complex, one can make a personal selection of signs from the total. There are simplified versions of full Kinetography, such as *Motif Writing*, designed by Preston-Dunlop (1963).

In addition to Kinetography, Laban devised signs to notate the dynamics of movement from his 'effort' analysis. These signs can be placed alongside the score, or notated as a separate graph. For detailed study of rhythm and timing, both the kinetographic score and the 'effort' graph are needed.

There have been various extensions of Laban's approach, notably Warren Lambs's Action Profiling, Movement Pattern Analysis and the work of Pamela Ramsden and others. In the USA, Effort-Shape was developed by Irmgard Bartenieff, with Davis, Kestenberg and others, working first at the Dance Notation Bureau, and then at the Laban Institute of Movement Studies, New York (see Bartenieff, Davis and Pauley (eds) 1970). The analytic methodology of Effort-Shape (now incorporated into Laban Movement Analysis) is also used as a basis for movement experience and training. Rhythm is central to the approach which is particularly concerned with the interaction of effort combinations with variations in spatial patterns (see Bartenieff and Lewis 1980). An important contribution is made to the study of phrasing (see also Blum 1987; Maletic 1983). Attention is given to ways in which phrases may begin, develop and end, and to how phrases are initiated and prompted by particular body action, use of symmetry or asymmetry and use of acceleration. 'Effort-Shape' is not a detailed notational method and is not specific about all features of rhythm, but use of the system can result in evocative descriptions of a full range of movement characteristics, including aspects of rhythm. It has been applied in various contexts such as in the Choreometrics Project (see p.104).

As noted in Chapter 2, Kestenberg has adopted notions such as 'flow' from Laban to note preferred patterns of rhythmicity in young children. She charts tension-flow along a curving line with a neutral centre line. Rise of tension is indicated by a rising line, lessening tension by a lowering line (1977, p.7). Kestenberg distinguishes between rhythms of tension flow as alternations in 'sequences of fluency and restraint in the state of the muscles in various parts of the body' and rhythms of shape flow, which 'organise the relationship of body parts in such a way that drives can be satisfied in transactions with objects' (1977, p.86). She also refers to the significance of gestural size (near or far from the body) in her definition of shape flow rhythm, which 'consists of alternations between growing and shrinking of body shape' (1977, p.90).

Abstract symbols are also used by a number of others, such as Loring and Eshkol-Wachman. 'Kinesiography', introduced by Loring in 1955, is potentially useful in studies of rhythm and timing for the attention it gives to dynamics, breathing and change of attitude from 'introvert' to 'extrovert' in performance. But it shows no way of fully recording rhythm and it has a cumbersome, eighteen-column staff. Better known is the mathematically based work and system of Noa Eshkol and Abraham Wachman, published in 1958 as *Movement Notation*. This system, soundly related to the structure of the body and process of moving, notates action in terms of degrees of rotation of any given movement.

Other methods

Examples of anthropologists who have made use of detailed notation systems for dance study and analysis have already been cited. Others in anthropology, dance, and in the field of non-verbal communication such as those quoted in Chapter 1, make use of various less detailed methods of noting movement patterns for descriptive and analytic purposes, including use of abstract signs, boxes, graphs, charts, frame-by-frame film analysis and drawings. Byers (1972), for instance, devised charts for movement and speech, with duration marked in seconds, to demonstrate aspects of synchronicity and shared beat or rhythm by two or more people. Valerie Hunt's movement behaviour scoring method includes 'patterns of energy; as well as shape rhythms' 'rhythm in movement' (force and time) with four headings: burst (explosive), sustained (smooth, continuous), undulate (wave), restrained (irregular, continuous), with three degrees in each (1968). In his interesting study of the African festival of Odwira at Akropong, Cole (1975) used an 'energy flow' model and form of notation which consists of a horizontal time line, read from left to right, with ritual intensity plotted below and elaboration or intensity of public display above the line. An aerial plan of the space used is also included (see also p.101).

The use of timing graphs is common in physiological and behavioural studies of various kinds. For instance, Kendon and Ferber (1971) plot observation of greeting behaviour on a graph, with a base duration line. Pitcairn and Schleidt employ graphs to record duration of dance pattern in their analysis of the Medlpa courtship dance in New Guinea (1975). Ryman and Rannie (1978) have made a quantitative analysis of aspects of the *grande jeté dessus en tournant* in ballet, making use of biomechanical methodology, including cinematographic analysis presented in the form of graphs (as well as body tracings and tables).

Frame-by-frame film analysis has been used by a number of observers, such as Kendon in his analysis of relationships between body motion and speech (1972). Kubik also devised a frame-by-frame system of movement notation to describe the action of Angolan boys' initiation ceremonies in Southern Africa (1977), transcribing patterns from film on to graph paper. The movement analysis is based on body use and changes in the direction of energy which Kubik terms 'corner-points'.

The focus on the use of time elements, rhythm and timing in this book does not include use of any one form of notation. However, it can be seen that for detailed structural analysis, a notational system is needed. I have used Labanotation in my own work from time to time, particularly in study and practice of historical and 'folk' dance, and this system is compatible with the approach to rhythm advocated in this book. Systems which notate floor pattern, such as in Feuillet and Cole, are obviously useful for recording aspects of spatial rhythm. For their emphasis on patterns of energy, Loring, Hunt and Cole's approaches are particularly helpful. Various inter-personal communication notational systems are useful analytic tools, such as Byers' (for synchrony), and Kendon/Ferber's and Kubik's graphs and frame analysis methods.

Contributions from anthropology
Rhythm in definitions of dance

> In dance...rhythm is transformed, heightened, manipulated, so that it becomes something larger and more effective than the ordinary rhythms that surround us in everyday life. (Royce 1981, p.2)

When anthropologists study performance (such as dance – as a component in ritual, for instance), they may examine it in terms of how it functions as social catharsis and control, in the transmission of beliefs and maintenance of social cohesion or in establishing cultural style, with time and use of rhythm and timing – as contributing elements (see Spencer 1985). Some have addressed the problematic topic of definitions of dance, and 'rhythm' is usually included in their definitions. Here are four respected examples as a representative sample.

Roderyk Lange emphasises rhythm as a shaping factor in dance. He makes a useful distinction between metrical and accentual modes of organisation, and refers to the recurrence of durational units as establishing rhythmic pattern (Lange 1975, p.31). Lange points out that these modes combine in many different ways and that accentual rhythm may result from energy output (dynamic accent) or from durational variation (agogic accent) (see also Riemann 1844).

Judith Lynne Hanna's definition of dance features 'intentional rhythm', which she describes as 'the organized flow of energy in time and space' (1979, p.19) – contrasting with the 'autonomic-interactional' rhythms of other human and non-human motor patterns (1979, p.72). Hanna states that the features she includes as 'rhythm' (tempo, duration, accent, meter) may be 'simple or complex, uniform or variable'. Studying material from the USA can sometimes be confusing for people unfamiliar with the word usage. For instance, Hanna refers to 'motor time' interchangeably with 'rhythm'. She describes 'accent' as we might in the UK, as 'the relative force or intensity with which energy is released' and meter as 'the underlying consistent numerical grouping of beats and accents' (1979, p.30).

Hanna, with Lange, emphasises recurrence as a salient feature of rhythm. She further describes metre, as an element of rhythm, more broadly as a 'basic recurrent pattern of tempo, duration and accent' (1979, p.245). Whereas Lange refers to recurring 'units', Hanna includes repetition of 'elements'. She stresses the patterned nature of rhythm with its alternations of 'relative quietude and activeness' (1979, p.28). The notion of alternation as a basis of rhythm is emphasised when Hanna defines a phrase as:

> the expression of a partial 'thought', a group of related movements in a pattern where there are alternations of activity (peaking) and quiescence (pose, rest, energy, diminution). A phrase has its own climax and is distinguished by rhythmic pattern and visual configuration of locomotion and/or gesture. (1979, p.259)

Elsewhere Hanna more briefly defines phrases as 'groups of related movements which have their own unity, perceptible start and stop, or climax' (1979b, pp.245–246).

Another definition of dance, and one that is widely adopted, is provided by Joann Kealiinohomoku. She, too, includes rhythm as a distinguishing feature: '[Dance] – a transient mode of expression performed in a given form and style by the human body moving in space. Dance occurs through purposefully selected and controlled rhythmic movements; the resulting phenomenon is recognised as dance both by the performer and the observing members of a given group' (1970, p.28). Kealiinohomoku considers that temporal design features of dance are those shared with music, and lists these as: duration, tempi, meters, rhythms (1976a, p.307). This anthropologist further defines rhythm in dance as patterns of energy output which include patterns of movement frequencies, accentuation and bodily impulses (1976a, p.26).

Drid Williams makes an important contribution in her definition, with an emphasis on dance as a 'rhythmically ordered', symbolic transformation of experience. She also includes reference to pattern, rhythm and time. A final example is that of Anya Peterson Royce who, with Lange and Hanna, in her definition of dance includes 'recurrent alternation of strong and weak elements' and repetition (1981, p.29). She suggests that the concept of rhythmic or patterned movement is basic to all dance definitions (1977, p.5).

Rhythm in the observation and analysis of movement in performance

Anthropologists have undertaken observation and analysis of movement in performance in various different ways. The approach to dance analysis proposed by Hanna is through a processual model of the idiom of dance as communication system in socio-cultural context. Hanna sets down the elements of the interaction process involved in performance, and places dancer, choreographer and audience in a causative framework which stresses feedback (1971, p.79). However, the limited causative stress of this model does not match the complexities of performance events in general. Turner's broader approach to performance genres and to concepts of time in relation to performance events provides valuable insights and a basis for further study of rhythm and timing in performance durational structure. He has directed attention particularly in ritual to phases of actions and the transitions between them (Turner 1977).

Cole's energy-flow model and study of the festival of Odwira was mentioned in relation to notation and may be considered further in this context. Cole notes the elaboration of public ritual display (the numbers attending and sensory stimulation) and ritual intensity which he concludes create 'an energy system'. He suggests that ritual intensity develops from the commitment of participants and religious significance attributed to the event. Cole describes the polyrhythmic time structure of the festival, and focuses on the importance of repetition as a structural device, suggesting that repetition is a fundamental component of the festival structure: 'Virtually everything is repeated on different levels: rituals including prayers, libations, sacrifices, and honorific gestures; musical performances; dance; isolable sculptures such as golden staffs, stools, swords and other items; processions; feasting; assemblies and speeches; ceremonial dress, jewelry, body painting and hairstyling' (1975, p.22). Cole mentions that temporal patterns recur throughout the week, with events being repeated simultaneously in family compounds. A principle of elaboration emerges: 'When repetitions and variations are multiplied, as they so often are in a festival, the principle of *elaboration* comes into play' (1975, p.23).

In Brink's study of West African Bamana drama and communication strategy, he includes reference to aspects of rhythm, especially tempo, in 'kote-tlon' performance (a type of satirical comedy) in which fast tempo brings the play's humour to a climax – and also considerably tests actors' skills. Brink further explains that to the Bamana, 'good' tempo is slow: 'Slow tempos in music and dance are said to put the rhythms and dance steps in order' (1980, p.24). On the other hand, he writes that fast tempos bring out 'kegunya' which can be translated as 'cleverness' or ability to decorate. 'Thus in the plays, slow tempi are used to order a play's theme and fast to exploit humour, "impolite" states, pain, abuse. It seems here that Bamana use tempi in a qualitative rather than in a quantitative, durational manner' (1980, p.25). Also, the theme of time underlies the drama which is the relationship between youth and elders. Brink comments that the Bamana have a concept of good timing: 'Actors who possess good timing are the ones who can sense when it is appropriate to pluck a 'funny thing' from the local gossip, imbue it with dramatic form, and by representing it in performance proclaim it as official public knowledge, or better, as official public stupidity' (1980, p.20).

Some anthropologists have included aspects of rhythm in detailed analyses of dance structure. Particular reference must be made to the half a century of dance research by the late Gertrude Kurath. Her work (already mentioned with reference to notation) includes studies of Iroquois, Algonquin, Ottowa, Menomini and Pueblo Indians' dance, and features observation of rhythm at different stages of her research. Vivid references to details of dance abound in her writing, from the Iroquois women who 'inconspicuously glide sideward in the wake of their gyrating warriors' (1951, p.126) to the 'relaxed pulsation' of the 'stamp step' of the Buffalo and Bear dancers (1964, p.64). Kurath encourages an experimental, flexible approach when she states that her observation procedure 'varies with each case, and [which] changes from year to year' (1974, p.36).[4]

Rhythm in cultural and dance style

Anthropologists have often suggested that use of movement in general is stylistically recognisable in a given culture or society, although they have usually not referred to many elements of rhythm in this context. However, in relation to dance, references are more detailed and wide ranging.

In early pioneering studies, Radcliffe-Brown and Evans-Pritchard, renowned in British anthropology, paid an attention to dance, which was unusual in their day. Radcliffe-Brown even commented on the part rhythm plays in the development of the aesthetic sense (1922, pp.250–251). He described the dances he saw on the Andaman islands, in the Bay of Bengal, and considered them to be socially harmonising and unifying. Features of rhythm he noted were actions of feet (in hopping), relationship to the beats of an accompanying song, musical notation of the rhythm, the dance track (round the circle of the dancing ground), and the step pattern used (1922, pp.28-32). Radcliffe-Brown stated that rhythm

4   Full reference to Kurath's material in this chapter and to that of many others is not within the scope of this book. For examples see: Kurath (1986), Kaeppler (1985), Lange (1975), Martin and Pesovár (1961), Proca-Ciorta (1971), Singer (1974) and Williams (1972a, b). Dance scholars from Rumania, DDR, Yugoslavia, Czechoslovakia and Hungary joined to discuss the development of a syllabus and basis for the scientific study of dance as 'ethnochoreology' under the auspices of the International Folk Music Council in 1972 (reported in Reynolds, 1974). They put forward suggestions for symbols for structural units of dance, variation, course of movement, relationship between dance and music. Tempo, metre and rhythm are included in their list of folkdance factors. Structural levels are listed as parts, sections, phrases, motifs, cells, elements. A method of formal analysis is described and various examples given of different dance forms.

induces individuals to join in – the power of rhythm acting from within and without – and encourages people to conform 'to the needs of the common activity' (1922, p.252). He stressed the 'rhythmic' element in dance, which he categorised as a form of play and means of group synchrony (1922, p.247): 'The essential character of all dancing is that it is rhythmical, and it is fairly evident that the primary function of this rhythmical nature of the dance is to enable a number of persons to join in the same actions and perform them as one body' (1922, p.247).

Evans-Pritchard presented a contrasting view from his study of the Sudanese Nuer (in North Eastern Africa) with an example of dancing as a common occasion for disharmony (1965, p.74). However, he stressed its socially integrative function elsewhere, when he remarked on the social importance and role of dance (1965a). Nuer life and use of time when Evans-Pritchard made his observations was entirely governed by caring for their cattle. This gave rise to a particular attitude to time which he identified in their movement style. Although he did not refer to use of time elements in detail, with an interesting similarity to Laban's way of viewing movement (see p.131) he characterised Nuer action as leisurely 'not fighting against time' (1940, p.103). Evans-Pritchard vividly refers to body parts in use, and briefly to bodily placement of rhythm in another study, in a description of Southern African Azande dancing: 'All the muscles of the body seem to be in action and the skin looks as though it accommodated a multitude of snakes … considerable latitude is allowed in variation of movement. Not everyone makes the same movements but they are all made to the same rhythm' (1928, p.450).

In the USA, Claire Holt, Gregory Bateson, Harold Courlander and Franz Boas were pioneers in the description and discussion of cultural style. They posed questions in their studies about movement style in relation to work actions, personality, dance and culture. They also provided descriptive references to rhythm in Balinese, Haitian, north west coast American Indian and Indonesian dance.

Of this group, Holt paid particular attention to features of rhythm in dance. In *Dance Quest in Celebes* (1939) and elsewhere, Holt recorded her observations of the many dances she witnessed, making use of her own form of notation. Her frequent references to time elements included for example: stillness, tempo, sudden action, control (1972, pp.75–79). Although often referring in a general rather than specific manner to 'rhythmic' elements together with diagrams of formations and figures, Holt was ahead of her time in including interesting and useful descriptive detail. For instance, in these notes about the use of a dance-costume scarf in Javanese performance there is a careful reference to the way in which body-extensions contribute to rhythm:

> The dexterity and subtlety of the pliable hands and fingers is further enhanced by the use of the dance scarf … Its loose hanging ends … are picked up by one edge

between thumb and middle finger, slowly led forward and sidewise [sic], thrown over the wrists, flipped open, tossed aside flying, etc., adding an ethereal quality to the relatively slow movement. (1958, p.119)

Holt noted rhythmic intricacy in Javanese dance, as distinct from the musical accompaniment:

The movements of the dance intertwine not only with the rhythms of the music. They flow, jut or vibrate in separate interlacing strands through the dancer's limbs. An arm may start to act and, as it continues to complete its pattern of motion, the head may join – by turning in the direction of the hand while a foot slowly moves forward and gradually causes the whole body to change its centre of gravity as hand and head pursue their own individual prescribed course. (1958, p.121)

Boas contributed an example of the significance of timing and tempo in a dance ceremony, when he described the winter ceremonial of north west coast American Indians:

suddenly the leader of the ceremonial enters the door swinging a rattle ... It is essential from this point on that neither the novice nor any of the singers make a mistake in the movement, rhythm, or song ... If any of them makes a mistake and beats time too fast or too slowly, the Fool dancers and Grissly Bear dancers, who police the ceremonial, become excited. Immediately the singers stop singing, and beat fast time. (1944, p.13)

Originally performers who made mistakes were killed, but this was changed to mock killing of an offender. Boas also referred to the significance of distinctive rhythmic variety evident in family 'ownership' of songs, and the belief that each of the clan ancestors received the spirit power in a slightly different form.

An extensive study of dance style is found in the cantometrics/choreometrics study of expressive behaviour by Alan Lomax, with Irmgard Bartenieff. This study describes pervasive, culturally distinct patterns in music and dance world-wide. Lomax's hypothesis was that 'danced movement is patterned reinforcement of the habitual movement patterns of each culture or culture area' (1968, p.xv). He set out to locate and map culturally distinct patterns in the manner of Murdock's *Ethnographic Atlas* (1967). The research team related synchrony in dance to the synchrony found in subsistence working actions: 'The degree and kind of synchrony found in a culture's dancing also will repeat the type of synchrony necessary to complete its community subsistence tasks' (Lomax, Bartenieff and Paulay 1974, p.204). Thus in this study dance is reduced to motor components 'characteristic and most essential to the activity of everyday' (Lomax 1968, p.224).

Reference was made to the rhythm of working actions in Chapter 1, and some dance as well as everyday movement may be influenced by habitual working actions. This is obvious in specific working-action dances and songs, which frequently imitate and accompany the work. In everyday movement it is seen in the walking action of women accustomed to carrying loads on their heads. But the work context alone cannot necessarily explain styles and forms of dance. In Lomax's study there is no emphasis on the cognitive aspects of dance or on dance as symbolic transformation of experience which we find emphasised in other anthropologists' definitions of dance. Also, there is little definition of rhythm and timing in the dance descriptions and although his colleagues developed the Effort-Shape system referred to earlier, rhythm is not emphasised in the coding and rating system. Nonetheless, this pioneering work is valuable and Lomax's focus on physique and body movement cross-culturally is important and still a relatively unexplored topic in relation to dance expression in anthropology.

A decade after Lomax, Judy van Zile represents the next generation of pioneers with her research into culturally acquired patterns of energy use (1977). This work is a considerable advance, and contributes to studies of the significance of the use of time elements in style and in learning dance. Students' problems in mastering alien dance style are due, van Zile suggests, to habitual, culturally acquired 'energy patterns' being different from the characteristic patterns of the alien style.

For 'energy patterns' we might substitute 'rhythm', and known for her studies of dance in Korea, Hawaii and elsewhere, van Zile's approach reveals considerable interest in various features of rhythm. In *Alarippu: A Choreographic Analysis* (1979) she provides clear description and movement analysis making use of Labanotation. A section on 'use of time' is based chiefly on noting counts, pulse, pauses, repetition, tempi. 'Rhythmic intricacy' is included as a feature, though not described thoroughly (1979, pp.14–16). Again, emphasising 'use of energy', van Zile raises the question of phrasing in dance and asks if punctuation is achieved through energy changes (1977, p.91). She suggests that measuring the energy level in pauses could reveal significant differences between different pauses.

Dance style has been described by Peggy Harper in various African contexts. She has also made particular references to the significance of rhythm in social and performance context in her description of the Nigerian Gelede masquerade ceremonies (1970, p.69). Several anthropologists have linked specific use of rhythm in dance with gender identity, and Harper perceives the Gelede dance movements to be an implicit synthesis of daily life action in a male dominated society. She points out, for example, that in the ceremonies the male mask performs powerful kicks, turns and strong swinging actions, and parodies women's movement. Harper makes useful reference to an important feature of timing seldom noted – the significance of preparation-timing. She was also alert to the effect of tempi: for instance, she notes the way in which rapid steps create excitement (1970, p.69).

In another reference to dance in Africa, Middleton (1985, p.175) also refers to gender identity when he indicates that differences in Lugbara dance patterns (from north western Uganda) signify the relative position of women and men in the society. Men characteristically leap and perform in groups, women tend to move gently but as individuals (like bush, wild people, say the men, in touch with spirits). Specific timing of dances is significant here too – performed 'when ordinary time has stopped'. Middleton suggests that Lugbara dance expresses structural conflicts and ambiguity; that dance is a means of resolving, changing, digesting conflict, or controlling emotion, such as grief. Here we are reminded that disorder in dance may be a means of coming to terms with it, as also occurs in children's play.

Many references to dance and ritual activities are found in John Blacking's studies of the Venda, in Southern Africa. In his introduction to Venda traditional dances, Blacking refers to tempo, how rhythm is placed in the dancers' bodies and again how one may observe contrasts in use of rhythm between the men and the women (1977b). One example indicates how even one feature of timing – beginning and stopping – may be significant and how observation of movement can aid understanding (1971, p.106).

Blacking was intensely interested in performance process, both as regards the performers and the audience. He includes reference to rhythm when he describes the 'shared somatic states' which can develop during performance events:

> Crucial factors in the development of cultural forms are the possibility of shared somatic states, the structures of the bodies that share them, and the rhythms of interaction that transform commonly experienced internal sensations into externally visible and transmissible forms. (1977a, p.9)

Those comments remind us of the references to synchrony and interaction in Chapter 1. We may recall here Malinowski's concept of 'phatic communication' (1948, p.315), and of the place of rhythm in collective action. For instance, as Shirogoroff remarks in relation to Siberian Shamanism 'The rhythmic music and singing, and later the dancing of the shaman, gradually involve every participant more and more in a collective action' (in Lewis 1971, p.53). In her account of southern African !Kung Bushman religious beliefs, Lorna Marshall states that the curing dance draws the people together more than anything else in their lives. She refers to rhythm during curing ceremonies. 'The clapping and stamping are of such precision that they give the effect of a well-played battery of percussion instruments producing a solid structure of intricate rhythm' (1962, p.248).[5]

Referring again to anthropologists whose definitions of dance have been cited, Hanna supports the view that rhythmic patterns characterising a group's dance style tend to be culturally patterned, but suggests that style may be determined by psychological, historical, environmental or idiosyncratic factors (1979b, pp.28, 30). Interestingly, 'focus' or 'projectional quality' is listed as an element of rhythm. Hanna is unusual in including this as an observational category within time elements of movement. She describes it as 'texture' produced by a combination of elements, particularly by the relative quickness or slowness of energy released by the performer (1979a, p.247). Hanna's studies of dance in Nigeria, West Africa in particular, illustrate the central place rhythm has in her system of dance style analysis (1979). Lange also has provided fine studies of dance style, especially from his fieldwork in Poland. In relation to rhythm, he makes useful comments on the significance of performance variation for instance and use of rubato in different social contexts (1970, 1977, 1996).

Based at the Cross Cultural Dance Resources Centre which she founded, Kealiinohomoku has specialised in cross-cultural studies of dance. There are references to rhythm in her studies of cultural and dance style, for instance in relation to Hopi and Polynesian dance (1967), and to African and United States Negroes (1976b). Kealiinohomoku attracted particular attention from the western dance world with her ground-breaking article 'An anthropologist looks at ballet as a form of ethnic dance' (1970 and reprinted many times – see Copeland and Cohen 1983, pp.533–549). This study considered many aspects of cultural and dance style.

Williams focused on ballet too, in a discussion of various 'grammatical' features of classical ballet style (1976). She draws attention to the rhythmic or dynamic terms which are used to describe movement in ballet, and to how the movement is dictated by rhythmic step patterns (polka, polonaise, mazurka, waltz, czardas, tarantella). Williams' valuable emphasis on the symbolically expressive nature of dance was referred to earlier. She also stresses the semantic significance of dance, describing it as action suffused with meaning. The significance of time elements in macro-structure is evident in Williams' approach: she states that meanings arise from the syntax, the ordering of elements to be noted as occurring both through time and simultaneously. Williams examines how synchrony, diachrony and panchrony apply to human actions and events (1976). Williams'

---

5   In a detailed study of Alaskan Eskimo Inupiaq dance, Johnston notes the prevalence of unison group movement which he suggests is a significant reflection of that traditionally egalitarian society (1990, p.200).

writing includes several clear descriptions of her experience of West African dance style in cultural context, with passing reference to rhythm (1968).

References to rhythm in aesthetic judgment of dance

Anthropologists have recorded local, indigenous aesthetic judgments about dance. These sometimes include reference to rhythm and timing. For instance, Keil in his study of the Tiv in central Nigeria, refers to the way they associate specific tempi and dynamics with particular dances: '*Girnya*, the traditional warrior's dance, should be danced quickly (*ferefere*) light on the feet (*gendegende*) with strength (*tsoghtsogh*) and rigorously, as a hen scratches (*sagher-sagher*) (1967, p.32). Also in Africa (the western region), Ruth Stone refers to a number of Kpelle remarks which indicate how performers should respond in both their dance and in the accompanying song:

> '*Mala na tee*', (cut the edge of the dance): the dancer should pause with a cut-off cue; '*Belei e ye*' (lower the performance): the performers should pause; and '*Belei aa pilan*' which indicates 'The performance has gotten down.' This means that the performers have reached a state of synchrony to allow the performance to enter the phase of '*ma yee*', where proverbs and certain highly valued aesthetic elements can be performed. (1981, p.17)

In his account of dance in Africa (with particular reference to Liberia, Dahomey, Nigeria, Cameroon and Zaire) Thompson describes the aesthetic significance of 'cutting the motion' in dance (1974, p.20). This means to present a sharply defined, well-timed beginning and ending to a dance, with clear body position. Thompson also refers to the time elements in his discussion of balance and the concept of 'cool'. This concept affects divers provinces of the artistic process and refers both to the inner state of the artist and to the character of the art product. Words used to describe 'cool' which relate to rhythm include: percussively patterned, harmonised, balanced, finished, calm, tranquil, gentle, moderate (1974, p.73). A further example of aesthetic significance ascribed to features of rhythm is provided by Kealiinohomoku. In relation to native American Hopi dance judgments she writes: 'A dance is considered 'not so good' if it is performed at too rapid or too slow a tempo... It is important for the performance to have the right number and length of songs so that the last song of a daytime performance is completed before sundown'. (1976a, p.131).

In conclusion, to summarise our findings: notators and anthropologists in this compilation have certainly drawn attention to a number of important elements of rhythm and timing. In their perception of rhythm, notators' special interests have led to particular observation of specific body positions and actions (such as a Renaissance bow or the steps known in jazz dance), metric patterning, duration, tempo, accents, pauses, tracks (the ground plan of steps, with changes of direction), gestural pathways and – to a limited extent in most cases – dynamics. More unusual, interesting features from some notators (who in the examples cited also happen to be anthropologists) include: paths (or flow) of energy, synchronicity and 'ritual intensity'. These are vital, captivating features of rhythm which are most evident in examples described, such as in the Shakers' movement, and in the traditional ceremonies of the Maring and the Yaqui (see pp.61–64 and Chapters 10, 12).

The anthropologists selected for their comments have likewise stressed a range of elements, some from a special interest in dance, one example from drama, and others from a focus on everyday life, ceremony or ritual. In addition to elements suggested by notators, we find particular mention of structural features of performed movement – motifs, phrases, alternation and repetition. Concepts, factors or elements of rhythm and timing less commonly referred to in studies include: rhythm seen in dance as a 'shaping' factor, as a stylistic element, and as a key element in human communication and interaction. Intriguing references are also made to rhythm in relation to focus or 'projectional quality' and with regard to intricacy in events. We read of the significance of moments of starting and stopping, bodily impulse and the infectious power of rhythm – a theme to which I return later, for instance in relation to rock and rave dance (see pp.190–193). As anthropologist Royce states, in dance: 'Our bodies are caught up in the rhythm and repetition whether we are performers or merely spectators' (1981, p.9). Movement rhythm and timing in the aesthetic judgment of performance is another topic mentioned which warrants investigation. All these references from both notators and anthropologists add to our understanding and store of knowledge. They broaden our view and make a useful contribution to a compilation and description of features, factors and elements of movement rhythm and timing in performance, through history and world-wide.

5

Contributions to the Study of Rhythm in the Theatre

In the 1890s the Swiss artist Adolphe Appia called his theatre designs 'rhythmic spaces': an exciting idea – it surely fires and extends the imagination about the possibilities of rhythm on stage. Indeed, rhythm seems to have been in the forefront of ideas in the European theatre and also in the USA in those days – in the late nineteenth and early twentieth centuries – especially in Russia and France. In this chapter I have adopted an historical perspective to share a miscellany of ideas from a number of pioneer theatre practitioners in drama and dance. It is a personal choice selected from a wealth of material which matches or has influenced my own approach to the subject. First, Stanislavski and Meyerhold have much to tell us about the striking use of rhythm and timing on stage and in the training of actors. Their insights and ideas on the subject are found scattered through their writings and in observers' accounts. Brief references to Copeau and Artaud represent stimulating ideas from France.

Since ideas about rhythm are particularly evident in dance, the survey of written studies from dance, although necessarily limited, is more extensive. An introduction to early dance history is followed with reference to Emile Jacques Dalcroze and Isadora Duncan – who made a particular contribution to rhythm and timing studies. Next, to bring us into more recent twentieth-century theatre work, there is an introduction to the ideas of Doris Humphrey, who wrote about and brought aspects of time and rhythm into her work in a distinctive and influential manner.

From these roots in dance history, later generations of dancers have developed ideas about rhythm in their own multifarious ways. Since Merce Cunningham has made perhaps the key pioneering contribution which broke with nineteenth-century forms to bring us into the present, the chapter concludes with particular reference to him and to some other contemporary theatre developments.

Drama

Theatre activity was especially impressive in Russia in the latter part of the nineteenth century, and until the Stalinist era. The most well known of a number of inspiring contributions to the study of rhythm during these years was made by Constantin Stanislavski, who stressed the inner organic nature of action. Rhythm was central to this concept and according to Stanislavski, it should be evident even when an actor was apparently motionless. In a seminar of noted Russian theatre practitioners, Toponkov recounted how Stanislavski addressed him in the middle of a scene: 'You are standing in the wrong rhythm!' (Litvinoff 1972, p.29). 'To stand and watch for a mouse – that is one rhythm: to watch a tiger that is creeping up on you is quite another one' (quoted in Toponkov *Stanislavski in Rehearsal*). Stanislavski emphasised that the actor should not lapse in any way during a pause in the acting: 'If you *drop out* of the life of your part during the pauses ... you will not gain the interest of anyone in the auditorium ... A pause on the stage is the highest point of stage art' (1950, pp.277–278).

Stanislavski had many ideas about the actor's use of rhythm in the development of a role. In a vivid description he explains one idea for an actor playing the part of a mentally unstable man:

> In a mentally unbalanced man the rhythm of attention is broken. The intervals of rest ... do not exist ... For him only the dashes exist, or in other words, attention, attention, and again attention ... a dance of thoughts without rhythm or control. He explodes in a series of disconnected thoughts – I am the Emperor of Abyssinia – I am a great musician – here's the stove – the mouse is on the table – I'm wearing French slippers – it is raining – and so on. (1950, p.141)

He stated that actors, working together in a performance 'must sound in one rhythm' (1950, pp.181–182) and it is clear from his writing that Stanislavski strove to develop actors' awareness of rhythm and timing both in ensemble playing and as individuals, particularly through practice in use of breathing, pause, metre and tempo. He saw breath rhythm as the basis of control and power on stage. Awareness of this was fundamental in his advice to actors:

> and it is only when it [breathing] is rhythmical that it renews all the creative functions of your organism ... but what happens to you when you are distressed, cross, irritated or when you fly into a rage? All the functions of your breathing are upset. You are not only unable to control your passions, but you cannot even control the rhythm of your breathing. (1950, p.142)

Stanislavski distinguished between rhythm as patterning of beats, and tempo pattern. He introduced a tempo rating system in which tempo was associated with life events. For instance, he indicated an increase of pace when characters were experiencing a disaster, and a decrease when they were about to die. Stanislavski took this idea seriously enough to include numerical marks of the beats-rating system (1–10) in the prompt copy. However, although he continued to include references to timing in his stage directions, he later found the rating system was artificial, and he abandoned its use.

In acting classes Stanislavski encouraged creativity and he devised training methods based, for instance, on use of tempo and metric beats. For example, students tapped out rhythm of different emotions and events such as grief, storms, headaches, ecstasy. 'Tempo-rhythm of movement cannot only intuitively, directly, immediately suggest appropriate feeling and arouse the sense of experiencing what one is doing but also it helps stir one's creative faculty' (1950, p.202). Stanislavski frequently included notes on features of rhythm when criticising actors – for example, he castigated them for lack of appropriate 'mad rhythm' and the 'bored faces and limp rhythms' in what as a result he pejoratively dubbed 'the so-called *Storming of the Bastille*' (1958, p.148).

The psychological component in human action was stressed in Stanislavski's approach to acting (see also Moore 1966, p.25). This was associated with the actor's awareness of an 'inner tempo-rhythm' for each role and for every part of a scene. Giving Hamlet as an example he writes:

> At the point when the hero … has to take a definite and strong stand there are no contradictions and doubts – one all-embracing tempo-rhythm is not only appropriate, it is even necessary. But when, as in Hamlet's soul, resolution wrestles with doubt, various rhythms in simultaneous conjunctions are necessary. In such cases several different tempo-rhythms provoke an internal struggle of contradictory origins. (1950, p.206)

Evgeny Vakhtangov, Stanislavski's assistant and former pupil, explains further:

> Rhythm must be perceived from within. Then the physical movements of the body will become subordinated to this rhythm spontaneously. The task of the school consists in training the pupil in this sensitivity to rhythm, and not in teaching him to move rhythmically … Every nation, every man, every phenomenon in nature, every event of human life – everything has its own characteristic rhythm. Therefore, every drama, every role, every part of a role, every feeling – has its own rhythm. Given the rhythm of a certain scene it will be played correctly. To perceive the rhythm of a drama is to find the key to its presentation. (1947, pp.121–122)

Vakhtangov developed these ideas about rhythm in his own fertile experimental work as a director. 'He found a different theatrical rhythm for each character' writes Sonia Moore, who was present at some of his rehearsals (1966, p.12).

Again in Russia, the wondrously inventive director Vsevolod Meyerhold evolved ideas about the continuity of action and scene on stage. He stressed the importance of rhythm: 'the essential thing is rhythm … how the actor breathes, how he walks, how he combines with the rhythm of other bodies and other movements on the stage ... how he embodies the rhythm of the play' (quoted in Kirstein 1935, p.32). And: 'the task of the actors of the future is to develop in themselves an awareness of time in their performance' (quoted in Ivanov 1973).

Meyerhold developed a process which he called 'braking the rhythms'. This concerned use of tempo and strict timing of pauses. Gausner and Gabrilovitch described the process in action in Meyerhold's 1925 production of *Bubus the Teacher*:

> The braking of the rhythms in *Bubus* makes it possible for us to discover that combinations of segments of time can acquire meaning. We were thus offered a new theatrical procedure of extreme importance ... the succession of body sketches would express nothing if they were not sustained by the *tempo*. It is the *tempo* which gives these mimed elements all their meaning. (from *October in the Theatre* (1926) quoted in Barba and Savarese 1991, p.90)

Meyerhold's working script was detailed and precise in notes about time elements. It specified duration of pauses, the tempi and time in seconds of actions and speeches, as well as timing of the all-important accompanying music. Indeed, impressed and influenced by Wagner, the rhythms of music pervaded Meyerhold's productions. This was evident as a changing pattern of rhythm in the flow of action, a subtext for the drama, underpinning and inseparable from the total work (see Leach, 1989).

Chapter 2 included some comments about reduction in stage space in relation to rhythm. Apparently Meyerhold explored the idea in his last great production, Gogol's *The Government Inspector*. 'The entire performance was concentrated on this small platform area [3.55 x 4.25 metres]. This restricted scene area obliged the actors to be extremely conscious of both their most detailed movements and the performance's general rhythm' (Barba and Savarese 1991, p.91). Stylised gestures and actions of all parts of the actors' bodies were an important feature of the production. Meyerhold had developed Appia's ideas of varying the planes and levels of the stage space, and for this show he designed a raked platform so that the audience could see the movement of the actors more easily.

Meyerhold aimed at increasing the degree of control in actors' movements. With this in mind he developed a theory of bio-mechanics and an athletic, gymnastic approach to movement training for actors with a timing basis of:

Preparation for action – pause –
the action itself – pause –
and its corresponding re-action. (quoted in Roose-Evans 1984, p.28)

He declared: 'performing is determined by the time principle' (quoted in Barba and Savarese 1991, p.91). And in a lecture about his experience of working on a film *The Picture of Dorian Gray* (1918) he stated: 'This rhythm with a capital R is precisely what imposes the responsibilities on the cameraman, on the director, on the artist and on the actors ... the task of the actors of the future is to develop in themselves an awareness of time in their performance' (quoted in Ivanov 1973).

In France in the first decades of the twentieth century, many owed a debt to Copeau for their training in experimental, radical theatre. As Roose-Evans explains, he stressed physical expertise in acting and he had 'a great sense of choreography'. But this 'developed organically from the text... He was deeply sensitive to the underlying rhythms of a text, the intervals of time and the elements in drama which were similar to music' (1984, p.55). These comments refer to Copeau's work at the Theatre du Vieux Columbier, Paris 1913–1914, 1919–1924. Stripping his productions to essentials, and at one time leading his troupe around Burgundy with a portable stage, Copeau developed the concept of *commedia dell'arte* with its use of contrasting masks which make increased demands on the movement-rhythm of the actors.

Antonin Artaud, a leading figure in the Surrealist movement in Paris, and influential in experimental theatre, placed movement centrally in his perception of theatre action. He too referred to elements of rhythm (1958, p.37). In his essays Artaud attacked the dominance of speech and verbal expression in our western culture. He showed his appreciation of movement expression in his description of Balinese performers: 'through the labyrinth of their gestures, attitudes and sudden cries, through the gyrations and turns which leave no portion of the stage space unutilized, the sense of a new physical language based upon signs, and no longer upon words, is liberated' (1958, pp.53–54).

Artaud displayed perception of elements of rhythm in Balinese performance: 'Repeatedly they seem to accomplish a kind of recovery with measured steps ... and on three final steps, which lead them ineluctably to the middle of the stage, the suspended rhythm is completed, the measure made clear' (1958, p.55). Artaud also noted how any costumes worn may contribute to the rhythm of a performance. For example, he observed the Balinese women's headdresses 'the crests of which tremble rhythmically, responding *consciously*, or so it seems, to the tremblings of the body' (1958, p.56).

Dance

The earliest references to rhythm and timing appear in western European dance history as description of social dances, with an emphasis on the accompanying music in relation to the dance; sometimes with a form of notation and advice to performers. Dancing masters such as Arbeau (1588), Feuillet (1701), Weaver (1706) and Rameau (1725) wrote manuals for the purpose of recording and teaching their work. Training, with skill and artistry demonstrated in performance, was taken seriously in the highly competitive social milieu of those days. And it was these social dances which were the basis of the first theatrical dance performance seen on stage.

There is evidence to suggest that early dancing masters considered rhythm and timing to be key elements in the desired manner and form of dance performance of their day. Of the five essential characteristics of dancers listed by fifteenth-century Domenico for instance, two are concerned with rhythm and timing: *misura* and *fantasmata*. *Misura* may be translated as both rhythmic control or order, and moving according to the music or 'measure', and *fantasmata* relates to both tempo and stillness: '"Fantasmata" is a bodily speed controlled by the measure of each tempo, that is, having made the movement in one instant, one must be all of tone, as if one had seen the head of Medusa (as the poet says) and in another instant putting on wings as a falcon which is moved to flight in fear' (Domenico, trans. Thomas 1978, p.24; Franko 1987). Linked with notational methods mentioned in the last chapter, studies generally pay attention chiefly to steps, metre and directions in space (floor patterns and partner or group formations).

Some comments from dance history research help us to envisage what the effect of cultural context may have had on the manner of performance of movement rhythm in the past. Emma Thomas in her study, for instance, includes reference to dance style as reflection of the image of man when she describes dance principles set out in the Renaissance: 'An awareness of these dance principles is absolutely necessary for performers attempting to work within the style of an earlier age when subtler gesture and balance, measure rather than heroics, controlled calm rather than emotionalism were more important considerations than they are today' (1978, pp.24–35).

In Switzerland, Emile Jacques-Dalcroze developed a system of co-ordinating music and bodily movement – 'Eurhythmics' – originally designed for training musicians but also used for developing aspects of movement rhythm and musicality in dancers. The emphasis was on music: 'Music is the only art, directly founded on dynamics and rhythm, which is capable of giving style to bodily movements' (1921, p.166), but Dalcroze considered duration, time, rhythm, pauses, counterpoint, phrasing and construction (form) to be common to music and dance. He distinguished between rhythm and time: 'A machine, however perfectly regulated, is devoid of rhythm – being controlled by time ... The submission of our breathing to discipline and regularity of time would lead to the suppression of every instinctive emotion and the disorganisation of vital rhythm' (1921, p.184). Although Dalcroze placed metre in the realm of time, he held that metrical regulation must be subservient to rhythmic impulses (1921, p.185). In an interesting cross-reference to the field of drama, Dalcroze considered that he was putting Appia's training suggestions into practice:

The special training for choruses proposed by Appia twenty years ago and since practised by us, aims at giving performers the necessary flexibility for adapting themselves spontaneously to all the rhythms, however complex, called into play by the inspiration and what we may be permitted to call the 'music' of the creative imagination. This education should be imposed likewise on conductors, producers and specialists in stage painting and lighting.' (1921, p.130)

Dalcroze saw rhythm as essentially physical, based on the action of heart, breath and gait. His training emphasised beat and metric patterns, with steps and gestures to match. He devised practical exercises in muscular relaxation, breathing, contraction of limbs, marching, arm gestures, division of beats, note values, pauses, rests, syncopation, anacusis, tempo, polyrhythm; he also encouraged rhythmic invention, improvisation and group work (see Enders 1941, pp.268–282).

Insights concerning the effect of temperament or personality on an individual's rhythm are found in Dalcroze' studies (1921, p.190). He also pointed out the potential of rhythm in effective stage presentation:

In the collective movement of a crowd we have to observe both changes and successions of attitudes … polyrhythm ought to play a highly important part in the training of stage crowds; not alone polyrhythm as applied to the chorus, but that formed by counterpoint between the gestures of the individual actor and those of the crowd. (1921, pp.128–129)

Isadora Duncan (who was born in America but taught and performed chiefly in Europe) tells us in her notebooks that 'The true dance must be the transmission of the earth's energy through the body.'[1] Indeed, Duncan's dancing and ideas about dance were rooted in the natural world and her chief contribution to studies of rhythm stemmed from this concern. 'My first idea of movement of the dance certainly came from the rhythm of the waves' (1927, p.9). It seems that Duncan immersed herself in sensing the flow of natural rhythms, of waters, winds, plants, living creatures. Duncan's much-publicised adoption of unrestrictive dance wear and bare feet, freeing the body for movement, served to increase rhythm and timing possibilities considerably. The soft fabric which Duncan used for dance wear accentuated rhythmic flow. Although Duncan herself danced on carpet she influenced the barefoot contact with the dance floor characteristic of modern dance, which led to more varied use of the feet in rhythm.

Sensing her solar plexus as a 'crater of motor power', central body impulse with motivation from the emotions was the source of Duncan's 'spontaneous expression of feeling' and use of rhythm (1927, p.75). Music motivated her too:

1   Duncan notebooks 1900–1903 (folder 141 New York Public Library).

her response to music released the ebb and flow of her dance expression. In private, Duncan worked in terms of the body's movement alone, without music. In these studies 'it was her hope to discover certain key movements, born of specific emotions, from which would flow of their own will, so to speak, related sequences of movement as natural reactions' (Martin 1968, p.136). This serious attitude to movement study and commitment to teaching was characteristic of Duncan and also thought to be crucial in the development of modern dance (see Siegel 1979, p.10).

In Britain and the USA from these early days until later in the twentieth century, in the field of dance education, the need for training in rhythm has been stressed. In this there was usually emphasis on features of tension and relaxation, use of the breath, energy fluctuation, metricity and phrasing. Attention was frequently directed to key elements of pulse, duration, tempo and accent as well as to sequential form factors such as repetition, variety, contrast, balance, climax and transition. These ideas were influential in the 1930–1960 era, especially in the USA. However, details of that educational material is beyond the scope of this book.

There were a number of influential pioneer dance artists who created and transformed modern dance in the USA, influenced by artists from Europe, such as Mary Wigman and Hanya Holm. From reports of the time, it is clear that the rhythm and beat of the new modern age penetrated the dance from the 1930s to the 1950s and beyond. There was evidence of this on stage in the work of Martha Graham, and later Alwin Nikolais and Anna Sokolow to name a few. As university dance pioneer Helen Alkire indicates, thought and change in relation to dance rhythm was in the air. She points out that modern dancers of this era 'were eager to find greater rhythmic freedom ... they found that the dynamics of rhythm were inseparable from expressive dance ... that emphasising changes in rhythm added excitement and power to movement... The fast-moving 20th century required that each person keep up with its urgent rhythmic pace' (1961, pp.7–8).

Doris Humphrey (1895–1958) was foremost among the modern dance pioneers in speaking and writing about rhythm, considering it to be of central interest and significance in all aspects of dance: choreography, dramatic expression, technique and teaching. 'Every movement has a rhythm, everybody has a rhythm, everything you do all day long has a rhythm, as people living also as dancers. Now as dancers we can expand the idea of rhythm, we can manipulate that too' (1951). As her autobiographer Selma Jeanne Cohen writes 'Of her generation in modern dance, Doris was probably ... the most sensitive to rhythm and phrasing' (1972, p.225).

Rhythm is 'the most persuasive and most powerful element, with the possible exception of virtuoso technique and dazzling personality' stated Humphrey (1959a, p.104). She listed five main sources of rhythmical organization:

breathing, heartbeat, peristalsis, action of legs supporting the body travelling through space, and emotions – 'surges and ebbs of feeling with accents which not only supply strong rhythmical patterns but are a measure for judging emotional rhythms in others' (1959a, p.105). Thus she developed her ideas about rhythm from observation of what she termed the natural movements of the human body – 'natural' here in the sense of movement in the body's muscular activity, response to gravity, need for oxygen and circulation of blood. Critic John Martin described her dance 'movement as emanating from inner impulse' (1965a, p.257). As is common in dance writing, Humphrey also used 'natural' to refer to the rhythm of everyday movements (as in walking, running) and to movements in the world of nature.

In a famous statement Humphrey referred to life (and dance) existing between two stillnesses as 'the arc between two deaths. This lifetime span is filled with thousands of falls and recoveries – all highly specialised and exaggerated in dance – which result in accents of all qualities and timings' (1959a, p.106).

An investigation of the relationship of the moving body to gravity appears to have initiated the rest of Humphrey's dance theory. The physical movement sequence in linked succession of 'suspension, fall and recovery' in relation to gravity was a characteristic central feature of Humphrey's dance technique teaching. We can see that this sequence relates to breath pattern (inhalation, suspension of breath and exhalation): 'There is a whole world of movement implicit in just this part of rhythm' (1959a, p.108).

[We may consider] the breath rhythm as the one principle of all movement ... a filling and expanding followed by a contraction in the dynamic sense, a continuous movement growing in tension followed by a letting go of tension which finishes with an accent. By combining these (three) elements of the breath rhythm consciously in various ways the whole dance may be evolved. (1934, unpublished ms)

Humphrey developed this idea as a dance impetus, with transference of action to different parts of the body and influencing the dancer's use of space.

Another important rhythmic source for dance, 'motor rhythm' (as it is generally called in the USA) was identified by Humphrey; that is, rhythm chiefly derived from change of weight from one foot or other part of the body to another, and locomotor patterns (such as walking, running). Again, she related this to her concept of fall and recovery. For instance, she stated that the action of walking (hip, leg, foot lowering/raising) is 'the key pattern of fall and recovery: ... the very core of all movement' (1959a, p.106). Humphrey also pointed out that since the change of weight can make a beat, metric rhythm can easily be developed from this, with use of accents. She made a clear distinction between breath rhythm and metric, or strictly counted-out rhythm: 'I think of rhythm as being of two kinds:

first what I call a breath rhythm and second what I call a metric rhythm' (1951). Passages in *The Shakers* exemplify this contrast powerfully, and I vividly recall how this was something Humphrey stressed when, towards the end of her life, she attended a reconstruction of this work in a London studio.

Group rhythm is choreographed powerfully in *The Shakers*, and Humphrey once stated: 'The group is my medium' (1929). As an observer, Cohen describes the inventive and complex group rhythm in another work, *With My Red Fires*: 'Rhythm was taken sporadically through the group – everybody had a different phrase length – my gosh, the stage was so jittery; and it was the rhythmic thing that did it. It looked like chaos – it was anything but chaos' (Cohen 1981, personal communication).

Humphrey described the pattern of dynamics in a rhythmic structure as a changing flow of energy:

the whole scale is subject to endless variation in tempo and tension ... slow-smooth with force; fast-smooth without tension; fast-sharp with tension (like pistol shots), moderate-sharp with little force (rather blunt), slow-smooth without tension (dreamy, sluggish or despairing) and so forth. (1959, p.97)

And in her discussion of the structural form of a dance, Humphrey again referred to energy and rhythm when she stressed the fundamental importance of phrasing in dance structure: 'this punctuation of energy is quite inescapable as a pattern ... this most fundamental of all shapes' (1959, p.67). She defined phrasing as 'the organization of movement in time-design' and a phrase as 'expenditure of energy at various rates, followed by a rest' (1959, pp.66, 67). And once more stressing the breath-energy base of dance action, Humphrey stated 'All our sense of phrasing comes from what may be expressed on a breath' (1951).

Humphrey's notes for a lecture on rhythm stipulated 'it [rhythm] must be sensed in muscular effort, not as mathematical beat imposed from without'. Furthermore, she insisted that for her, phrasing and rhythm was essentially centred in body movement, rather than derived from any given music. Her choreography was designed in relation to the music but not necessarily finally determined by it: 'The rules of movement do not always coincide with the music and it is a matter of judgment as to how to treat it so that both keep their integrity and both keep the dance moving forward' (1951).

In a programme note for *Water Study*, a group dance with no accompaniment, first performed in 1928, she wrote:

Probably the thing that distinguishes musical rhythm from other rhythm is the measured time beat, so this has been eliminated from the Water Study and the rhythm flows in natural phrases instead of cerebral measures. There is no count to hold the dancers together in the very slow opening rhythm, only the feel of the wave length that curves the backs of the group. (quoted in Cohen 1972, p.85)

Thus, Humphrey was essentially concerned with dance as an independent art with distinctive rhythm and timing – 'subject to laws of its own' (1959a: 135). Her instructions to students about creating dance with music emphasised this:

> Make a structure that does not merely rest like a bird on a wave on the music, but is in flight in itself. To carry the simile further, as though the bird were moving above the water and touching it and tipping it – so that when you look at the whole thing there is a relationship but they are not identical – they are two different things going on at the same time. (1950 class recording)

It is interesting to trace the trends, recurrence and changes in ideas about rhythm through the generations as various allegiances shifted and modern dance developed. For instance, some of Humphrey's concerns recur in the otherwise very different work and ideas of Merce Cunningham (1918–   ).

As dance critic Marcia Siegel stated, 'Cunningham was the first to explode the old concepts of stage space, phrasing, sequence, and determinacy in dance' (1973, p.248). In relation to rhythm and timing, the dance technique which he developed, initially to meet the demands of his choreography, is designed to develop a dancer's control, precision and split-second timing, readiness for the physically unexpected, and sensitivity to a wide range of tempi and intra-group events. Dance critic Arlene Croce described what she saw as a new dance technique and new dance vocabulary. She noted the marked and distinctive rhythm and timing content especially in the use of tempi and weight transference:

> he is the only choreographer working outside the ballet who has found a way to move with security of expression at great speed... incredibly rapid shifts of weight and direction of pace on the ground...When you see the whole Cunningham company hitting clear bursts of rhythm with all their fast little feet ... and when the frenzy of the action and the austerity of the dancers' control combine to give an effect of slow movement speeded up, then what you are seeing is the eloquence of a new vocabulary. (1968, p.25)

Cunningham's choreographic ideas spring from and are about movement, not derived from psychological or narrative source. In his work with dancers he requires them to sense time and rhythm as coming from within their own bodies, rather than as imposed from without. Thus, as with Humphrey, use of energy contributes in a distinctive way to Cunningham's concept of rhythm, energy which he describes as 'geared to an intensity high enough to melt steel in some dancers ... fusion at a white heat' (1955, p.37).

This choreographer's approach to the use of metre, as well as to the relationship of music and dance, take Humphrey's ideas a stage further. Metric patterns can be identified in the movement his dancers perform, but the choreography is not based on these. Cunningham feels strongly that the nineteenth-century music-based metrical rhythms of ballet are inappropriate for his work. He believes:

> dancers can depend on their own legs, instead of on the music. So I let them dance, instead of coming from an outside source – prompted by music – the dance comes from the movement itself. Or from a sequence of movements, each of which is built upon another. And the rhythms come out of that, rather than from dependence on musical structure. (1979 May 9 interview)

The innovative composer John Cage's collaboration with Cunningham notably emphasised the autonomy of each art. In the past 'The idea was that the music kept everything together and one danced on it, or to it; interpreted it ... [the musician was asked] to come in like a dressmaker and fit some music to the dance' (Cage 1980 lecture, Goldsmiths' College, London).

Unexpected effects of timing in Cunningham's works arise partly as a result of his innovatory methods of choreography: for instance, he and Cage became known for their application of chance methods in composition to determine dance structure, including selection of type of action, sequential order and spatial patterning. Cunningham again speaks out strongly against nineteenth-century forms as a model when he is discussing timing in structure:

> These consist mainly of theme and variation, and associated devices – repetition, inversion, development and manipulation. There is also a tendency to imply a crisis to which one goes and then in some way retreats from... More freeing into space than the theme and manipulation 'hold up' would be a formal structure based on time. (1952, p.150)

Thus, as noted in Chapter 2, Cunningham's dance time structure is based on duration: the one common feature Cunningham and Cage recognise in the dance/music relationship.

Always adventurous and open to new developments, Cunningham's thinking was influenced by the advent and use of electronic music: 'I know for me one of the things that changed my thinking about time very much was electronic music because I suddenly realised that I couldn't count that in the way that I had counted conventional, metrically arranged music' (1979). Thus working usually with a stop-watch, Cunningham measures phrases in terms of the time their movement takes, rather than in the counts or beats of conventional practice. As he has said:

> time can be an awful lot of bother with the ordinary, pinch-penny counting that has to go on with it, but if one can think of the structure as a space of time, in which anything can happen in any sequence of movement event, and any length of stillness can take place, then the counting is an aid towards freedom rather than a discipline towards mechanization. (1952, p.151)

Cunningham referred to his concepts and working methods in relation to time in a lecture about his piece *Torse*. In it 'there are no cadences. There are no traditional ways of changing from one thing to another, [the dancers] just go'. Each dancer frequently pursues a seemingly independent track of changing energy, speed and direction, so that different rhythmic patterns occur in each track simultaneously. In discussion of the work Cunningham expressed a liking for everyday rhythms and for group movement with similar action content but not necessarily in unison, 'as seen with animals or birds' (London, 20 February 1977).

Notions of perspective and significance or hierarchy of certain stage areas such as solo centre of front do not constrain Cunningham's use of stage space or spatial rhythm: '*any* point, wherever *anybody* is, is of interest' (interview May 9 1979). His dancers primarily cue in relation to each other, to each other's movement rhythm and timing, and group interaction. Cunningham's work even frequently gives the impression that pieces begin or continue off stage, or are taking place simultaneously on and off stage. In fact his pieces have left the stage entirely in his explorations of television as a choreographic medium.

Cunningham is also in the forefront of experiments with computerised choreography: 'pushing at the frontiers of dance for four decades' as the introduction to a television programme about *CRWDSPCR* (pronounced 'crowdspacer') described him.[2] We saw in the programme how the grid of figures moving on the computer screen influenced Cunningham to invent new steps, gestures and rhythms. "The computer opens the eye to detail" he said.

It was something of a relief to notice that despite Cunningham's fascination with the computer he still gets as much of a kick as ever out of everyday rhythms. Gazing down at the river from his studio windows high above Manhattan, he told us: 'There aren't many boats, but when they come it's a great pleasure. When I'm teaching in the late afternoon, I often look out the window to see if one of those large cruisers that carry many people to the Caribbean is coming down the river very slowly – and the rhythm is so different from what's going on in the dance class it adds a surprise element.'

To conclude, the multi-track approach to rhythm on stage which Cunningham characteristically adopts (with or without the use of computer software) frequently brings a high degree of variety, intricacy and complexity to his choreography. For example, speaking about his work *Events* Cunningham stated that he tries to allow: 'for as much in that period of time as I can – as many different kinds of complexities as I can get into that time. Sometimes there are single things, sometimes there are multiple things' (interview 1980).

2   *CRWDSPCR* first performed 1993. *Summer Dance* BBC2 TV, 4 August 1997.

Other contemporary theatre developments

The use of television, computer technology and the subject of performance complexity brings us right up to date. It plunges us into the theatre world of the late twentieth century, where especially in dance, it seems that 'anything goes'. In drama too, theatre work has become increasingly diverse. This chapter is not designed to provide an account of the use of rhythm and timing in present-day theatre developments, but some references here, in addition to the few made elsewhere in the text, are needed.

Particularly obvious examples of focus on the use of rhythm and timing in contemporary theatre are to be found in Robert Wilson's work (in the USA – also sometimes seen in Europe), and in that of the Wooster Group in New York. For Wilson the passage of time seems to be an abiding theme. Merging drama, ritualised action, scenic effects and music, he has explored unusual structural form and varied use of timing, with some influence from his work with autistic and brain-damaged children. This exploration has included use of slow motion, as in *Deafman Glance* (1971), considerable extension of performance duration, as for example in *The Life and Times of Joseph Stalin* (1973) which lasted 12 hours, and sometimes surprising, sudden actions and lighting changes as in his production of Marguerite Duras' *La maladie de la mort* (1997).

In common with other experimental theatre groups, the practice of the Wooster Group has been to take months for the preparation of ensemble-performance projects, devised and developed by the company with director Elizabeth Le Compte. During their shows, sequences with varied rhythms have been included from diverse sources, such as black stand-up comics' routines, vaudeville-style dancing, real-life timing (an actual telephone call to a food take-out service was made on stage in one production), extracts from political debates and other excerpts from programmes seen on TV screens, on stage. From the realisation that we no longer inhabit a culture centred on one idea, the company presents a number of rhythms such as these, simultaneously in their works. Narrative structure is non-linear, and without transitions between episodes. In *LSD,* during an idiosyncratic version of Arthur Miller's *The Crucible,* the group used excessive pace and cartoon-like imagery to subvert audience expectations and to generate the feeling of hysteria in the play. Particular use of elements of rhythm and timing is inherent in their presentational style, even to the extent of threads from shows being picked up and developed in later productions. During past decades others in the USA too, such as Richard Foreman with his inclusion of still tableaux, false starts and repetition, or the Bread and Puppet Theatre's rhythm of changing, thought-provoking images, have expanded notions of rhythm and timing in theatre movement.

These and other ideas have been seen in the approaches of European and other directors also. For instance, Kantor, Grotowski, Tomaszewski, Barba,

Mnouchkine and Suzuki (Tadashi) are well known for their challenging and exciting work as well as for rigorous actors' movements training methods which have pushed theatre expression, with varied use of rhythm and timing elements, to further limits.

In the earlier part of the century, the subject of rhythm in theatre movement was largely neglected in Britain. Interest in text rather than movement prevailed. Now, with influences from overseas and perhaps from contemporary dance too, a more movement-based approach is sometimes evident. It seems then, that perhaps this may be an appropriate time to draw attention to movement-rhythm and timing in the theatre, and for a rediscovery of the work of early pioneers in both drama and dance – and to consider how this relates to contemporary developments.

We can see how those pioneering representatives from the world of theatre lead us from the past into twentieth-century practice, and an important new emphasis may be discerned. The core of Appia's view of stage design was that it should relate to the natural scale of man/woman, and the ideas and theories of these working-directors, dancing-masters and choreographers bring us closer to the performer's experience of rhythm. With the repeated stress from Stanislavski, Isadora Duncan and the rest, on physical features such as inner organic rhythm, rhythm initiated by central body impulse, breath, pulse, and muscular action, the actor, dancer, moving person is brought vividly to the fore. Set within the design environment of Appia's 'natural' scale and 'rhythmic spaces', we are vigorously reminded how use of elements such as tempo and pauses, and fluctuations in energy or in the tension-release continuum, may contribute to actors' characterisation and to the expressive range of dancers. This can be seen in the work of individual performers and in the power and imaginative orchestration of groups on stage, as well as in the variety around us in everyday life.

Suggestions about factors of rhythm and timing in the structural form of performance in the work of the artists described, range from the traditional to the innovative. Of the ideas presented perhaps the most radical – seen fully expressed in the pronouncements of Doris Humphrey and Merce Cunningham – are the distinction made between metric and 'natural' rhythm, and the idea that we should consider movement rhythm in its own right, independent of music. In addition to his innovatory work with television and computers Cunningham expands our view of the expressive, dynamic potential of rhythm and timing in his ideas about the democratisation of stage space (with its inevitable effect on spatial rhythm), and about duration, rapidity – 'split-second timing', simultaneity and complexity: 'Things in life are changing ... if people are going to stay alive ... they're going to have to deal with complexity' (Cunningham quoted in Jowitt 1977). And Cunningham's approach is certainly one of 'staying alive'. His example encourages us to be adventurous, innovative and daring.

The concept of a physical language of movement emerges from the work of these pioneers – further developed in contemporary theatre experimentation, and rhythm and timing play a significant part in this. Rudolf Laban was a key figure in the development of the concept, bringing the world of movement to the attention of a wider audience, not only in the theatre. His approach to rhythm and timing is described in the next chapter.

6

Time and Rhythm in Human Movement
Rudolf Laban's Contribution

Movement therapists, management consultants, dance notators, some theatre people and probably most movement teachers are familiar with the work of Rudolf Laban. Countless numbers have based their practice on his discoveries about the principles of movement behaviour, while others have derived inspiration for research from his concepts: (see Bartenieff and Lewis 1980; Gellerman 1978; Kagan 1978; Lamb 1965; North 1972; Pforsich 1978; Preston-Dunlop 1981; Sweet 1978; Youngerman 1978 – to name a few). Laban's teaching and approach to time and rhythm in human movement has been influential in the development of my understanding of the subject, and this chapter provides a survey of his approach.[1]

Rudolf von Laban was born in 1879 in Bratislava, Czechoslovakia. Interest in movement, rhythm and nature – and in links between these – developed in him at an early stage. In a memoir he refers to his movement response to a sunrise when he was just 15: 'I moved from sheer joy in all this beauty and order; for I saw order in it all…And I thought, there is only one way I can express all this. When my body and soul move together they create a rhythm of movement; and so I danced' (1956, p.9).

As a young man, Laban travelled and studied architecture and the arts in Paris; then, in 1910 he founded a community centre for dance and other arts with a summer festival, at Ascona, Switzerland. This was to be a base for his experiments in movement and dance on which he worked with other artists, of whom perhaps

---

[1]   In brief, to acknowledge influences which led to my own Laban studies: first, as a University of Bristol Drama Department student in the 1950s on our summer course at Dartington Hall, I was impressed by Laban-trained Geraldine Stephenson's performance and work with us there on Yeats' *Plays for Dancers*. Later Veronica Sherborne was the fine teacher who introduced me to more of Laban's approach when she taught a session for the Drama Department, after which I attended her evening classes. Training at Laban's Movement Centre came next, and opportunities to observe and work with a number of Laban-trained teachers. A teaching appointment at the Centre followed ten years later.

the best known were Mary Wigman and Kurt Jooss. By the 1920s Laban had developed ideas of 'movement choirs' and dance-dramas for group participation. He directed many performances and established dance schools, which were led by former students in a number of European cities. In 1928 his *Schriftanz*, a method of movement notation which he invented, was published.

Although Laban also worked as a choreographer in the theatre, he sought a form of movement expression which was closer to nature, a form which was markedly different from the ballet and other stage dance of his day. He was seeking *Bewegungskunst* – movement art, and a modern form of dance, which became known as *Ausdruckstanz* – dance of expression. In Germany this was developed with his pupils, notably by Mary Wigman in stage performance and in her teaching, and elsewhere by other dance pioneers such as Gertrud Bodenwieser in Vienna (who acknowledged Laban's influence).

Laban's life in Germany ended in 1936 when his work was banned by the Nazis. He moved first to France and then to England in 1938, where he lived until his death in 1958. The work in industry, education and notation with which his name is now chiefly associated, developed further during that time.

Even as a student, I recognised Laban's exceptionally clear understanding of the significance of time elements and rhythm in movement expression, which he applied in imaginative ways. His approach was certainly unusual in England in those days. I recall taking part in a work based on ideas from Shakespeare's *A Midsummer Night's Dream* which he devised and directed. His view of the fairies was a far from pretty one. He had us imagine and adopt individual rhythmic patterns of grotesque, demented gremlins with sharply jerking elbows and knees. At a rehearsal when we were still wearing the long skirts from the previous episode in which we were representing members of Duke Theseus' court, our appearance as the weird, spooky 'fairies' was enhanced by Laban's sudden inspiration to have us pick our skirts up from behind and whisk them over our heads, where they remained for the scene – an unconventional, outlandish sight from front or behind. A striking effect was created from individually varied rhythmic phrases which agitated the skirt-cloaks in a bizarre rhythmic counterpoint. The change from the preceding stately slow movement of the court to a realm of unpredictable magic, provided a fine lesson in the effective use of contrasting time-worlds on stage.[2] From a survey of Laban's books and papers, it can be seen that his writing is informed by the practical understanding of

2   Contrasts and range of performance experience were emphasised in the various dance-dramas which were part of the curriculum in those days. One basis for this was the idea of differing performance modes which provided themes. These were identified as: lyrical, rhythmic-dynamic, grotesque, dramatic, mimetic, ritualistic. Characteristic use of rhythm and timing in each clarified the difference between them.

movement expression – whether on stage or off – which may be glimpsed in that example.

Fundamental connections between posture, energy use and period, cultural or contextual style were noted by Laban, and he emphasised the significance of rhythmic content in relation to these:

> In certain epochs, in definite parts of the world, in particular occupations, in cherished aesthetic creeds or in utilitarian skills, some attitudes of the body are preferred and more frequently used than others ... the selection of and preference for certain bodily attitudes create style ... The finer shades of style will only be understood after a thorough study of the rhythmic content of the attitudes in which a definite series of effort combinations has been used. (1950, pp.88–9)

The approach to rhythm in both solo and group movement interaction which Laban articulated remains valid still: 'Solo dance is a duet between the dancer and his environment, or the dancer and his inner world... More concrete is the play and inter-action between people in a group in which rhythms of fleeing and following, of sympathy and antipathy simultaneously appear and therefore become more powerful' (unpublished MS). He was thoroughly conversant with the process of rhythm in dance, and he understood the performer's experience of it.

In the last chapter Doris Humphrey's focus on dance rhythm as distinct from music was described, an idea developed later by Cunningham and others. An important feature of Laban's understanding of rhythm in dance, and as with Humphrey one unusual at the time, was that he too considered it as a subject in its own right, essentially different in many ways from the concept of musical rhythm:

> Rhythm is experienced by the dancer as plastic (three-dimensional). Rhythm is not for him time-duration divided by force accents, as one tries to interpret this concept in music. Rhythm is the law of gesture, according to which it proceeds at one time more fluently and at another time less fluently and its sequence in space within a sequence of time (duration), as a result, tensing and detensing (relaxation) originating within the body whole. (quoted in Bartenieff 1980, p.55)

That dance training and expressive movement in performance has been influenced by Laban was evident in the work of dance artists such as Wigman, Holm, Jooss, Leeder – not least in their use of time elements. With these and other associates, he developed ways of training the dancer. One fundamental action stressed was that of moving from the centre of the body and stretching out into space. There were also related exercises derived from the rhythm of alternating bodily tension and release. As John Martin wrote: 'Throughout the studios of Germany you will hear the phrase "Anspannung und Abspannung" over and over again – the ebb and flow of muscular impulses. It was perhaps Rudolf von Laban who was primarily responsible for this emphasis' (1933, p.32). And I can vouch for the echo of such phrases in our training. However, Laban's chief aim with students was to develop the fullest possible range and extent of movement vocabulary and use of rhythm, rather than any one particular style. He was concerned to discern and bring out the individuality and creativity of each class member. As a teacher, I hope I never forget his immediate, positive response to a student who expressed an innovative fresh idea: 'Try it!'

Laban presented a broad, encompassing view of movement. He investigated the principles of movement which underlie the complexity and surface detail. Observation and analysis of these principles at work in human movement were the foundation of his pioneering approach. This provides a basis, not only for movement and dance training, but also for movement therapy, for vocational guidance and for the study of work efficiency. By adopting Laban's approach, it is possible through observation to acquire a detailed picture of the rhythm and interplay of movement elements that constitute what we might call signature characteristics of the movement-personality of an individual. This approach can be applied to the study of a movement style too, such as we see in the performance of a particular traditional folk dance.

The method of movement observation, with its codified vocabulary and notational method which Laban developed, was clearly a marked advance on general unsystematic description and the use of idiosyncratic language. 'In calling rhythms wild or soft, frightening or appeasing we do not give more than a very general idea of the mood they evoke' (Laban 1950, p.68). Laban did much to remove the weaknesses of limited generality and inexactitude in the description of rhythm.

Fascinated by human movement and committed to all aspects of its study, Laban was especially alert to the significance and power of time elements in performance and of the need to examine these:

> Rhythmic movement is the basis of play and art ... The actor on the stage shows in his rhythmic movements a great variety of efforts which are characteristic for almost all shades of human personality ... In watching dancing, our interest is focused upon the visible efforts forming the rhythm expressed by movement. In a similar way we can discern the rhythm in the efforts of any working person ... We can gather the meaning of a movement and though it seems difficult to express it in exact words, rhythm conveys something by which we are influenced; we may be excited, depressed or tranquillised. (1948, p.xiv)

Laban applies a broad concept of rhythm to choreographic inspiration when he writes of rhythm in the world: 'The vision of the world as an arrangement of rhythmical vibrations on a vast scale, of waves and dynamic streamings, might prove to be a powerful incentive for future choreographers' (unpublished ms.).

This description could well be applied to one of the movement choir presentations referred to earlier, and which Laban himself continued to devise in later days with Lisa Ullmann. I well remember the experience of 'dynamic streamings' on those occasions, and Ullmann herself makes references to rhythmic content when she writes of her own first experience of seeing a Laban-led 'movement choir':

> There were groups of men with strong and vigorous rhythmical movements countering the women creating smoothly flowing patterns, there were dramatic moments when one group seemed to imprison and subdue another one and when finally at first a few and then more and more dancers emerged from a maze-like entanglement in a pulsating rhythm of joy and harmony. (1956, p.5)

As indicated in Chapter 2, definitions of rhythm frequently include reference to metricity. This can derive from a musical approach to rhythm. Although Laban's concept of movement and dance rhythm differed from a purely musical one, he certainly valued and used music extensively in his work. He had a particular interest in metric rhythm, which is associated with music and with classical poetry. In discussing metric rhythm he frequently referred to classical Greek practice with its basis in a combination of time duration and accentuation. Varied moods were thought to be evoked by the six 'fundamental' rhythms of trochee, iambus, dactylus, anapaestus, peon and ionian. This seems close to ideas about energy fluctuation in relation to *anima, animus* etc. (see pp.25–26) and it was also thought that they suggested gender difference. For instance the Greeks referred to the 'feminine' trochee or the 'masculine' iambic pattern, and Laban followed this model (see Laban 1950, pp.130, 129–131). (For further explanation of metricity see Chapter 7.)

Incidence of accents, irregular (or mixed) metrical form and duration had of course been studied before. But for me, one of Laban's major contributions to the study and practice of rhythm was his recognition of non-metric or free forms of rhythm. Non-metric or free forms are those which are 'elastic' in their use of duration, erratic in their use of accents, and not framed in bar-lines or measured in lengths. They are governed more by the fluctuation, increase and decrease of energy flow and dynamics than by other rules, such as those derived from western classical music.

A further contribution made by Laban was to the study of phrasing in dance and movement. He emphasised the role of increase and decrease in the use of movement elements in 'shaping' phrases. In particular he referred to the effect of fluctuation in the output of energy, in the rate of movement, in the degree of extension in space and in the stability/lability continuum.[3] This idea of energy

---

3   Readers familiar with developments of Laban's work in the USA, will notice differences in word usage. For instance in the USA 'lability' is sometimes referred to as 'mobility' which in the UK has the more general meaning of 'free to move' (O.E.D.).

fluctuation was incorporated in Laban's teaching about rhythm in phrasing when he stressed the expressive difference between the adoption of an 'impulse' or of an 'impact' pattern in motifs and phrases. An 'impulse' (so-called 'feminine') pattern is that of the trochaic accent pattern (that is: long–short, with an accent and more output of energy placed at the beginning of the motif or phrase). Patterns which adopt the 'impact' (so-called 'masculine') iambic (short–long) pattern have an accent placed at the end of the phrase. He sensed 'more impetuosity in the first one and the expression of a more languid mode in the second one' (1959, p.21).

Since Laban's ideas about rhythm were bound up with his concept of motion factors, a brief summary of this now follows. (At this point readers may prefer to proceed directly to an application of these ideas in a dramatic context (*Dr. Faustus,* below), and then if they so wish, refer back to the theoretical basis which follows here). Four motion factors common to all movement were distinguished by Laban as 'weight', 'time', 'space' and 'flow' (inseparable in practice, but isolated for study purposes). All are present to a greater or lesser extent in any movement. These factors are more commonly understood quantitatively. Indeed they are used quantitatively in movement: weight, as a measure of strength or use of muscular energy; time, as a measure of durational length; space, shown by degree of angle in gesture or floor pattern; flow, the degree of continuity or controlled pausing.

However, the analysis, although not unrelated to the quantitative aspects, was especially concerned with the qualitative – always more difficult to describe. Broadly speaking the qualitative 'weight' range of expression is from strong or powerful through all the variations in between to delicate or gentle; 'time' extends from the suddenness of an unexpected action to lingering, sustained movement. 'Space' or spatial quality in movement ranges from an extravagant, roundabout pliancy at one extreme to a more directed, economical linear focus; 'flow' from freely going movement to a held-back restraint. Here the focus is on what Laban called a person's 'inner attitude towards' use of the four motion factors, which may, to a varying degree, be one of resisting or of yielding.

Indeed, Laban frequently referred to the relationship between inner feeling and the outward form of movement expression, which includes the pattern of rhythm. For example, he stated 'The fighting against or indulging in motion factors forms the basic aspects of the psychological attitudes of hatred and love' (1950, p. 116). He also indicated how particular combinations of movement elements might be correlated with certain states of mind or with mood, and showed how this was evident, not only in general bodily movement, but also in the small 'shadow' movements of which we are even less aware.

When applied, these ideas are dynamic and it can easily be seen how they relate to characterisation in drama. Two of the Deadly Sins in Marlowe's *Dr. Faustus* provide a contrasting example. Awareness of the motion factors and qualities of the constituent movement elements with particular reference to rhythm may be applied to envisage and make suggestions about some possible aspects of their characters and movement. First, Wrath: urgent, attacking self and others, forceful, roaring and snarling; sudden and impactive in phrasing, moving with vehement steps and stamps, perhaps using space in both a wild, round-about whipping manner and also with a direct thrusting energy; rushing and fuming, lashing out at phantoms – never achieving satisfaction; flamboyantly free at times, at others, strictly contained – but ready to burst forth and threaten at the next opportunity, or before it: 'I leapt out of a lion's mouth when I was scarce half an hour old; and ever since I have run up and down the world with this case of rapiers wounding myself when I had nobody to fight withal. I was born in hell' (*Dr. Faustus* lines 735–738).

Wrath contrasts with Envy who appears next in the scene, possibly entering with sly, mingy, impotent steps and certainly relishing a narrow, mean-spirited attitude. Envy nurtures a limited self-absorbed outlook; perhaps somewhat impulsive in phrasing, experiencing life as a fruitless, ever-unresolved journey; existing on the continual treadmill or rack of wanting to outdo and have all and more than everyone else, but with none of the wit or intelligence to achieve anything. There is some of Wrath's sense of angry frustration and self-flagellation here, but it is a less overtly powerful anger. Envy is always gazing outward and craving an escape from the inner torture, the invidious, grinding ache; the eyes of Envy devour the possessions and talents of others, but really just glimpse an unattainable shining, slippery surface of things – snatching at the air and opening the hand only to see its emptiness, and even the spaces disappearing between the fingers. We can imagine the sharp, piercing, viciously jabbing actions which perhaps sometimes degenerate into a painfully intense, sustained stare or twist of pain: 'I am lean with seeing others eat. O that there would come as famine through all the world, that all might die, and I live alone! Then thou should'st see how fat I would be. But must thou sit and I stand! Come down with a vengeance!' (*Dr. Faustus* lines 743-747).

Thus if actors apply Laban's ideas to a role, they may be helped to develop characterisation strongly and effectively. They may also come to a closer understanding of differences between characters, and also of how inter-personal communication takes place (in everyday life as well as on stage). This approach can be applied when considering how situations and events may be developed in performance. Indeed, Laban indicated that specific use of rhythm distinguishes the nature of performance: 'It is the arrangement of the efforts of everyday life into logical yet revealing sequences and rhythms which gives a theatrical performance its special character' (1950, p.91). This is an interesting and rare focus.

Laban's theories developed throughout his life and were formulated in both German and English and translated in various ways in different publications. This, together with varied use of his terms by others, can be confusing. The term 'effort', as used by Laban and by those who have adopted his approach, can refer to several aspects of human movement. Rhythm is central to the concept.

In Laban's terminology, 'effort' could mean the energy content of action, in the first instance in relation to inner motivation, as in 'the inner impulses from which movement originates' (1950, p.10). He also used the term in relation to the visible evidence of effort in human exertion, and in relation to the time and rhythm patterns which arise from this:

> A person's efforts are visibly expressed in the rhythms of his bodily motion. It thus becomes necessary to study those rhythms, and to extract from them those elements which will help us to compile a systematic survey of the forms effort can take in human action. (1948, p.xi)

The term 'effort-action' was originally used to distinguish working action from dance action. Laban identified six different 'effort-actions' by combining each of the motion factors of weight, time and space in terms of a blend of contrasting movement qualities.

Reference was made to the physiological basis of rhythm in Chapter 1, and contemporary biological and physiological assumptions were a basis of Laban's research into 'effort-recovery' movement patterns which he related to 'the rhythm of life'. He used the metaphor of the interdependent food-procuring cytoplasm (for male rhythms) and the reproducing nucleus (for female rhythms) thus:

> If it is assumed that the rhythm of life consists of an alternation of male and female functions as they become visible in unicellular being and that the co-operation of the two rhythmically opposite poles works on the evolution of the chain of life, perhaps one comes nearest to a definition serviceable for our research on effort and recovery. (1959, p.21)

Laban stressed the significance of recovery in relation to action, 'one of the most important aspects of the great number of rhythmical alterations observable in Nature' In class, this idea was applied in many ways in action–reaction partner and group work. Attention was drawn to the particular use of motion factors during recovery: 'which is not simply a fading away of energy, but ... contains a set of elements of movement which momentarily help to dissolve those of the main action, thus preparing for its effective repetition' (1959, p.18). 'Recovery' can also be thought of as a form of transition to a fresh action. Laban here again drew attention to an aspect of movement phrasing, to patterns in sequential development. In his instructions for observation of rhythm he advised that there is 'much more [to be] observed than a series of single movements. The investigator endeavours also to trace the relationship between the movements' (Laban and Lawrence 1945, p.1). Thus it can be seen that observation of the constituent elements of motion factors is not only fundamental in a Laban-based analysis of the dynamic content of rhythm, but also the basis of his method for study of expressive energy use in phrasing.

Use of personal and general space is included in Laban's analytic scheme, and he recognised ways in which spatial aspects of movement contribute to rhythm. 'One can discern space-rhythms, time-rhythms, and weight-rhythms. In reality these three forms of rhythm are always united, though [any] one can occupy the foreground of an action' (1950, pp.127–128). Laban drew attention to the inter-relationships of dynamics and spatial use. He alerted people to the possibility that there might be latent expressive meaning in the use made of directions and gestural shaping in space, combined with use of time and force (1966, p.31). He also related 'space-rhythm' to 'effort-rhythm', showing, for example, how certain effort sequences can promote particular gestural designs in space.

Laban explained that 'space rhythms' arise from the related use of directions which result in spatial forms and shapes. 'Two aspects are herein relevant; (a) the one in which there is successive development of changing directions, and (b) the other where shapes are produced through simultaneous actions of different parts of the body' (1950, p.128). Laban's exploration of geometric forms in relation to movement in space is well recorded. As students, our sense of spatial orientation developed through imagining ourselves moving in the centre of larger-than-life-size versions of these forms. Some of these were constructed from long, thin poles for our practice. We were encouraged to discover that movements in dimensional directions promote stability (i.e. directly up–down, side-to-side, forward–back), those in diagonal directions, lability/mobility. The implications of these ideas for the use of time elements in performance is suggested in the following extracts from a compilation, made by one of Laban's assistants, Gertrude Snell Friedburgh, in 1929: 'dimensionals always induce restriction … contrast with … the pure diagonal, which is charged with movement intensity to such a degree that the moment flows on in an unrestrained manner' (quoted in Laban 1966, p.208).

Other aspects of spatial rhythm to which Laban drew attention, included the 'calming' nature of movements in one plane, and the 'rousing' effect of those using three-dimensional pathways. He explained how some gestures in space have the effect of restraining flow of action, while others promote it. For example, returning to the starting point of a movement or gesture restrains the flow of action, whereas progressing to somewhere different in space promotes the flow (1966, pp.208–209). Laban sometimes referred to stylised forms of fencing and sword-play, with their contrasting gestural patterns of curves and thrusts, when he pointed out that rhythm is also derived from the different ways in which the body contracts and opens out in space.

Contracting and opening, tensing and releasing – the '*anspannung und abspannung*' referred to earlier – are examples of key movement-rhythm activities favoured in Laban-based training. They offer a student balancing, harmonising bodily experience which at the same time are designed to expand movement range and vocabulary. Another fundamental action sequence related to these and which was stressed in the body training we received as students was 'Gather and scatter!' When we heard that phrase resounding through the studio, it meant we had to direct our energies, arm gestures and bodily intention inwards towards the body centre, and then take a reverse gestural path and open out, with palms and inner surfaces of the arms turning outwards. Perhaps readers can picture how this generated curving figure-eight patterns in the arms. The sequence was frequently performed with transference of weight in the legs, with inward–outward figure-eight gestures in alternate legs which were synchronised with opposite arms. This then could develop into energetic travelling as we flung ourselves across or around the room, on a bounding 6/8 rhythmic pattern.

Laban's ideas on space-rhythm were in tune with theories about the cosmos prevalent in the thinking of his time. He frequently spoke of movement as universal flow, or as he once wrote, 'the stream of life and growth' (1948, p.8) The ideas and theories were linked with his concepts of space harmony, and with his interest in patterns of natural growth and crystalline forms in relation to human movement.

> Our mind seems to conceive and understand that the same laws rule not only the construction of living beings but also the structure of all inorganic matter and its crystallisation. With this discovery the whole of nature may be recognised as being governed by the same choreatic laws, the laws of inter-dependent circles. (1966, p.26)

The circle (*reigen* in German) was viewed as the archetype of universal order – 'the *reigen* is a unity which embraces everything ... up in the immensity of space of the endless solar systems, up to the equally immense play of the small atoms, the same order is present, the *reigen*' (1920, p.38). We may be reminded here of the so-called whirling Dervishes for whom circular motion leads to a form of cosmic union. Students' training included varied experience of dancing in circles and in curving lines – waxing and waning, as well as practice in the rounded or steeply rising, falling, opening, closing movement-rhythms of spatial studies.

Thus Laban brought cosmic dimensions to the personal act of dancing, more usually to be found in some form of religious or liturgical dance, or in ritual context. It is clear from his writing that he thought of dance as an expression of divine power (1920, pp.101, 146) and of movement in general he writes: 'We should never forget that every gesture and action of our body is a deeply rooted mystery and not a mere outward function or trick, as many people regard it in modern times. It was thus that tumbling or standing on the head could once have been a sacred play' (1966, p.54).

When we read of all this now, the ideas seem related to some of the latest thinking of environmentalists, Gaia theorists, contemporary 'sound-scape' musicians, post-atomic physicists and other artists and seekers. Many of Laban's statements, once pejoratively dismissed by some academics as mystical, unsubstantiated or lacking in supportive evidence, would not seem out of place in more recent, well-received writing today. For example, see Berendt (1988), Capra (1996), Moore (1996).

Laban's approach in practical movement context also appears related to examples of dance we see today. Some of the work in 'post-modern', 'contact-release' and 'new dance' since the 1970s has been strongly reminiscent of the movement exploration and dance experience of students at the Laban Centre in the late 1950s. At that time there was virtually no support for 'modern dance' in the theatre in England.[4] Classical ballet dominated as the preferred performance dance style. Laban was seen as much an innovator then as he had been in the Europe of 1910. In relation to time and rhythm in human movement, in many ways he still seems like an innovator today. His ideas on the subject remain valid and useful, and even now there is still much to be learnt from them.

Conclusion

Since, Janus-like, he encompassed both in his work, the focus on Laban's approach takes us from the ideas and theories of Part I to the domain of practice in Parts II and III. Furthermore, Laban's special interest in movement observation leads us towards the particular subject of the next chapters.

We have seen in Part I that movement-rhythm with timing in performance is essentially an integrated process which develops from a mix or blend of different elements. The outcome depends on the circumstances and given conditions, as well as on the performer's intention and utilisation of energy in time and space.

Ideas and comments from the wide range of sources cited in Part I are incorporated and expanded in the exposition which follows. The focus now is on the practical context of performance with a delineation of factors and elements which generate, influence, shape and order the structure of rhythm in any performance event.

4   With the notable exception of critic A.V. Coton.

PART II

Looking and Seeing

7

Description and Classification of Time Elements in Performance Events

A Synthesis of Approaches

> Every movement has a rhythm, every body has a rhythm, everything you do all day has a rhythm, as people living, also as dancers. Now as dancers we can expand the idea of rhythm, we can manipulate that too. (Humphrey 1951)

> Rhythm is an aesthetic organization of phenomena or events ... structured in time and/or space. (Nicholls 1992, p.146)

> A performance of a play is an alternation of dynamic and static moments, as well as dynamic movements of different kinds. That is why the gift of rhythm seems to be one of the most important a director can have. (Meyerhold quoted in Schmidt 1980, p.155)

In these statements a choreographer urges us to expand our idea of rhythm, while an anthropologist and a theatre director draw attention to the significance of its structural features. If we are to pursue these and other ideas satisfactorily, in order to observe and study rhythm, it is necessary to look at its features systematically and in some detail.

It is not easy to study the use of rhythm in complex performance events. I am reminded of my own unsatisfactory attempts to identify various features on many occasions, when watching the Polish Gardzienice Theatre Association's highly creative work for instance (such as *Avvakum* or *Gathering*) which so powerfully integrated all aspects of movement-rhythm and timing with voice and imagery. It was experiences such as this which prompted me to undertake a detailed survey of the subject.

As a beginning, and in order to organise observation effectively, it is necessary to distinguish factors and related elements of movement-rhythm and timing as clearly as possible. Drawing from the material presented in Part 1 as a basis, I suggest these factors and elements may be identified and broadly classified to address the key issues of *where, how* and *when* the rhythm is located, and how the environment may influence proceedings. These do not comprise separate or discrete sets of factors – elements of rhythm may relate to more than one set. Observation of these suggested factors and elements can provide a useful general impression of the main characteristics or features of rhythm and timing in a performance event. (For full analysis a more detailed classification, notational method and fully developed rating method are required.)

Body and space. Where the rhythm is located in the performer's body structure, and in the space.

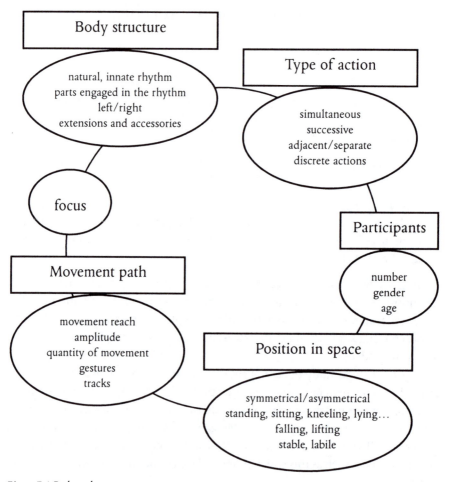

Figure 7.1 Body and space

To begin with the obvious, we recognise rhythm in movement events through observation of the human body (the performing instrument). If more than one person is performing (such as in a duet, trio or larger group) we also recognise

Figure 7.2 A unique world of timing and rhythm: when in action, attention is drawn to undulating patterns and accents in the variously jointed arms and hands. The movement and dramas of Javanese puppets fascinate many western theatre artists.

rhythm in the interaction. Movement of participants in a larger group generates group orchestration of rhythm. When participants gradually gather together in a dance, scene or ceremony, the growing accumulation of people is a form of rhythm (as in a Shakers' custom, see Chapter 2).

The skeletal-muscular structure of the body provides the physical frame which offers the potential for movement rhythm; gender and age of participants may be influential factors. Bodily range and capabilities determine outcome. The degree of mobility we have in our joints, the length of our limbs – together with the pull of gravity – affect our movement. In order to develop their performance, dancers may need to compensate for a particular body type. A physiotherapist with whom I was discussing this, drew a clear distinction between short, stocky dancers and those who are tall and long-limbed, pointing out that the 'natural' preferred physical rhythms of each are entirely different. Whatever our body type may be, the shared fact of our two-limbed, right–left structure generates rhythm. I remember Laban remarking in a light-hearted moment in class that perhaps rhythm began because early humans became tired of standing on one leg!

Figure 7.3 A length of fabric adds to the rhythm of a dance, during rehearsals for an Asian Mela festival in east London.
Source: *Mark Turner*

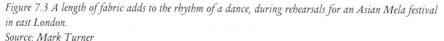

In drama, dance or ceremony, extensions to the performer's body or accessories may contribute to rhythm, and together with the bodily action promote varied time-patterns of co-ordination. For instance, performers with long hair sometimes swing it about in a lively, patterned way as part of a dance. Choreographer Alwin Nikolais was famous for the moving body extensions in his works such as the elongated head-gear in *Imago*, or the elasticated curving cloth inside which dancers moved in *Sanctum*.[1] Thus items such as banners, billowing lengths of fabric, clashing swords, assertive threatening sticks, lighted candles, or even

---

1   In a powerfully expressive example, sharp lines of cloth, worn and pulled in different directions by the soloist, emphasise the grief-stricken mood of Martha Graham's *Lamentation*.

animals held by performers, may need to be observed as part of the pattern of rhythm. In Alaska, Athabascan women dancers use feathers 'to extend movement into space' and Tlingit ceremonial dance features the spinning of tassles on dance gloves (Johnston 1992, pp.222, 295). The long sleeves of a Japanese or Chinese dancer are sometimes used almost like additional limbs, and mark the rhythm when little other movement is taking place. Wolz has written of the use of extensions to the body such as this in Japan, where, in performance, 'so much movement is simply a manipulation of very elaborate costumes, which sometimes even inhibit movement ... The manipulation of properties is also a very important source of movement' (1971, p.34). Men dancing with chickens, grasping their wings, was observed by anthropologist Linda Shanson during Mexican wedding festivities (1978), while I myself found that the feather head-dresses of the Maring dancers in New Guinea generated an intricate counterpoint (see Chapter 11). Dorothy Ray supports the notion of paying attention to these performance aspects; describing items worn by an Eskimo dancer which made an important contribution to rhythm in the dance she witnessed, she writes: 'As important as gestures in the dance was the movement of undulating feathers and appendages on masks and clothing, or in the hands' (1967, p.25).

As noted in Chapter 1, a basic form of rhythm is realised in the body in the processes of breathing, heartbeat or pulse and peristalsis. In the survey from drama and dance studies, we have seen how some artists developed choreographic and training ideas from these processes. Instinctive, spontaneous physical reactions to

Figure 7.4 Body positions: gestures and changes of position may generate rhythm.
Source: Liane Payne

situations and events may be thought of as an aspect of body timing, such as occurs in startled reactions of fear.

It has often been suggested that in dance, performers base their use or measurement of rhythm, consciously or unconsciously, on these natural or innate rhythms (see Martin 1965a, p.68). Dalcroze made a significant contribution here; and perhaps Agnes de Mille's 'inner pulse' refers to the same factor:

> The true artist will develop a sense of rhythm complex and subtle, not just the mechanical reflex to a downbeat, but a sense of shape and dynamism in musical phrase and dynamism in gesture, and an inner pulse that lies beneath all these and that is the true life beat. The last is essential; without it all the rest is useless. (1963, p.82)

As Doris Humphrey and others have shown, phrasing in movement performance has a physical basis and may be related to breathing in a variety of ways. Dancers' phrasing may follow or be shaped by a performer's breath pattern, especially in non-metric sequences (for explanation of metricity, see pp.153–155). Inhalation is frequently associated with the start of a phrase and exhalation with the ending of a phrase (or phrase-section). This is a breath-time pattern which is also required in the actor's delivery of clause or sentence. Also, as with breath, our movement cannot be evenly continuous; it includes necessary rhythms and phases of preparation, action and recovery which contribute to performance structure. (For further reference to rhythm in performance structure, including phrase, phase etc. see pp.160–163).

Muscular contraction and release, which we see most noticeably in working actions or in sport and gymnastics, has its own rhythm. Another obvious body action which generates rhythm is that of walking or stepping in various ways. Indeed, in classical Greece the range of dynamic intensity in movement was thought of as generated largely by the physical action of *'thesis'* (the foot touching the ground) *and 'arsis'* (the foot lifting) (see Aristoxenus, 1959 orig. *c.*370 BC). The dancer's sense of what would be termed 'beat' and 'upbeat' in music (as well as 'strike' and 'rebound') is associated with this. Particular body actions like swinging, swaying, vibrating, bouncing, whipping, punching, skipping (with weight transference) tend to produce distinctive rhythm. A young child's pleasure in the mastery of a skipping pattern frequently extends even to the extent of insisting that an accompanying adult join in.

Changes of body position, direction and level in space, generate rhythm. Features of symmetry and asymmetry in body position and action can affect rhythm, with the balancing effect of the former and the uneven characteristics of the latter. As demonstrated in Chapter 6, Laban developed particular ideas about space-rhythm. As he stressed, an aspect of body-use in space in relation to rhythm concerns stability and lability. Stable body action, where the body's centre of

Figure 7.5 Holding on: lability anchored by stability – a dramatic moment of arrested motion from an East London Dance workshop performance.

gravity is directly above the base-support (usually hips in relation to feet) tends to promote regular, steady rhythm. Labile, off-balance or tilted action, where the centre of gravity is shifted away from directly above the base-support, tends to promote irregular, varied rhythm.

Spatial factors which contribute to rhythm operate in relation to the movement of individual performers, and to the movement orchestration and spatial disposition of groups. Theatre directors can display inspired crafting of the orchestration of movement rhythm in group action and interaction to provide exciting theatre experiences. I am reminded of sequences such as the scene of unexpectedly imminent departure from the governor's palace in Brecht's *The Caucasian Chalk Circle* when harassed servants rush and dart about with varied degrees of efficiency, packing the governor's wife's possessions at her imperious, somewhat erratic behest. Or I think of the interaction of the eccentric, sometimes threatening mountain king's trolls in Ibsen's *Peer Gynt.* A degree of rhythmic complexity on stage can bring life to less agitated, more peaceful sequences too, such as in the scene of Cerimon's healing care of the storm-beaten victims in Shakespeare's *Pericles.* Here a range of calming rhythms infiltrates the stage as some servants wrap and enfold the unfortunate victims of the turbulent night in blankets, others perhaps gently wind soft bandages while Cerimon applies the soothing balm of ointments, and the victims comfort one another. All this is made the more telling after the violence and uneven rhythmic attack of the preceding storm scene, and creates a rhythmically varied prologue to the unifying, rhythmically focused discovery of the chest, washed up on the shore, which contains the temporarily inert Marina.

We can note if actions and accents are occurring simultaneously or successively in a performer's body and across a group of performers. Simultaneous actions shared with partner or group may be synchronised. The movements may be the same, that is, in unison, or they may be complementary, contrasting or in counter-rhythm. (In the movement of an individual, this applies to accents or actions in different body parts.) There are striking examples of group unison action in the popular Irish *Riverdance* shows. All those sharp little knees hitting the air together! And the rows of perfectly synchronised crossed legs, heels and toes. Spatial rhythm is also generated in this example from the contrast between the erect, vertical body carriage and up–down emphasis of steps, and the fast, even, horizontal lines of the dancers travelling across and around the stage.

Actions and accents may be located successively in adjacent body parts. For example, in an individual performer, 'successive adjacent' would describe a sequence in which accents occur in the right shoulder, then right elbow and finally wrist and fingers. Successive movement travelling through a group of performers can be likened to a rumour spreading. A succession of actions or accents may be located in body parts (or among a group of performers) which are not adjacent, but are separate. For example, in an individual performer 'successive, separate accents' would describe a sequence in which accents occur in right shoulder, left elbow, right heel.

The path of movement in ground track or in gestures has a rhythm component which may be emphasised, as in the *Riverdance* example. The angle employed at a change of direction (in gesture or floor pattern) 'colours' the rhythm. The use of wide angles or curves brings forth a different rhythmic pattern from the use of narrow angles. Spirals, twists and zigzags are a development of these possibilities. Different spatial pathways referred to here can induce different moods, of course, depending also on use of other movement elements. A circle, for instance, can appear to have a more calming effect than does a zigzag's sharpness.

A gestural trace-form through space or a ground track which returns to its starting point tends to have a restraining effect and promotes security, whereas one which arrives somewhere new tends to promote less restraint. The latter contributes irregularity, and perhaps more vitality, to the rhythmic pattern.

A further spatial factor which has a bearing on rhythm is range of gesture or movement in respect of the individual's reach space, as well as in the general acting area. Anthropologist Claire Holt noted the expressive power of expansive,

Figure 7.6 Spatial rhythm: people far apart and close together – contrasts in the use of space are emphasised here by the tension in extended arms and by varied directional focus. Members of The Royal Ballet in Kenneth MacMillan's Anastasia.
Source: Douglas Jeffery

large gestures in a Javanese dancer's personal reach space, which, combined with 'stately, regular rhythm of his gestures', made him 'an unrelenting force, impersonal, impassive' (1967, p.101). Also, the quantity or amount of movement both in personal reach space and in general acting area contribute to rhythm. This is especially interesting to observe when performance space is limited, as noted in Chapter 2. A dancer's use of space may be limited or expanded in various ways. McPhee provides another example from his observations of Balinese dance. Here he describes space limited vertically through the dancer's constant use of flexed knees and lack of elevation, and of the stylistic significance of the movement:space ratio:

> The Balinese dancer moves within a narrow frame, out of which he never steps. It is in the narrowness of this frame, and the amazing life and freedom created within it that the beauty of his dancing lies... The dancer never leaps ... he remains firmly on the ground, moving across the surfaces by a controlled shift of

weight from one foot to the other, the free foot raised an inch above the ground or grazing it as it moves to the next position. The normal slow advance is accomplished by the free foot moving out in an arc and returning to center ahead of the other. (1948, pp.186–187)

The direction in which the rhythm of the movement is projected, or its focus, contributes to spatial aspects of time-use and rhythm in performance. Whether this be towards an audience, to fellow performers or to sky, earth or meditatively inward, it is likely to have different expression and significance.

Development of action: How energy is used and when features of rhythm and timing occur.

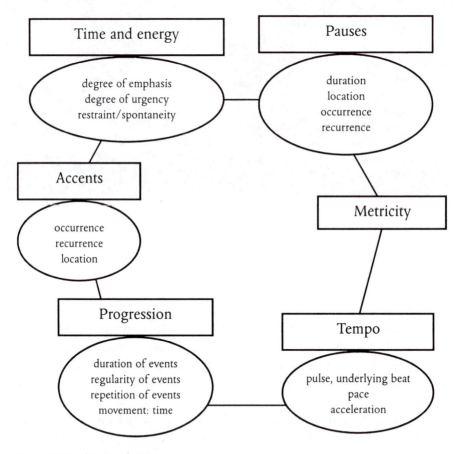

Figure 7.7 Development of action

To summarise, rhythm develops in performance action through fluctuations in energy and with the use of accents, pauses, tempo and duration.

Accents are an important feature in the patterning and dynamics of rhythm. They attract and direct attention. Accents may be spatially and dynamically

Figure 7.8 Use of rhythm evident in a back view. Spatial rhythm: the angle at the knee is offset by the balance of the horizontal arm with its firm energy – perhaps there is a hint of softer energy in the dancer's left hand. The downward focus of head and eyes contrasts with the onward and upward direction of the leap; sharp accents in toes and in stretched and flexed knees. The bunch of hair adds quirky a-rhythmic detail. Dancer Catherine Quinn in Siobhan Davies' The Art of Touch. *Source: Hugh Glendinning*

limited, or located in small body parts but nevertheless they may be important stylistically and expressively, such as in the eye movements of Indian dance. A relatively small but characteristic and distinctive accentual feature of modern dance pioneer Martha Graham's dance performance was the sudden movement of her mouth opening, on an emphatic gesture or muscular contraction, as in a gasp. Related to her own idiosyncratic way of breathing, and probably an involuntary movement, this was nevertheless part of the whole rhythmic expression of her performance. An example of the use of accents as a feature of style in dance is provided by McPhee, who describes use of accented movement in hands, eyes, shoulders and head as a predominant characteristic of Balinese dance:

> The hands ... move alertly to the syncopated accents, or vibrate rapidly from the
> wrists ... Eyes are slewed first to right and then to left to stress certain rhythmic

accents. Accents may also be marked by a slightly raised eyebrow … The rapid shoulder quiver (*engejen pala*) and slight shifting of the head from side to side with neck erect (*engota*) are a feature of many dances. (1948, pp.187–188)

Accents occur in a number of different ways both in the performer's body itself and in the use the performer makes of the performance space. Thus a gesture, step, turn, jump or change in dynamics may be accented, 'standing out' from what it follows or precedes. Change of direction, entrance (or exit) of performer, contact with other performers, use of objects or performance environment (for example, movement up a flight of stairs) may be accented. However, let us be aware, as far as we can, of cultural bias in our assumptions. For instance, as Pantaleoni points out in his discussion of Anlo dance drumming, it is a particularly western characteristic to 'attach to dynamic stress a major role in the rhythmic organization of an ensemble' (1972, p.62).

Particular, regular placing of an accent can generate specific kinds of bodily action. For example, an accent every two beats may promote a march. In dance, every three beats may promote a swinging movement – especially if associated with a drop, lift, lift action. There are of course exceptions. A three-beat pattern is the base of the well-known triplet 'walk' in Graham-based dance technique (but a flowing quality does result from the pattern); 3/4 is the metre of a march in Rameau's *Hippolyte et Aricie*, Act V, and of Schumann's march of the Philistines of culture in *Carnival*, but perhaps he used the metre for an intended bizarre emphasis. Dotted rhythms (unequal division of beats within the bar) promote other distinctive actions such as in the skipping referred to earlier. Irregularly recurring accents produce an uneven pattern. Depending on the context and whether combined with other dynamics, this may generate an uncertain mood, or perhaps it may have an aggressive effect. A repeating pattern of irregularly recurring accents may be termed 'irregular' yet 'constant', but a pattern of irregularly recurring accents, continually changing, may be termed 'irregular' and 'inconstant'. Further reference to metricity is included later in the chapter.

Contributing to rhythm in an exciting way, syncopation is another use of accents where stress is displaced from an expected regularity, in metrical terms essentially avoiding the 'downbeat'. (For example, in 4/4 time, emphasis on beats two and four instead of one and three, or on halfbeats. From *synkope* (Greek): to cut short.) It is sometimes referred to as emphasis 'off' the beat, or more flexibly, 'around' it, in African music, for instance (Chernoff 1979, p.48). Accents occurring frequently, very close together, may be referred to as 'dense'; if they occur sporadically or spread apart, 'sparse'. Frequency of accents can be a strong mood indicator when combined with other movement elements that affect dynamics. For example, many accents occurring near each other – with a particular combination of other elements – can create or contribute to a mood of excitement, perhaps eroticism, urgency, even panic. Accents placed erratically can be exciting too, or they may produce a disturbing, strange or even frightening effect. Placing single accents in different parts of a sequence or phrase can create different dynamic effects. If an accent occurs at the beginning it initiates the phrase as an 'impulse'; if at the end it provides an 'impact', an abrupt conclusion (see also Laban p.131). Use of accents by a particular performer may indicate a leadership role, or reveal a system of cueing rhythm and timing in a performance.

The moment of pausing, or of stopping, movement may be a form of accentuation and may alert attention, especially if it happens unexpectedly or is preceded by a sharp, strong movement. This is clearly illustrated in a further description of a Balinese dance from McPhee:

> Rhythms are taut and syncopated throughout, and filled with sudden breaks and unexpected accents ... Dance movement is not conceived in a single broad, legato line, but continually broken by fractional pauses that coincide with the breaks in the music: on these the dancers come to a sudden stop, and the eyes of the spectators focus momentarily on a motionless sharply defined pose. (1948, p.160)

Stopping movement may serve as a punctuation mark, or make a particular intentional statement in the context of a performance, or extend and result in an ending. For a pause to appear heightened is dependent on what precedes it; alternatively, a pause may draw attention to what follows. Hutchinson Guest (1981) includes use of timing as one of four distinctive stylistic features of the Bournanville (ballet) style (the others being use of body, space and dynamics). Hutchinson Guest particularly notes accented use of pauses: 'Bournanville punctuated his movement phrases and sentences with pauses in a most interesting way ... suddenness – unexpected abruptness – often occurs as an ending where an unusual pose occurs' (1981, pp.146–148). We can distinguish between pauses during phrases or sequences of movement and pauses which define and mark the end of a phrase or sequence.

Significance of pauses may be likened to the Japanese concept of the spaces between the lines of design being as important as the lines themselves – or even more important than the lines: lines as containers for spaces, pauses as containers for movement. Small, preparatory movements can create the effect of a slight pause which draws attention to the gesture following, and may make it seem larger in scope. Balanchine described the importance of pauses in relation to music, but his words are equally applicable to pauses in movement: 'A pause, an interruption, never means an airless space between two noted sounds. They are not simply a nothing ... life goes on in each pause' (quoted in Goodwin 1973).

Thus pausing, or even stopping movement for a while, can create a variety of effects and promote tension as well as calm not only in dance, but in stage acting as well as in ceremony. A pause or more extended period of stillness may be used as a foil to contrast with movement. In dance there is an obvious and well-known instance of this in the popular MGM film musical classic *The Belle of New York* (1952). In an ocean-view scene, the background static pose of a group of promenading bystanders serves to highlight the lively rhythmic patterning of Fred Astaire and Vera-Ellen's duet in the foreground. There is a striking, expressive example in recent dance work – American Bill T. Jones' *We set out early... visibility was poor* (European premiere 1998). The theme of the piece is a group's life journey towards the millennium. Strong contrasts in the use of rhythm and timing are evident throughout. But during the final moments, as the work nears its climax, there is a particularly effective extended sequence when one dancer (who has emerged as a hero-figure) stands quite still, alone down-stage, as if in contemplation of the future, while the other nine dancers of the company are in constant motion as they move across the stage behind him in a close-packed, happily rapping, hip-hopping, throbbing cluster, perhaps representing the pulse, energy or busy-ness of ever-passing or past life. Placing, number and duration of pauses may be significant. In the context of ceremony we learn, for instance, that when Princess Mary visited Henry VIII, sixteenth-century court etiquette demanded three pauses (during which she would curtsy): the first on entering the presence chamber, the next in the middle of the room, and finally on reaching the monarch (Wildeblood and Brinson 1965). The two minutes' silence and stillness at the Cenotaph service in London on Remembrance Sunday indicates honour, respect, mourning, national pride.

We can relate stillness in movement to silence in speech. In western Apache culture, moments of silence are associated with situations involving ambiguous or unpredictable relationships (Basso 1970). It is interesting to examine similarly the use of stillness in different contexts and situations. Behnke's study of silence includes comments which can usefully be applied to stillness in movement performance (1977, 1978). She refers to the expressive use of silence, for example, 'an angry silence', 'the silence of outrage'; as well as to silence as the 'source of things' in meditation and religious tradition. Silence with stillness is a feature of the Quakers' form of worship, for instance. (See also Lasher 'The pause in the moving structure of dance' (1978).) The ratio of both accents and pauses to time duration overall is a further element to consider, and one which may certainly affect the mood in a performance. Frequent, irregularly recurring pauses may have an uncertain or hesitant effect, or if the recurrence is regular, pauses in the movement may contribute to a more relaxed, calm mood.

Shared metre and pulse are characteristics of west European time-keeping in music and dance; elsewhere the process varies. For instance, Pantaleoni draws attention to a different source of timing in Anlo dance drumming. A high, relatively soft bell sounds a repetitive, asymmetrical pattern to which dancers and other players relate individually: 'The players neither follow a beat nor build additively upon a small, common unit of time... Performers may derive from the play of the bell a feeling of pulse ... but this feeling of pulse is not the primary source of timing' (1972, p.62). Hall contrasts the African Tiv use of the beats of four drums, each for different parts of the body, with the common European use of one beat (1976, p.78). 'Marking time', in terms of movement as well as metaphorically, indicates simply walking on the spot, making no progress.

Alternations of accented and unaccented movement and of short and longer actions generate a basis of rhythmic pattern in phrasing. Alternation of short and longer actions is a basis of metric patterning in movement as in music, or as in the morse code. This is a form of accentuation through use of duration – durational accent – known as 'agogic' (Riemann 1844).

Metric pattern, based on a discernible regular pulse, is a pattern dependent upon the contrast between 'long' and 'short' movements governed by the given pulse and within a given time-frame. As emphasised in jazz and tap dance, the pulse or beat underpins the structure and unifies an ensemble. Being 'in time' or 'keeping the beat' means that the moving person is holding correctly to the regular pulse, the beat of the metric structure. Some people, even trained dancers, can find this difficult.[2] The pattern may be repetitive (motifs repeated) or changing (successive motifs of different metre), which is commonly termed 'mixed' metre. 'Cumulative metre' consists of successive increase or decrease in arithmetical progression of the number of beats in each motif (or bar 'measure' in transatlantic terminology). 'Resultant rhythm' occurs when two or more different metres performed simultaneously result in another one. Ancient Greek practice provides the west European basis of this procedure, with patterns selected and often repeated from the following motifs, which interestingly also correspond to Indian Sanskrit metres (from Fox Strangways 1914, p.196):

Greek		Indian Sanskrit
iambus	— ——	laga
trochee	—— —	gala
dactyl	—— — —	bhanasa
anapaest	— — ——	salagam
spondee	—— ——	gaga
molossus	—— —— ——	matara
amphibrach	— —— —	jabhana
antibacchic	—— —— —	taraja
cretic	—— — ——	rajabha

2   Dancers have been known to infuriate instrumental accompanists by counting aloud as they design a sequence to enumerate an order of actions, of varied duration; that is, not counting in the regularly spaced, metric order of musicians.

tribrach	— — —	nasala
pyrrhic	— —	lala
bacchic	— —— ——	hamata

Note: One beat 'short' duration; two beats 'long' duration.

The Greeks attached expressive significance to the use of metric patterns, using (for instance) the iambus to convey what they considered to be masculine energy and the trochee for femininity. The dactyl was used in performance for solemnity and the cretic for excitement or terror.

Strict use of metric pattern in dance form predominates in west European social ballroom dance, which we sometimes also see in theatre performance context. The 3/4 of the slow waltz and the 'quick, quick, slow' pattern of the quickstep are instances of this. Particular use of metric pattern may contribute to a specific dance style or be characteristic of historical period. For example, the particular characteristic of the fast nineteenth-century waltz was the movement flow and lack of restraint generated by its 6/8 metre. It was interesting to note that the first production of Pam Gems' version of the nineteenth-century classic *Camille* in 1985, successfully realised a sense of period – until the waltz, which was performed in the later, slow 3/4 version. Another familiar use of 6/8 in dance is in swinging action (that is, in a drop, lift (lift), drop, lift (lift), use of weight which differs from the side to side regularity of a pendulum swing). In British ceremonial, use of metric pattern prevails most noticeably in marching: spondee base for a slow march, pyrrhic base for a quick march.

When we observe performance events we must be on the alert for both unison and non-unison action and for more than one metric (or non-metric) organisation which may be occurring simultaneously. Synchronicity does not necessarily involve sharing a metric pattern, but it is likely to mean a shared sense of pulse or beat. To note Stern's comments here: 'Congruent synchronous movements tell you that the humans involved are in a situation of relatedness. In fact, one way to diagnose some kinds of psychotic behaviour is to observe how out of synchrony the affected person is ... Moving together is one of the things that defines a collection of people as a group. The group stops being a group when a person stops sharing movement patterns or rhythms with others' (Stern 1973, p.124).

In western European dance of the early Renaissance, the rhythmic variety and texture which arises from polymetric rhythms is a notable component of the style, and uses a wider range of time values than those listed above. This style makes considerable use of syncopation and of beats divided in various ways, triple as well as duple time, and incorporates the six rhythmic modes of medieval musical practice:

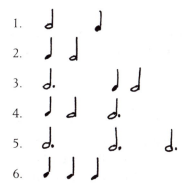

Arbeau noted the rhythmic characteristics of dances of his period in 1588. For example:

Pavane:

Tordion:

Allemande:

Courante:

Much folk music and dance exhibit varied use of metricity. For instance, in traditional Macedonian dance interesting use is made of irregular subdivisions of the beat. In a dance of the Ewe people of Ghana more than one metric pattern is used simultaneously and repeated extensively. An example of a basic rhythm, notated approximately (from a workshop in Ewe dance, Africa Centre, London):

New York choreographer Nancy Zendora gave me a fine example of metric patterns varied in another way which she had experienced in Haitiian spirit-possession dance: 'the feet take up a side-to-side three beat pattern, the hands cross in front of the body with a two beat pattern while the spine and head ripple in a continuous phrase, more like a swinging 6/8 – this signifies mounting by Damballah, the ritual snake spirit' (interview, June 1997).

A non-metric movement pattern is one which cannot be metred or counted in the way outlined above. There is no discernible regular pattern or set of patterns of that kind in non-metricity. The movement follows what seems an erratic, unpredictable and free pattern – as occurs in conversation, or even in the kinetic constructions of artist Alexander Calder. Pauses of varying lengths are likely to be included, and metrically unrelated accents. There is no obvious recognisably constant pulse on the surface, but a very slow pulse may be found underlying what appears as rhythmic dissonance.

It can be argued that sections of non-metric rhythm occur in passages of acceleration and retardation or rubato in otherwise metrically patterned movement. However, the difference here is that such passages simply represent an elastic approach to the presence of the beat, which may give a spontaneous, improvisatory impression, but it is not a fundamental cancellation of the metric beat as would be characteristic of non-metric rhythm. There is a relationship here to Laban's concept of 'flow'. Release and arrest of flow, its liberation and control, and the varying degrees and conditions between extremes which contribute to dynamic intensity, may be registered as key aspects of non-metric rhythm.

Tempo of movement (alternatively referred to as pace, speed or rate) may be judged from the number of beats, steps or other actions which are performed in a given length of time, such as in the traditional west European beats-per-minute-measure of metronome marking used in music, with considerable leeway permitted in execution:

Rate		Approx. number of beats per minute
(Very slow)	*largo*	40–90 MM (metronome mark)
↓	*larghetto*	70–96 MM
↓	*adagio*	97–126 MM
↓	*andante*	127–156 MM
↓	*allegro*	157–184 MM
(Very fast)	*presto*	Over 184 MM

Of course a beat may be established without recourse to metronome or clock-time. As Chapple explains: 'The beat is built up from the length of each action and the interval of silence or inaction in between, the summation of which establishes the tempo (or pace) of the individual pattern of behaviour' (Chapple 1970, p.39). In Chapter 4 there was reference to Stanislavski's use of beats in theatre training and rehearsal. The practice continues in theatre work today, such as in waiting for 'a beat' before delivering a line or making an entrance, (see reference to Billie Whitelaw in rehearsal, Chapter 2, p.53).

Sense of pace and judgment of speed varies from one person to another. Characteristic use and sense of tempo varies from one era and culture to the next.

McLaughlin (1970, p.31) summarised findings on sense of pace and judgement of speed in early 1970s British culture, as:

Very slow	Below 30 (bpm) MM
Slow	30–50 (bpm) MM
Moderate neutral	50–95 (bpm) MM
Fast	95–240 (bpm) MM
Very fast	Over 240 (bpm) MM

This is a useful beginning but ambiguous: is 30 'very slow' or merely 'slow'? Comparisons of both everyday and stylised forms of behaviour in different countries have illustrated cultural variation (see Hall 1959). In many places and contexts, slow tempo and an extended duration are characteristically associated with solemnity, dignity, respect. Duration of applause may signify degree of approval (Alistair Cooke saw fit to report that Senator Dole received an eight minute standing ovation when he resigned on 11 June 1996: *Letter from America* 16 June 1996). People are often prepared to wait a long time for the arrival of star-performers or other high-status persons. Anthropologist Monica Wilson refers to the significance of duration in East African Nyakyusa burial rites – prestige is indicated at funerals by the number of days the drums play (1957, p.31). Wolz describes use of slow tempi in traditional Japanese dance, and particularly in Bugaku, where:

> movements are extended in time to give the viewer an opportunity to enjoy every subtle gesture. Economy of means and leisurely contemplation are important aspects of all Japanese art ... Bugaku's association with the Imperial Court, with its strict hierarchy and formality, is reflected in the solemnity and dignity of the dances... The combination of these solemn, dignified and ritualistic qualities creates a special, almost hypnotic atmosphere. (1971, pp.2–3)[3]

Alternatively, brevity and rapidity may be associated with frivolity, even superficiality (not allowing time to go deeply into a matter or to 'give due consideration'). A vivid example of utmost speed is seen in the arrival of the Nigerian Igede *Ogirinye* (warrior association) mask at a funeral ceremony.

---

3   In his *Journal* Paul Claudel comments on how the use of slow tempo in Japanese Noh acting can make a range of interpretations possible: 'The slowness of the gesture makes all interpretations possible: for example, the woman wants to cry and so moves her hands up to her eyes, but this action can also be the image of her grief, which she brings closer so as to see it better. She seems to draw up the water of her tears, the weight of the pain, then comes the withdrawal from the cup of bitterness which she has drunk, the abdication from life,' (23 February) (quoted in Barba and Savarese 1991, p.257). Also see other references to extended duration pp.74–75.

Running at full tilt represents 'a great warrior who is so fast that he can hardly be seen, and by extension, so too death, which also appears unexpectedly among the living' (Nicholls 1984, p.73). Anthropologist Leach has referred to pace as one of the most widely distributed major constituents of human ritual sequences (1961). See also Hall (1959, 1966, 1976).

Novelist Kundera maintains, 'our period is given over to the demon of speed, and that is the reason why it so easily forgets its own self' (in *Slowness* 1996, p.115). Indeed, in our high-speed western urban culture, the excitement, risk and tension of rapidity is prevalent. In the rhythm of movement performance perhaps this is most obviously evident in television programme style. In the theatre, shows such as *Starlight Express* even bring the ever-increasing rate of roller-skaters to the stage. The desire for speed dominates advances in technology. Performance artist Laurie Anderson, long experienced in the use of technology in performance, goes further: 'it's like you're in a race against speed itself' was her comment about present-day tempo and what can become an addiction to the latest computer technology (*The Speed of Darkness* Royal Festival Hall London 30 June 1997). In contemporary dance since the 1970s, forceful, sometimes risky rapidity – which makes considerable technical demands on the performer – has been a popular component of dance style. Cultural and personal preference may be seen to influence use of tempi. Habitually preferred tempo, and differences between judgment of tempo when watching or when performing, should be taken into account when observing the use of tempo.

'Slow' – performing each movement through an extended time-duration – may be a demanding test of control or balance. The performer's 'inner attitude' to energy use, referred to previously, assists the performer here if a sustained (a 'time' movement factor in Laban's terminology) and restrained (a 'flow' movement factor in Laban's terminology) attitude is adopted. 'Fast' – performing a number of travelling steps or other successive movements in a short duration of time – is a more demanding test if these are large movements or of varying pattern. Sometimes tall, long-limbed dancers find fast, intricate movement difficult but in terms of preferred tempo it is misleading to assert that physique is a determining factor. Training and practice overcome many physical limitations. As McLaughlin states, albeit in a different context: 'There is no evidence that short-legged conductors habitually set faster tempi than lanky ones' (1970, p.33).

Tempo, after duration itself, provides an on-going frame for the detailed patterning of rhythm and appears to be one of the more easily recognised elements of rhythm. Perhaps this is because we are familiar with a characteristic use of tempo in individuals or with its distinctive use in social and everyday life. To refer to Kundera's *Slowness* again, his premise in the novel is that speed is linked to forgetting (a person trying to forget something walks fast), and slowness is linked to memory (a person may automatically slow down when trying to remember something). Particular usage may be expected or criticised in different contexts; for example, in the culture in which I was educated, to be 'a slow learner', 'a fast talker' or 'a fast worker' were all pejorative terms – elsewhere they might have been considered praiseworthy characteristics.

Different tempi may occur simultaneously in a performance. This will be manifest in the distinctive tempi of different characters in a play, for instance, while there will also be an overall sense of shared tempo in the whole production.

Changes in tempo may involve changes in pulse and in body tension. These changes contribute to expression and characterisation in dance and drama, and to excitement or calm in ceremony. Different speeds, acceleration and retardation can promote different moods or expressive results. This is partially implied in musicians' terminology which is sometimes used in relation to dance. The terminology (OED) can indicate the kind of bodily tension with which a musical instrument is to be played, such as:

vivace	in a lively manner
allegro	in brisk time
largo	in slow time with broad dignified treatment
staccato	abrupt, sharply detached
legato	smooth, without breaks
sostenuto	sustained, prolonged

These terms relate to metronome markings but there is considerable leeway permitted in execution (e.g. *allegro* 158–184 MM, *largo* 40–60 MM). *Rubato* indicates occasionally slackened or hastened tempo – literally robbed or stolen time.

A nervous or excited condition may lead to the adoption of either faster or slower tempi (affected by pulse) even to a total standstill ('paralysed' through fear) – 'the pulse of a healthy person is regular, but accelerates or decelerates under the stress of physical or psychological experience' (Neuhaus 1973, pp. 30–31). Byers directs attention to an aspect of the possible significance of tempi in movement expression:

the same movements … of gesturing, walking, changing postures, etc. … take on a new effect to the observer if they are performed either more slowly or more quickly than usual. This might be seen as signalling a new state … or tiredness, illness, depression on one hand or excitement, frigidity, or restlessness on the other. (1972, p.42)

Fluctuation in tempi may indicate or support change of mood or change of situation. Deceleration may indicate depression, time for thought, a peaceful mood, or menace. Acceleration frequently occurs as excitement builds, at the end of a folk dance, for example. Or it may occur in a thriller, for instance, with dramatic tension gathering as the victim becomes increasingly afraid. Nketia provides an example of a common use of acceleration – to induce a state of ecstasy – in the African *Yewe* cult of the Ewe (1975, p.221). Also, in Sinhalese curing ritual, 'the dancers spin ever faster around the arena, carving elaborate patterns in the air with flaming torches' (Kapferer 1973, p.15) – using acceleration and spatial rhythm to drive out demons.

A number of features of rhythm may contribute to a growing or lessening sense of urgency or power in a performance as in accelerating or decelerating tempo, or with more or less strongly marked accents. A performer's use of energy makes a particular qualitative contribution here. Laban's concept of 'inner attitude' to energy use may be applied in this context. 'Inner attitude' relates to the performer's intention which initiates or provokes the use of energy in the movement, and promotes dynamic expression in performance. The expressive outcome of 'inner attitude' to use of energy is displayed through a blend in rhythm of time, weight, space and flow elements, particularly significant in dramatic characterisation. As theatre director Paul Baker states: 'Rhythm is a combination of tempos and tensions which come from physical, emotional and philosophical tracings, from attitudes towards life' (1972, p.102). A performer's inner attitude to time and energy use may also be evident during stillness – perhaps observed as degrees of intensity. Zeami's handbook for Japanese actors advises that the actor:

> must be careful not to lose his intensity even down to the deepest recesses of his heart at such times as the moment after the end of his dance, song, dialogue, gesture, etc. The feeling of concentrated intensity in the depths of the actor's heart is sensed by the audience, and thus the silent pauses are made interesting. (quoted in Nakamura 1971, p.51)

Accents, pauses, tempi and duration in the micro-structure of a performance, all contribute to the punctuation and total duration of an event. That is, they contribute to the way in which the segments or phases of action develop and build up in terms of motifs, phrases and longer sequences in varying conditions of complexity, to form the macro-structure of the event. Seen in another way, we may distinguish two levels of structure in performance – micro-structure (performers' moment-by-moment use of elements of rhythm and timing, observed to the level of motifs and phrases) and macro-structure (time and rhythm in performance structure overall, observed from the level of motifs and phrases through to complete events, series of events and wider contexts such as a series of annual festivals). The emphasis of the mode of classification and categorisation delineated in this chapter is on micro-structural features of rhythm and timing. However, comments on features of macro-structure now follow.

Structural analysis of the pattern of time use and rhythm throughout a performance event can be in terms of its syntax, of constitutive counted-out units and the sequential and thematic development, a method analogous to grammatical analysis. That is, one action unit = a word, a movement motif = a word cluster, a section of a movement phrase = a clause, and a phrase = a sentence. To distinguish one fixed action pattern from another requires criteria with which to separate them – the process of 'sequential demarcation' (Altman quoted in Chapple, 1970, p.33). Following established practice in structural analysis of movement, single movement units may be defined by one-directional focus or focal point (to allow for circular pathway) and/or body part in action. They are thus primarily distinguished from each other by change of focus or active body part, and may be further delimited by accent. For further explanation of structural analysis of movement, see Birdwhistell (1952), Kaeppler (1972), Pesovár (1976).

A unit may be termed 'single' if only one occurs at a time, or 'compound' if two or more units occur in the body simultaneously. 'Motifs' consist of two or more units and normally include at least one accent and change of direction in space, focus or dynamics. It is difficult to define their length precisely, but they do not usually consist of more than four units, or take longer than a full inhalation or exhalation of breath. In choreography, a dance motif is usually considered to be the smallest compositional unit capable of development (since simple repetition of one action is not normally considered as development).

A motif repeated or developed, or several different motifs or actions connected together, may comprise a phrase. Dalcroze has suggested that 'every set of gestures in logical succession constitutes a phrase' (1921, p.162). 'Logical' requires further definition, especially if the definition is to be applied in contemporary choreography, where, as in contemporary music, traditional ideas of phrasing do not necessarily apply. However, there is a sense in which the actions of a phrase 'belong' together through some compatibility of style, action, idea, theme or mood and use of energy in the progress of the movement. A phrase may have an independent character, although one phrase may be designed as a response to the previous phrase or to lead on to the next until the end of a sequence or section of action. Transitions are often fluid. Also, among a group of performers, there may well be overlap of phrasing.

We see again how the various factors or spatio-dynamic characteristics of rhythm inter-relate, since phrases may be initiated in a number of different ways. For instance, a phrase may begin with a marked change of focus, direction, dynamics or action, or with a change of body parts in action – as when one phrase ends in a contracted position and the next is initiated by a limb extension. Phrases may be concluded by a change in use of dynamics or by a pause. The significance of pauses as boundary markers usually increases as one proceeds to longer structural units – a short pause may mark the boundary of a time and rhythm phrase, a longer pause the end of a sequence, section or scene. Lengths of phrases may relate to tempo: for instance, in his discussion of the form of Japanese Bugaku court dance Wolz points out that phrase lengths are 'eight beats for slow pieces, four beats for medium tempo and two beats for faster pieces' (1971, pp.19–20).

Breathing pattern, together with the notion of 'shaping' movements and flow of movement energy through time and space, is central to phrasing, most noticeably in dance. Changes of weight in body action (as in steps, jumps, rolls and so on), placing of accents, pauses, variation and fluctuation in use of dynamics, spatial direction and movement amplitude all contribute to the shaping and patterning of a dance phrase. Dynamics and accents may be used to shape a phrase by drawing attention to the beginning, a central section or ending of a phrase, or in keeping an even level throughout (see references to Laban and Humphrey, pp.130, 119; Blum (1987) and Maletic (1983), for the dynamics of phrasing identified in more detail; and see the reference to an aspect of phrasing in Japanese performance practice, p.53). Thus a phrase may be considered analogous to a sentence and divided into sections (analogous to clauses), though it is usually more difficult to discern separate phrases and phrase sections in movement than it is to recognise sentence structure. Movement phrases in drama and in ceremony may be discerned more readily when they follow a text or sequence of ideas, with clearly defined entrances or exits; and they may be pointed by use of objects or furniture.

Repetition is a common organising agent in movement patterns. It can bring a sense of security and a form of coherence to the whole. We frequently see children relishing the fun of repeating rhythmic movement – predictable and contagious, it is enjoyed by adults too. Motifs in dance can be repeated to reinforce mood, indicate character or to emphasise communality. Alternatively, they may be brought back later in a work in various ways. We can use or observe different kinds of repetition: it may include exact or distorted versions of the original motif or phrase. Variations include echo or partial repetition. Repetition can be used sequentially to accumulate further material (as in the nursery ditty 'The House that Jack Built'). A litany form uses a repeated pattern of words as a refrain.

In the macro-structure of a dance or ceremony, the rhythmic pattern accretes in many different ways through a variety of compositional means. In these examples, A, B, C, D each represent a unit: repetitive series, A A A A A; varied series, A A1 A2 A3; contrasting series, A B C D. A particular form of a repetitive series is the rondo (sometimes termed 'periodic', A B A C A B A (and variants). It may be seen that notions of symmetry and balance are related to series such as these. A series may take a cyclic form (A B C B A), a mirror form (A B C D C B A), or if performed by more than one person, a canonic form:

$$(A \quad B \quad C$$
$$A \quad B \quad C$$
$$A \quad B \quad C)$$

Less definite or regular series may be recognised as consisting of varied or contrasting units. Cross-cutting complexities of patterns and randomicity may emerge from repeated viewings.

Structures such as those described are usually more evident in dance or ceremony rather than in drama. However, sometimes repetition of elements may be readily discerned in drama too – in poetic or surreal work, as a thematic device or perhaps for comic effect. For example, repetition is an unusually important component in Caryl Churchill's two linked one-act *Blue Heart* plays (1997). With bizarre, fantasy elements and some accelerated action for emphasis, tensions in family life are reiterated again and again in *Heart's Desire*. The opening action and lines are repeated 11 times at different times (followed by varying amounts of the rest of the script). In *Blue Kettle* the con-situation of a son meeting his (pretended) biological mother is repeated four times, and a meeting with his real mother ends the play. With 'A' representing one of the meetings, this results in an A A B A C A D A structure.

Repeated gestures may be a particular feature of an actor's performance – for emphasis, or perhaps in agitation or as some habit or eccentricity of character – or simply as part of the action. In films, Peter Sellars' obsessively repeated restriction of his arm's involuntary urge to salute in the Nazi manner during his appearance as the doctor in *Dr. Strangelove*, Stan Laurel's uncertain scratch of the head in baffling situations and the distinctively repetitive ways of producing a gun from a holster in a Western, are obvious examples.

Extended use of repetition can be monotonous, but its particular use may be a stylistic characteristic in dance, for instance in Laura Dean's choreography where she has used repetition of steps, turns. It can induce a trance-like state. It is usually significant in ceremony. Use of repetition can generate an intensity which is different from everyday life. For instance, movements designed to banish the evil spirits thought to cause illness, are repeated over and over again with increasing power during curing ceremonies in many parts of the world.

Environment: Location of the performance event and its affect on rhythm and timing.

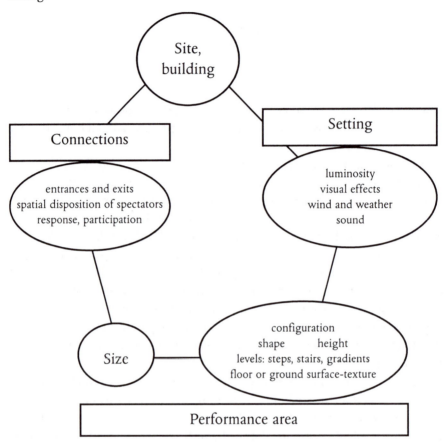

Figure 7.9 Environment

I remember witnessing designer Bruno Santini's instructions to actors during rehearsals for a touring production of Shakespeare's *Pericles*. When the company first saw the splendid, wooden hexagonal floor of the set, he told the actors to move around it thoroughly. He asked them to sense and appreciate the space, not forgetting the area high above which was contained by six long outwardly angled masts. The actors were urged to 'experience' the surfaces, to notice the shapes and angles of the planks, to make varied use of the flights of steps. All this, so that they could respond to, fully explore and make subsequent effective use of their stage environment – Appia's living 'rhythmic space'. Thus 'the environment' is considered here as the physical circumstances in which the performance takes place. They frame and may limit, extend or complicate the possibilities of performance time-use and rhythm. (See also Roose-Evans' 'Making of a Ritual' in

Passages of a Soul 1994.) The performance-frame conditions the expectations and perception of the audience, marking off time and place – like the enclosing of a picture by a frame. In a BBC interview the painter Patrick Heron remarked on the importance of edges in looking at pictures: 'The eye is always going to the edge and bouncing back into the painting.'[4]

The observer should note the size of the performance space and of specific areas used within it in relation to spatial factors of rhythm such as the ratio of movement to space. From the simple carpet of Peter Brook's early company travels to the theatricality of Noguchi's vibrantly interactive sets for Martha Graham,[5] configuration of shape, levels and height of the stage influence rhythm and

Figure 7.10 Auditorium, circus ring, stage and orchestra pit: movement-rhythm in all parts of the house. The tiered spectators partly encircle and look down on the action in Astley's Royal Amphitheatre where an equestrian act is in progress, with lively action on the stage and in the ring, accompanied by the musicians.
Source: Courtesy of Victoria and Albert Museum

4   Interview *Omnibus*, BBC TV, 13 March 1983.
5   Sets which included items such as the shining wire sculpture of many waving strands under which Medea ferments and into which she steps (in anguished pride) at the end of the *Cave of the Heart*, or the scarlet cloth pathway for Agamemnon's return in *Clytemnestra*, later used ceremonially as curtains to reveal his ritualised stabbing to death.

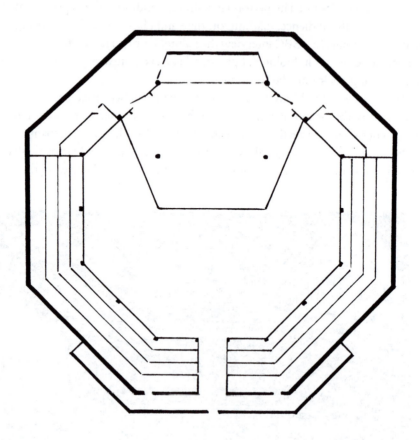

Figure 7.11 Plan of an Elizabethan playhouse – 'thrust' stage presentation. The parallel lines indicate the arrangement of seating and the blank space between seats and stage was where the 'groundlings' stood. This is a theatre design which brings the rhythm of the drama forward into the auditorium and encourages actor–audience interaction.
Source: Liane Payne

timing. Movement on the traditional nineteenth-century west European 'picture-frame' stage 'reads' differently from 'in-the-round' staging and the time and rhythm orchestration in the space is likely to differ in each case. Other stage shapes include 'thrust', in a full form of which spectators are ranged round three sides of the action, and 'avenue' – spectators face each other on opposite sides of the action. Deborah Warner adopted this form for her 1996 production of *Richard II* at London's Royal National Theatre. As an audience member, I found this form of staging induced an increased sense of participation in the action, almost as if we were sitting in judgment on the king, ranged adversarially as opposing sets of witnesses to his downfall. The long avenue shape of the performance area was reminiscent of a tilting yard of the period.

Figure 7.12 Promenade performance staging: a moment in Noah's ark from Tony Harrison's Royal National Theatre production of The Nativity *– Noah (Howard Goorey) and his wife (Edna Dore) with other actors. Use of objects contributes to the rhythm of action: the umbrellas in use as billowing waves surrounding the storm-tossed ark generated a lively rhythm. The audience clustered round the acting area defined its limits. The informal, fluid nature of promenade staging provides changing, irregular outlines to the acting area and influences the audience–actor relationship and rhythms of interaction.*
Source: Douglas Jeffery

Different levels of the performance floor or ground in the context of theatre or ceremony may affect the use of time elements – well illustrated by Fred Astaire in performance on film, or by Meyerhold's incorporation of flights of steps in his staging. New concepts of rhythm and timing were brought to the London stage in the memorable 1973 production of Lorca's *Yerma*, presented by the Nuria Espert Company, in which all the action took place on a trampoline stretched in different ways during the production. If the stage is steeply 'raked' or ramped, the force of gravity may affect the performer in various ways, with a bearing on the use of rhythm. The performer may either go with or against a natural flow and tempo induced by the slope. As Santini mentioned during his advice to actors in the previous example, the height of the performance space above the floor may also

Figure 7.13 Changing levels of dancers with body extensions leaning towards and away from one another as they work together in an ensemble of rhythmic interplay. Lighting contributes to the rhythm in this episode from Mantis, *performed by The Dance Theatre of Alwin Nikolais (from Nikolais' Imago – a full length work in eleven parts).*
Source: Douglas Jeffery

be significant in relation to spatial rhythm, a concept which was realised and made famous in Craig's theatre designs.

The texture of the surface of the performance area can affect use of time elements and rhythm. If an event is transferred from an outside location on rough ground to an indoor location with highly polished floor, the conditions and limits for use of time elements and rhythm have altered fundamentally. Pina Bausch is a choreographer well known for her use of different surface textures on stage, including earth (*Rite of Spring*), leaves (*Bluebeard*), flowers (*Carnations*) and water (*Arias*).[6] The Dance company Pilobolus, visiting Sadler's Wells Theatre, London,

---

6   When water is used it not only affects performers' movement-timing – it may also contribute irregular rhythm-patterns of scattering drops and splashes. For a supreme example, see Gene Kelly's 'Singing in the rain' film sequence.

1985, used a plastic stage-cloth flooded with water, on which they skidded and slid, carrying weight on various parts of their bodies – obviously the surface influenced their use of rhythm and timing while it also added to the company's distinctive stylistic feature of unconventional body use. In England, further examples were demonstrated in contemporary dance work such as in that of Jackie Lansley and Rosemary Butcher, both of whom have made use of outdoor locations with surface-textures varying from sand or rough stones on a beach, to hard cement. In the theatre, Peter Brook's production of *The Ik* featured a stage covered with peaty earth, and more spectacularly, his production of *The Mahabarahta* played on a beach of sand with a canal of water and real fires lit. Choreographer Geraldine Stephenson provided me with an example of how an unexpected change in stage surface texture caused her to alter features of the dance she had designed for a production of *The Winter's Tale* in Birmingham 1985. After rehearsal on a smooth studio floor and expecting a similar stage floor surface, she had to adapt rhythm and timing considerably to adjust to a rough, uneven surface of the stage design.[7]

As indicated in earlier chapters, connections between performers and spectators, between stage and auditorium, location of entrances and exits (on stage and in the auditorium) affect spatial rhythm. The comments made concerning performers' floor pattern and ending positions in the preceding section on spatial factors of rhythm may be applied here. Symmetric or asymmetric use can be made of the performance area and may be assisted or generated by location of stage entrances and exits.

The spatial disposition of spectators is primarily determined by the shape of the performance area. However, the degree to which spectators may participate in or contribute to the timing and rhythm of a performance may be affected by associated aspects, such as their proximity to performers and ease of access they may or may not have to the performance area. Innovatory directors have experimented widely with these aspects of performance, even to the extent of timing the entrance of spectators, one at a time, in this example from an Off-Broadway 1969 New York production by the Performance Garage's *Makbeth*: 'Spectators had to enter a door on Wooster Street, go upstairs over the theater, pass through a complicated maze one at a time, and descend down a narrow, steep stairway into the theater' (Schechner 1977, p.254). In Tony Harrison's Royal National Theatre's promenade production of *The Nativity* (1985), spatial rhythm – with the power of the circle predominant – was evident in the scene of Christ's birth. Participating members of the audience, bearing lighted candles, gathered in

7   Choreographer Twyla Tharp has described the effect of ground texture on rhythm during the preparation of one of her works: 'The controlled sustained lowering of the weight through the feet comes from creating *The Fugue* on grassy fields and softly padded beds of lichen, textures that promote different speeds and transitions' (Company programme notes 1998).

an encircling cluster. As the scene drew to a close the light-bearing hands converged in gentle, uneven flickering patterns of rhythm over the birth beneath.

An obvious display of how the setting, lighting and other visual effects may contribute to the overall performance rhythm is presented during the transformation scene of a traditional British pantomime. In contemporary dance such effects are most marked in works by choreographer Alwin Nikolais, for example. Describing *Somniloquy*, the critic Siegel writes,

> Instead of accepting the stage patterns traditionally implied by the wings, the cyclorama and the edge of the stage, Nikolais has divided his stage horizontally into an almost infinite number of planes by the use of a scrim and bands of light. The action takes place within any one of these areas, or in more than one area at a time. The lights and projections can make the spaces appear and disappear. (1968, p.214)

The piece contains many and varied design ideas, including dancers' use of flashlights and in the final scene a projected image of white dots with a repeated switch of focus. There are many other vivid examples in Nikolais' work. Loïe Fuller is to be noted here as a pioneer in the theatrical use of the rhythm of light and fabric. From the dramatic shock of a sudden black-out to the quiet ending of a fade, designer Lauterer is one artist who urged the considered use of light in relation to time:

> When light is used in any other way than as time, it is used in sheer economy in lieu of paint and the labor that attends it, and hardly ever in our modern theatre do we see light used honestly and properly, which means as time, because that is what it is, essentially – it is time.' (1969, pp.66–7)

Visual effects of many kinds may add to the rhythm and timing of a performance in theatre or ceremonial context: for an example of the latter, Nelson comments on visual effects and use of scenic devices in the Eskimo Yukon River Doll Festival. Large hoops were hung in the kazgi (ceremonial house) halfway between floor and roof. Tufts of feathers and down were attached to these and to the many rods hanging from the central roof hole and fastened to the upper hoop at equal intervals:

> These hoops and rods represented the heavens arching over the earth, and the tufts of feather were the stars mingled with snowflakes. The cord suspending the rings passed through a loop fastened to the roof, and the end passed down and was held by a man sitting near the lamp. This man raised and lowered the rings slowly by drawing in and letting out the cord in time to the beating of a drum by another man sitting on the opposite side of the lamp ... This movement of the rings was symbolical of the apparent approach and retreat of the heavens according to the conditions of the atmosphere. (1899, p.496)

Figure 7.14 Vertical rhythm – an aerial spectacular: performers atop flexipoles swoop and swing to a background rhythm of flags stirring in the wind outside the Royal Festival Hall, London. Australian company Strange Fruit *in* Flight. *During this summer 1997 show, unison swaying action contrasted with random accents and patterning of acrobatic movement, high above the ground.*
Source: James E. Graham

The use of dry ice to create the effect of drifting mist is a popular stage effect, but in another example from ceremony, smoke, fire and fireworks are components of the rhythm of a celebrative rite during the Santa Fe fiesta, New Mexico, held annually in November – the burning of Zozobra (Old Man Gloom). As one witness told me:

> Fire spread closer and closer to the effigy of Old Man Gloom until it began to consume him, and by this time the whole of the hill was a smouldering mass. The fire reached his hind-part and then up went the fireworks. It was a brilliant display and continued amid cheers until Old Man Gloom was gone. Gloom was gone and the fiesta was under way. (Bruce, personal communication 1986)

The release of doves during the Pope's blessing in Rome provides a further instance.

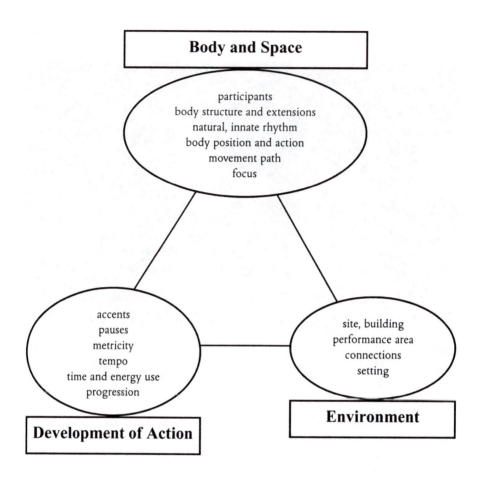

Figure 7.15 Movement-rhythm and timing: summary test of factors and elements.

Finally, the effect of wind on rhythm pattern can be noticeable in many outdoor performances, affecting flags, plumes, costume. This was considered sufficiently important to be generated electronically for an effective display of flags during the British ceremonial 'hand-over' of Hong-Kong to China, 30 June 1997. In the theatre, a wind machine produces various effects. A most striking example was its use in the creation of a vast snow storm which appeared to fill the stage and advance towards the audience as the small figure of Russian clown-performer Slava Polunin struggled against the density of whirling flakes (*Snowshow,* Hackney Empire, 1996).

To conclude, movement rhythm and timing develops from a mix of spatio-dynamic characteristics and continuity-pattern variables. It is suggested that these develop from combinations of the body, space, action and environmental factors described in this chapter, and as summarised in Figure 7.15.

8

Suggestions for Training in the Observation of Rhythm and Timing

Even if we don't make theatre, we are theatre. To be theatre is to be human, because only humans are capable of observing themselves in action. (Boal in Delgado and Heritage (eds) 1996, p.35)

I suspect we all have characteristic ways of perceiving movement. I know that after all these years there is no such thing as being able to see what no one else can see – its just a matter of persistence, motivation to really get into the observation, and readiness to see new details each time you look! (Davis 1973, p.19)

The concept of rhythm is a conceptual tool. When we use this tool and assorted technology to examine it, we can arrive at another level of process description. (Byers 1972, p.9)

Observing movement in detail is not a skill which comes easily to everyone. We can see the process at work when a child who has this aptitude registers and imitates the movement of an adult. The classroom imitation of a teacher may develop into the expertise and art of a stand-up comic, or be stored in the observation-bank of an actor.

As a model for characterisation, an actor may study the movement rhythm and timing of an individual in everyday life. Assuming the movement habits and characteristics accurately – which may then be exaggerated or emphasised by repetition – is essential for the success of a stand-up comic's routine. For instance, delighted recognition and applause rewarded Eddie Izzard for his imitation of Prince Charles' occasional habit of lightly checking his cuffs between thumb and forefinger, just before making a speech. This action has a distinctive, repetitive rhythm which through effective observation was captured in Izzard's portrayal. (Eddie Izzard at the Albery Theatre London, March 1994).

For teachers, observation and response to what is seen is a continual process. Generally speaking, the better or more efficient and thorough the observation, the better the teacher. Of course, rhythm and timing elements in an actor's characterisation, in the classroom or in everyday life, are only one aspect of

Figure 8.1 Observing the rhythm of writing. An English-speaking Sri Lankan friend notices that her thought and behaviour patterns are different when she writes in her native Sinhalese. This she ascribes to its flowing, predominantly rounded letters and to the resultant rhythm in the act of writing. She also thinks this relates to a characteristic non-linear mode in aspects of Sri Lankan people's behaviour and interaction. ('To wish you a happy birthday')
Source: Kumari Liyange

movement behaviour. But as examples in earlier chapters have indicated, these elements are a significant component in movement and dance, and they offer a useful basis for movement observation practice. Thus in this chapter the features and elements of rhythm and timing which have been described are considered in application to the practical situation of movement work and its observation. Throughout this study the writer has attempted to emphasise the integrated nature of movement expression and of rhythm itself. However, the suggested elements of rhythm and timing are listed separately as a reference check-list at the end of the chapter.

Different contexts and study purposes determine the kind of observation to be done. These factors affect the amount or level of detail required and the form of analysis which may be needed as a result of the observation. Full analysis of the rhythm and timing content of an event, be it drama, dance, ritual, ceremony or other event, requires a considerable amount of detail. However, this chapter has a limited objective. Advice on methodology and procedure for fully detailed and analytic academic studies are beyond the scope of this book. The purpose here is to interest beginners and to enable them to make a start, and perhaps to improve any observational skills others may already have. The suggestions include mainly simple, basic starting ideas for observational tasks we can all set ourselves if we want to develop our skills, as well as some suggestions which present a more difficult challenge.

A useful pre-requisite for movement teachers or anyone else who wishes to develop skills in directed, detailed observation of movement, is a basic anatomical knowledge of the kind usually acquired by dance students as part of any effective training. That is, as a basis for recognition, knowledge of the taxonomy of

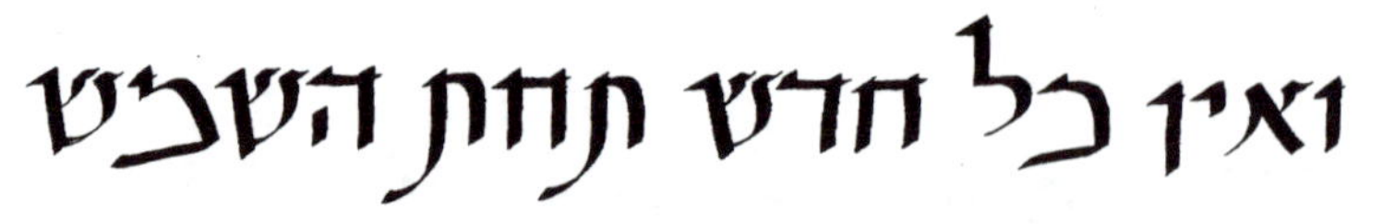

ואין כל חדש תחת השמש

Figure 8.2 As if hewn from stone, but with a flowing hand and pen: an ancient writing rhythm. An example of the Hebrew Yerushalmi or Dead Sea Scroll script in a modern version: 'and there is nothing new under the sun' (Ecclesiastes 1:9).
Source: Meg Nellist

movable parts of the body, action of joints and muscles together with an understanding of the physical features of momentum, force, velocity, acceleration and gravity.

Looking and seeing: a young teacher may be nervous and too concerned with 'the content', really to *see* the details of the action, or in the case of rhythm, precisely how different parts of the body were involved, particularly in the torso and all-important body centre. Movement in arms and legs is more obvious. The eye needs training and practice: observing movement involves the visual and kinaesthetic perceptual systems, whereby the individual is required to look with heightened perception and clear purpose.

A relaxed, easy attitude during observation, without pressure to produce results, is beneficial. As zoologist Frazer Darling stated when describing his experience in observing deer:

> It takes time for the eye to become accustomed to recognise differences … the observer must empty his mind and be receptive only of the deer and the signs of the country. This is quite a severe discipline calling for time and practice … soak in the environmental complex of the animal to be studied until you have a facility with it which keeps you as it were one move ahead … In this state the observer learns more than he realises. (quoted in Chapple 1970, p.6)

Observational skills are dependent on visual competence, kinaesthetic sense memory which informs one's response, experience and practice. Swift, non-judgmental response to what is seen in a given context, and immediate recognition of movement elements is also required. And observers need to be able to identify and distinguish rhythm and timing from other movement features.

Figure 8.3 From hand to hand: a graphic artist's view of 'juggling rhythms in space' – wavy lines, zigzags and loop the loop provide a simple reminder of some of Laban's ideas about spatial rhythm. Source: Liane Payne

A beginning may be made by scanning the whole scene and noticing its main characteristics in terms of use of space, dynamics, physicality; and at the same time allowing for whatever features of rhythm are prevalent to make an impact. What do you notice first? Just as when looking at a painting, recognition and responses to its visual rhythm will differ, so when viewing rhythm in movement, we do not all see it in the same way. Perhaps there may be something about the use of time or rhythm which strikes you as particularly interesting or unusual in the context. Variations in tempo, acceleration and deceleration are usually readily discernible. If you are looking at a choreographer's work, can you distinguish characteristic use of any aspects of rhythm or timing?

Here is an example from my own experience of observing dance. Once described as 'a wondrously strong, fast, slouching hell-cat of a dancer' (Croce 1976, p.122), choreographer Twyla Tharp has stated 'Dance is like a bank robbery; it takes split second timing' (1977). I certainly found this characteristic most evident in Tharp's own work, in the use of rhythm and timing in her early pieces from the 1970s. Of course individual pieces of work differ, but to take one example by way of illustration: *The Rags Suite*. This is an eight minute piece in

Figure 8.4 Outline traces here suggest how changes of direction with timing of gestures may contribute to movement rhythm.
Source: *Judith Greenbaum*

three sections, for two dancers. It is set to piano music: Scott Joplin – *Fig Leaf Rag*; Mozart – *Variations in C major kv265*; and Scott Joplin – *The Ragtime Dance*. Let us just consider elements of rhythm in the style of movement (that is, as distinct from rhythm and timing features in the partner relationship, in the use of stage space and in the macro-structure of the piece). Characteristics of rhythm which I noted included the following. There was varied deployment of accents and varied intensity or degrees of vehemence in their use, performed in different body parts, and often in more than one part at once. Deborah Jowitt vividly described this aspect of Tharp's dancers' movement: 'They twist and shudder lightly as if something were crawling on their spines' (1973). It seemed like playing tricks, perhaps. Indeed, the overall mood was carefree, fun-loving. Quirky use of accents which occurred irregularly during phrases, with marked use of syncopation, contributed to this atmosphere. Spatial rhythm was noticeable too, with extremes in use of stability and randomly tilting lability, of symmetry and asymmetry, and in range or size of movement gestures. Small movements were frequently stressed, which drew attention away from predictable climaxes. Clearly etched changes of direction promoted spatial rhythm. The tempo varied, and movement was often rapid, with fast, staccato footwork or surging, open swinging action which contrasted with sudden freeze-holds. Sections of expansive gestures, slashing turns and off-balance lunges were set against motifs of little twisting steps, jiggling hips and shoulders, or calmer phrases, with softly folding arms (as at the ending). A propulsive, continuous flow of energy at different tempi induced vitality, and a feeling of 'get up and go!'

There was a strong sense of dancing with the music, but the music was not necessarily matched precisely by the movement. Both metric and non-metric patterns were adopted. A sharply pointed sequence following the beat of the music might continue with one of seeming casual, nonchalant movement, across the beat. Regular movement motif-patterns, sequences and action-phrases were part of the structure, such as a sequence of falling, followed by rolling out of the fall, then rising, turning, and a surprise ending with a step or two. Sometimes a clear metric pattern was adopted, such as in a slow, quick, quick, slow succession of steps, reminiscent of ballroom dance patterns; pre-dating by many years Tharp's later choreographic work based on this idea. The overall drive of all aspects of the rhythm-patterning of the action had the effect of impelling the dancers to the end of a phrase with unusual skitterings, swoops, scuttles, dives and turns of many kinds: risky, subtly syncopated action which contrasted with precise arrivals 'on a dime'.

Dance company member Colton described the physical experience of performing in Tharp's early works: 'our muscles must keep the proper balance of tension and relaxation so that the dance appears to be held together, not by counts but by magic' (quoted in company programme notes, 1986). This writer suggests that use of elements of rhythm other than metrical counts made a major contribution to that 'magic' and to the dance style. (Photographs which illustrate Tharp's style of this period are included in many books about contemporary dance. For instance, see Siegel 1991, photographs 6, 22).

The on-going nature of Tharp's dance-action, the variety and complexity in the use of rhythm and timing features made a strong impression, and were innovatory features of dance style at the time. As Marcia Siegel commented: 'Tharp uses the classical movement vocabulary with distortions, changes, interpolations … she mixes the order of energies, starting fast and ending slow … she evades climaxes that have been working out the same way for generations' (Siegel 1974).

Sometimes the challenge of observing a whole dance or scene of movement can be daunting. Limited objectives at the start may help. For instance, if you want to figure out the pattern of beats or accents in a dance, a basic, obvious exercise is to notice when the feet (or other body parts) contact the ground, and note what pattern emerges. It may be that the dance follows the metric pattern of accompanying music, or it may have adopted a non-metric rhythm which goes across any regular beat. Another simple idea is to select one part of the body for its involvement in rhythm. In a dance, perhaps the arms often swing and beat the air, initiate phrases or accent the movement in a distinctive way. In a ceremony, stillness may be an important key: when does it occur? What part of the ceremony does it mark? Perhaps it is a sign of particular respect.

Some of the suggested categories such as frequency of accents or of pauses require a rating system. A simple approach is to note the extremes at either end of a range, or presence of the feature or element as low/high on a scale of degree. This is sufficient in the general kind of observation for which these suggestions are designed. Alternatively, in relation to a particular element, ask yourself: 'Can I

Figure 8.5 Visual rhythm: an emblematic pattern.
Source: Liane Payne

see lots of this, a little or is there none?' Or very broadly: 'When is it slow, when is it fast?' That is, notice contrasts or alternation in the use of elements of rhythm.

Skills in observation of movement rhythm and timing may be stimulated when you have enjoyed performances and may wonder how the directors or performers achieved their effects. The use of timing is perhaps at its most obvious in comedy. A televised compilation of the work of a favourite comic actor is a useful source of material for practice. Questions to ask about a theatre performance might include: How is rhythm used to build a relationship with an audience? How does an actor manipulate an audience through the use of rhythm and timing to generate response? Take a look at the ways rhythm and timing may function during performers' interaction. In an ensemble, can you detect a movement cueing system? Do teachers use the same techniques? Perhaps consciously at first, but of course unconsciously later in their careers when techniques have been established. Are you able to distinguish different elements of rhythm in audience behaviour such as during an actor's comedy routine? Frequency, speed, pulsing and synchrony of people during laughter have been studied (Mair and Kirkland 1977; Brodzinsky 1977).

Although time elements are ever present in movement, the degree to which they are stressed, developed or arresting in a performance (with use of rhythm), varies. A powerful or particularly captivating scene may alert and prompt you to consider the extent to which the effect was achieved through a director's use of time elements. One experience of this occurred for me during Yukio Ninagawa's production of Terayama's play *Shintoku-Maru* (Barbican Centre, London, 1997). Clear, varied use of a remarkable number of the elements suggested on the check-list at the end of this chapter was evident throughout the production. Indeed, the potential and theatrical power which resides in skilled utilisation of these elements was strikingly demonstrated. For instance, one dream-like scene, which developed into a nightmarish whirl of movement, was particularly memorable for contrasts in the deployment of environmental, spatial rhythm and in the use of rhythm in the development of action. Briefly, in darkness at the beginning of the scene, several inconspicuous, crouching figures gradually began to enter, slowly pushing low boats, which were filled with flickering candles. Steadily gliding, the boats changed places across the space and moved around. In the semi-gloom, a contrasting procession of very high, precariously balanced fringed canopies, golden palms and other objects hanging from slender, swaying poles encircled the stage. Then during the subsequent development of action, there was a further strong contrast. The movement rhythm of an isolated, young boy (the central character in the play) was violently disturbed by a series of cross-cutting, irregular, non-metric, accented rhythms. These sprang from the individual movement patterns of wild, grief-wracked women, who zig-zagged headlong about the central area of the stage with flailing arms and clutching, tearing hands, doomed ever to mourn and seek their lost children. In the first example, the use of slow tempo and the exaggerated low/high and direct/circling spatial rhythms considerably heightened the mood of dream-like, surreal mystery. In the second example, the movement-rhythm of the women not only contrasted with that of the boy but also heightened the audience's sense of his inner feelings, since in the scene he is mourning and seeking his own dead mother.

Rhythm and timing elements as characteristic or stylistic features of choreography, individuals (dancers, actors, other performers, politicians – or your acquaintances) as well as cultural signature may all provide subjects for the practice of your growing skills. Variations which occur in different live performances of a work may be a focus of study. The function and use of rhythm and timing in the various phases of the performance process is an intriguing topic (rehearsal/performance/post-performance). Ways in which performance usage of rhythm and timing relates to everyday usage and to perception and attitudes to time – and how these vary cross-culturally – are yet to be fully investigated.

In a large, busy observational situation, beginners are advised to restrict and frame their observational field and to develop eye-movement speed in ranging this. Depth of field, background as much as foreground, and a full sideways scanning can be included. In some cases one particular performer may be observed; in others, an impression of the pattern of rhythm of the group in general. If several observers are working together, each may watch one performer, or single elements of rhythm or timing in use by one performer.

I encourage students to use any notation skills they may possess and to explore and experiment with various modes of notation and recording their observations. They may, for example, make use of freehand drawing as Kestenberg advises:

> Rhythm consists of the recorder's freehand drawing of the increase and decrease of muscle tension during movement. It is based on the observer's kinaesthetic mirroring identification with the observed subject. The tracing must be done with free-floating attention while at the same time one has to judge the rate of increase of tension, the degree of the intensity reached, and the frequency of fluctuations of tension during a given sequence of movement. (1977, pp.4–5)

As in the development of any skill, practice in observation best proceeds from the simple and relatively familiar, to more complex and less familiar observational tasks. It is worth taking advantage of any occasion or situation for inconspicuous observation practice; for instance, when sitting opposite people on train or bus, or watching people on television. If you have access to video, make use of that, especially with the sound turned down. Study movement in nature too. The free patterning of boughs in the wind, the varied regularity and irregularity of waves as they approach the shore and recede; animals and birds – the sudden precision of the sparrow's head, the slow relentless sustained progress of a predatory heron.

In my own experience with students it has been found helpful to undertake preliminary work on recognition of fieldworkers' own preferred patterns of rhythm and timing before unfamiliar patterns from other cultural areas are experienced or observed. As Kestenberg states: 'preferences for certain rhythms tend to distort kinaesthetic perception and reproduction of another person's movements' (1977, p.5. See also Hunt, as recorded in van Zile 1977, p.93). Preconceptions, prejudice, and seeking or seeing only that which confirms held views are dangers. Bambra warns us of this: 'Movement is inevitably interpreted by each observer in terms of his own knowledge and his inbuilt perception of movement. What we observe is readily coloured by our own understanding, experience and convictions' (Bambra 1966, p.41). Also see studies of perception such as Kafka (1957) and Newtson (1971).

Training in movement observation ideally should include practical class experience of movement. Even at a rudimentary level, some appropriate movement training can stimulate the requisite kinaesthetic awareness in would-be observers. In his Anthropology Department at the University of Virginia, Charlottesville, Victor Turner advocated and experimented with practical movement experience for anthropology students. During a study visit, the example in which I participated took the form of an improvised version of a ritual event based on Turner's Zambian Ndembu ethnography. From movement experience of this kind, Turner argued, fieldworkers' understanding would grow, proceeding from 'lived-through' experience:

> At the very least, potential fieldworkers would begin to grope, in a more than cognitive way, towards an experimental or 'inside view' of the other culture. They would also learn something about reflexivity, since they would be learning about themselves and their own values and modes of assigning meaning even as they attempted to grasp and portray those of the other group. (1981a, p.9)

However, it was noticeable that a number of the students in the group I joined, clearly lacked movement experience. This affected their participation and concentration detrimentally.[1] Practical movement training may also facilitate a fieldworker's participation in dance activities of any community, often an essential

---

1   Turner was receptive to my suggestion that the students would have become more readily involved, benefitted more thoroughly from the experiment and been better prepared for the subsequent analytic session, if they could have had some movement class work and observation training beforehand. The suggestions for movement rhythm observation and training have been endorsed by anthropologist Allison Jablonko: 'I consider anthropology will have a big breakthrough when movement classes will be offered to anthropology students so their learning will not be limited to verbal-mental channels, but will include the physical experience of different culture rhythms. Thus, a more concerted study of rhythm and timing, as J.G. [Janet Goodridge] is in the midst of, will provide vital tools for improving cross-cultural contacts, both in teaching dance and in preparing anthropological fieldworkers (whether film workers or not) to "find" themselves more readily (or not at all) in their field location' (unpublished ms., 1978).

Figure 8.6 Street carnival rhythm. Informality within processional structure. Banners and mobile costumes add to the rich patterning and rhythms of the Notting Hill Carnival, London.
Source: Simon Ashmore Fish

feature of social life (also suggested by Kurath 1952, p.53; Hood 1971, p.35; Blacking 1973, p.81; Koning 1980, p.417). And what Spencer has termed 'some kind of tool kit for movement observation' is useful to the ethnographer in the field. (Spencer SOAS Seminar, 7 January 1984). Training in movement observation remains relatively neglected in the fields of drama, dance, anthropology and in teaching, despite the work of psychologists, ethologists and movement practitioners.

The suggestions put forward here are in the nature of work in progress, and are not intended as a categorisation or method 'set in stone' or to be imposed on anyone. In fact, given the persistence, motivation and readiness recommended by Martha Davis at the beginning of the chapter, the best training is that which is done by individuals for themselves. One way of undertaking this is through posing and exploring questions for ourselves – an endless process. One of the most experienced movement observers in the field, Ray Birdwhistell, was always asking questions. For instance: 'How do we isolate, differentiate and measure a body motion? What are the initiation and end points of a particular motion or motion sequence?' (1970, p.170).

Figure 8.7 Observed in nature: a long, slow rhythm of widening lines on a sea-snail shell.
Source: Annabel Rees

If repeated viewing is possible, additional features of rhythm and timing may be observed each time. As already indicated, for detailed study a number of viewings of the work or event are required. However, a useful general impression may be obtained from one viewing by a practised observer. During my own experience of observing rhythm it has usually been apparent from one viewing which characteristics were emphasised or significant; for example, during an Indian Kathak performance it was possible to note a number of recurring elements of rhythm and timing, as well as to supplement these notes by recalling other features after the performance.[2]

On this occasion, the process of observation was aided by several factors. There was a usefully limited viewing range because of the reduced performance area which is characteristic of Kathak dance style. Much of the dance took place

2   This performance was by Alpana Sengputa, Leyton Town Hall, London, 26 March, 1981.

Figure 8.8 The skirt swirls to continue the rhythm: Alpana Sengupta, Kathak dancer, in performance.
Source: Mick Taylor

on the spot, with occasional figure-eight or circular floor patterns. Front-focus to the audience predominated. Also, a strong dance–music relationship and synchronicity between the dancer and the musicians served to reveal and emphasise many features of the rhythm, making them more obvious.

Provided by sitar and tabla, the music matched the pattern of the dance which retained metric patterning throughout. The relationship between the music and the dance was most evident in the shared use of pulse-divided beats, with the dancer's feet marking a constant pulse. There were occasional rapid passages of dance movement which elaborated the beat. These movements were further accentuated by the four-inch wide bands of bells which the dancer wore round her ankles. Not only the ankle bells but also the richly coloured, fluid silken skirt were adjuncts which added to the rhythm in torso, hips and legs. Pauses were used at times. The dancer would sometimes arrest her movement very suddenly; here the swirling continuation of rhythm in the skirt softened the abruptness of the stop.

Since the dancer was positioned centrally, and facing the audience for extended periods, with repetitive use of starting and ending positions and gestures, again observation was a relatively simple matter. Given the predominantly frontal view, it was more possible than usual to note the small action-rhythms of hands, feet, neck, eyes and eyebrows. There was often a clear flow of action from the eyes to the hand and seemingly back to the head. (After the performance I wondered if maybe this related to the adage, well-known in Indian dance circles: 'The eye follows the hand, and the head directs the eye, and the heart directs the head.') The performer's inner attitude to time and energy was perceived as emphatic and intense, and there was a strong driving flow of rhythmic action throughout. Tempo varied from medium to fast (judged on a low/high scale of degree), with bursts of speed and use of acceleration.

There was emphasis on the use of rhythm in the dancer's personal space. Arms, in which much of the rhythm resided, were predominantly held above waist level, at shoulder height, sustaining the flow and as it were 'holding the reins' of the rhythm and timing. This position of the arms again afforded a usefully limited visual range for observing the pliant, successive rhythm in the hands and the symmetrically balanced, curving, or sharply direct arm gestures which extended from near to full reach in the dancer's personal space, sometimes with an alternate right, left rhythm of the arms. With complementary action in the legs and feet, sometimes it seemed as if the arms were juggling the rhythm in the air, pointing or smoothing the varied pattern of beats and accents.

Accents were both regularly and irregularly placed and increasingly frequent as each section of the dance proceeded. Body parts stressed and accented in use, were feet (especially in the flatly placed stamping action and use of heels), hands (wrists, fingers, thumb and forefinger particularly), arms, neck, head, eyes, eyebrows and smiling mouth. There was also accented use made of changes of direction, especially in turns towards the musicians and also towards the audience, and in pivot turns executed by the dancer in place. Each of the main sequences of the 22 minute dance built to a climatic concluding section: vibratory action in the legs followed by the dancer turning ten times on the spot, with pivot steps.

Throughout her performance, the dancer gave the impression of totally inhabiting the rhythm of the dance and of the music. It was alive in her centre, and she in the centre of it.

This miscellany of first impressions from one performance provided an introduction to the use of some features of rhythm and timing as a basis for more detailed subsequent observation and study. Following Bartenieff, 'summary images and the outline can be valuable aids to the researcher in the process of full movement analysis' (1984:7).

It is always useful to have feedback and constructive criticism. For this purpose, on this occasion I was able to have comments from an advanced student of Kathak dance, Linda Shanson, who supplemented my notes with reference to her own experience of the rhythm and timing components of the form and style. Shanson first pointed out that traditionally the area used for the dance was even smaller than in the performance I had seen. It used to be performed solely in an intimate 'chamber' setting. Performing artists have now adapted the form for larger spaces.[3]

Concerning the use of the feet and legs: Shanson demonstrated important differences in the ways in which the weight is directed more or less strongly into the ground through the feet, which I had not noticed. Furthermore 'there is significance attributed to the earth and use of the feet in relation to signs of respect'. The vibratory action observed in the legs is to give an illusion of the valued appearance of 'shimmering'. It is produced by the action of a beating flat-foot, heel, heel, and is clearly emphasised in the ankle-bell sound. Here, as in other comments, the advantages of obtaining notes from someone who has had personal practical experience of a movement style were evident: a spectator may not identify physical sources of rhythm as clearly as a performer can. About the use of sudden stops in the dance: 'These are for dramatic emphasis or as a high point on the first beat of a new sixteen-beat cycle.'

Shanson commented that the glancing action of the dancer's eyes 'are particularly significant as they address Krishna – as if looking at the beloved'. The use of eyebrows is apparently a distinguishing mark of Kathak, and in any further observational study it would be important to note this specifically and in detail. Using eyebrows individually is considered to be more alluring than when they are used both together, simultaneously.

There was an interesting amplification of my observations about hand movement when Shanson quoted her teacher Binju Maharaj, an undisputed master of Kathak. During classes he had described the movement of the hand in various ways: 'as if water is on it ... as if water is dripping off it ... as if blessing ... as if two friends are meeting ... as if riding a horse'. In another comment about rhythm and timing in the hands and arms, during turns the aim is a spiral effect in gestures. This pattern starts in a hand and arm gesture and circles on, spiralling around the body as the dancer turns. According to Shanson, this is very clearly observed when the dance is viewed from above. Commenting further about

3   After the performance I was told that one training method is for the student to practise the steps within the confines of a small square of bricks in order to achieve the necessary retention of placement and reduced use of general space.

rhythm in the neck, Shanson informed me that 'the rhythm is decorated with the neck – these are known as 'adami' movements'.

Shanson was convinced that rhythm in Kathak dance is a form of expression: 'There is an aesthetic operating ... it is clearly a dimension of expression as well as motivation ... it brings out the masculine and the feminine'. And to quote Binju Maharaj once more: 'The dance is never purely abstract – there is always some meaning in it.'

The observations about rhythm in this example are endorsed and further supplemented by Devi:

> The predominant style of Kathak dance is *Nritta* – pure dance, footwork is its distinctive characteristic. The beauty of Kathak dance is the perfectly harmonised plastic patterns of the arms and curves of the body that give visible expression to the rhythmic patterns of the feet. Variations in tempo, permutations of the timing cycle in cross rhythms, rapid turning movements and sudden still poses, are the technical formulae of Kathak. Flow of movement, grace and poise are its aesthetic qualities. (1972, p.168)

Full involvement as a spectator, together with a kinaesthetic awareness and empathy, stand the observer in good stead during later recall. In some cases, the more understanding an observer has of an event, the better the observation. In other cases a fresher, sharper result may be obtained from attending an event without preconception. If recording or note-taking is feasible at the event, this should be done efficiently and without attracting attention. Practice is required in making notes while watching movement, especially in a darkened theatre or outside at night, and preferably with no glances away from the action.

In many contexts, recording or obvious note-taking may be inappropriate or inadvisable. In such cases, as in my study of the Yaqui Easter, memorisation is the only possibility, with repeated viewing if there is the opportunity for this; and with any notes made as soon as possible after the event (see p.219). As Scheflen (1965) advises, repeated viewing is necessary in order to see repetition of specific behaviour. There is then the chance to examine clusters of elements or features; and to discern regularities, complementariness, contrasts and inter-relationships. However, the difficulty of discernment should not be under-estimated. Let us remember that at an advanced level, and in an academic context, Scheflen and his associates undertook several years of study of repeated viewings of one filmed psychotherapy session!

Through practice in movement observation, definition of chosen categories can become more precise. The ability to perceive a full range of elements of rhythm and timing and structural features may be developed. Attention span increases. Awareness of the details of patterns and of the complexity of movement rhythm also develops over time.

The experienced observer develops a more refined judgment and also learns to perceive use of several elements in combination, or a particular configuration or overlapping patterns of elements. In relation to observing layers of patterns, when rhythms overlap in the movement of an individual performer, Hutchinson Guest offers useful comments to would-be notators which illustrate the expressive potential of body-timing:

> For example, in a formal bow, the inter-related timing of the head movement and the accompanying torso bend will provide a very different message according to whether the actions occur completely simultaneously, or whether there is only a slight overlap. The head may start first and the body later, or the head participation may come through the torso bend or only near the end. With each such variation the expressive effect is subtly altered. (1984, p.21)

Hutchinson Guest goes on to explain how an action delay in one body part may express different attitudes. For example, if the torso and head bow simultaneously – 'a gracious bow'. If the torso bends first, the head after – 'reluctance' or 'a lack of true respect'. In more advanced studies, mapping layers of patterns of rhythm in group movement superimposed on each other as a complex set, might be the challenge.

This chapter is mainly concerned with looking at live performance, but film directors' use of rhythm and timing is a fascinating study in its own right, and it is interesting to notice how the suggested factors and elements relate to film. Also video or film if available, can be a useful observational study-aid – and is certainly recommended for in-depth work. Since tempo is a crucial factor of rhythm, in general it is necessary to retain tempi of the original during repeated viewings. However, using video with speed variation control during repeated viewings can be useful. Through accelerating the tape, attention may be drawn to the patterning of certain structural features, such as use of accents and aspects of spatial rhythm and phrasing. Also, boundaries of phases, phrases and sequences of movement tend to emerge more clearly when the tempo of the tape is increased. Movement detail in complex sequences can be noted more easily through decelerating the tape.

In addition to the observation of rhythm and timing elements of a performance event, the wider context of the event may be a focus of interest. An observation study of rhythm and timing in a relatively limited context may perhaps unexpectedly lead you further. Here is an instance of what I mean by this and how a development may occur, as a final example. I was pursuing an interest in features of rhythm and timing and their effects in rock and rave dancing. At first, the observation of movement rhythm and timing was my only concern. My attention had been drawn to the essential features of non-stop continuity of action, duration, beat, tempo, repetition, specific body involvement and step patterns – as well as to the popularity of the movement style with an enormous number of young people. Brief comments on these features now follow.

Experience of holiday-makers abroad pre-dated and influenced the development of rave in England. With reference to the non-stop continuity of action and extended duration of events, Adam Heath remembers dancing through the night, non-stop, on Ibiza in 1987: 'We were there to dance! And dance, and dance and dance! And not stop!' (quoted in Collin 1997, p.52). At Longstock in 1991, one of the notorious all-night festivals attended by many thousands, the Spiral Tribe sound system was 'never slacking, never slowing' (Collin 1997, p.201).

The incessant beat and pulse of the music was picked up in the movement of a crowded dance floor: 'The dance floor was something special … [it] would be pulsing' (McKenna 1996). Or as reported in *The Sun* 17 August 1988: 'On the packed dance floor, youths in surf shorts stripped to the waist flailed their arms to the pounding beat'. And as Julia Franks, a former rave events promoter, now working as a therapist with ex-ravers, assured me 'we are certainly dancing in time with the beat!' and also, when I asked her what 'dancing well' entailed, she replied 'dancing in time … keeping with the beat'. A number of writers have drawn attention to the significance of the beat in ecstatic or trance-dance: 'the rhythmic beat of every dance movement [is] the most essential method of achieving the ecstatic' (Sachs 1937, p.25). So as we probably could have guessed, in rave events, the power of the beat is paramount. Furthermore, it relates to the heart-beat. The music is timed to take account of this. The House music prevalent at raves has a particularly fast beat and as Franks commented, 'there's something about the heart-beat going faster that gets the whole thing going more'.

When I asked Franks about step patterns, she was adamant: 'It isn't about steps – it's not about being a great dancer!' And as she went on to explain, there is a sense of release, of casting off restraint in the style of moving. Dave Roberts, speaking of his 1988 rave dance experience, bears this out: 'The music was so crazy. The dance you danced to, it wasn't posed, it was joy' (quoted in Collin 1997, p.84).

Concerning environmental factors which relate to rhythm and timing, the visual component at rave events, including lighting and other effects, such as dry ice shot through with laser beams, makes a considerable contribution to the rhythm. The timing and beat-pattern of these effects are a striking feature of raves and club events. For instance, Collin describes the 'jerking bodies synched to the strobe and the metronomic beat', and the 'relentless' strobe light (1997, pp.61, 74). When I enquired about this, Franks assured me that the rhythm of the lighting is important; it is specifically designed to complement and synchronise with the rhythm of the music.

Meerloo wrote of the 'contagious quality' of rhythm (1962, pp.70–72). The extent to which rhythm is 'caught' through each of the senses – hearing, sight, touch – is a further area of investigation. In his work on interpersonal synchrony, Condon suggested that it is established by sounds (Condon and Ogston 1971). Stern and others have suggested it is accomplished by people perceiving an underlying pulse and joining it (1973) – but how is the pulse perceived?

'Too-fast music could cost nightclubs their licences' (10 December 1996). Newspaper headlines and reference in the press to the 1996 code of practice for dance venues alerted me to the particular significance of tempo and changes of tempo in club programming. The London Drug Policy Forum was advising clubs to include periods of music in their programmes which had a slower beat and tempo. Thus an initial consideration of rhythm and timing features began to suggest the need for a wider focus.

Medical experts had become increasingly concerned about the physically damaging effect of over-heating, induced partly by the continuous fast music and rapid beats, and accentuated in the body by the accompanying movement. This, as Franks had told me 'increases the effect of Ecstasy and develops into the altered state aimed for ... House [music] perfectly complements Ecstasy ... It's fast ... You need to get your heart going to get the effect of it [Ecstasy]'. And in *Mixmag* July 1994 we read: 'They pushed the tempo further to see how high they could take the music.'

It is well known that drug use has always been part of the scene since those early Ibiza days – when apart from anything else, the majority of participants thought they needed 'something extra' to help them last the night. But information from the London Drug Policy Forum and elsewhere indicated that if a movement rhythm and timing study was to proceed adequately, a thorough investigation of the effect of the different drugs in use would be required.

Franks pointed out that Caribbean music and dance has had an influence on developments in Britain. For instance, she had witnessed DJ track mixing in West Indies' sound systems before it had begun at raves in England. And more interestingly in relation to tempo and to slowing the tempo, she had seen DJs use their judgment and introduce a process of interruption when the temperature and pace got too hot. They would repeatedly stop the music after a few phrases and then start it again, only to stop again, to cries of 'Play it! Play it DJ! Play the music!' Despite the excitement it provoked, Franks found that this procedure had the effect of physically cooling and slowing people down. However, the code of good practice for safety at dance events in *Dance Till Dawn Safely*, published by the London Drug Policy Forum, warns that 'an abrupt and unexpected cessation of music or sudden change of tempo could inflame an already highly charged situation' (1996, p.10).

The features of rhythm and timing with regard to group movement in rave events connects with group movement in other contexts. The nature and significance of the unison action which occurs, and of the group synchronicity which is so enjoyed at rave events; the links of these and other features with the use of movement rhythm in religious cults, in spirit healing, trance-dance or possession rituals of various kinds are obvious topics for further study.

It can be seen that, as in the case described, if observers and researchers are to extend their studies, it may become essential to investigate the reasons for an event, as well as to study the form and function of rhythm and timing features within it in more detail. Information about traditional and innovatory features may also be gathered. This material may be obtained both directly and indirectly from the people concerned. Also, as Kealiinohomoku has pointed out, it may be useful to note not only what is said but also what is not said about an event – just as one may observe what is not done as well as what is done in, or because of, an event (1976a, p.343). It is suggested that Kealiinohomoku's and Lange's check-lists be referred to for background features of an event (Kealiinohomoku 1972, pp.245–260; Lange 1985).

Although to follow Kurath's expert example, observational procedure may vary with each case, (see reference p.102) at an appropriate stage some initial procedure for observation and assessment should be clearly established. This is of course particularly important if comparative studies are to be undertaken. Increased recognition of the elements of rhythm and timing as well as awareness of process and interaction in movement rhythm develops over time. Results of observation can be analysed to discover frequency and persistency of use of certain elements of rhythm. Particular features, regularities, complementariness, contrasts, inter-relations and causal relations in use of rhythm and timing, as well as range in use of elements, can be examined. See Scheflen (1965) for further comments. For detailed study, considerable practice and perseverance is required, as Condon indicates: 'I spent a year and a half studying 4½ seconds four or five hours a day, before I could see interactional synchrony' (1982, p.55). Condon's study is an example of an extremely detailed, painstaking form of movement observation in the service of advanced academic analysis.

Recognition and clear description of features and elements of rhythm and timing at the micro-structural level is a first stage of observation, and has been the main objective of these suggestions. Analysis and interpretation of data as well as detailed study of the form and function of rhythm at the macro-structural level is for a further stage of development. A full movement notation score would be needed for more detailed analytic study. Principles of order and implicit rules governing various forms of performance may emerge at that stage. This method for identification and description of suggested, selected elements of rhythm was

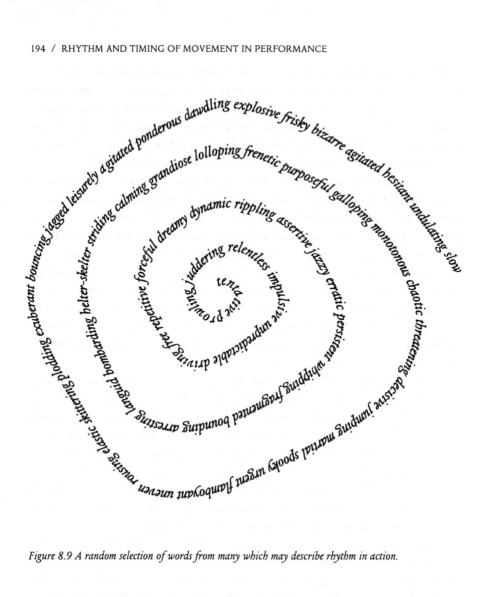

Figure 8.9 A random selection of words from many which may describe rhythm in action.

devised in order to pursue the study of performance rhythm and timing at a descriptive level.

Check-lists of factors and elements of rhythm and timing in movement[4]

> He that has eyes to see and ears to hear may convince himself that no mortal can keep a secret. If his lips are secret, he chatters with his finger-tips; betrayal oozes out of him at every pore. (Freud 1908, quoted in M. Cox and A. Theilgaard 1994, p.238)

---

4   The check-lists provide a summary of the exposition in Chapter 7. Also see comments, p.157.

Introduction

Disadvantages of a mode of categorisation or check-list are acknowledged by the writer. For instance, if this means fitting perceived behaviour into pre-determined categories it may be considered that this process over-simplifies and distorts the material (see Davis 1977, p.60). However, for serious study a system of some kind is needed when faced with the complexity of movement behaviour, and for comparative purposes. In such cases it has been found that the suggested check-lists aided focus on particular aspects of movement-rhythm and timing.

Fellow observers' responses influenced the writer in devising the form of categorisation and the suggested check-list. Both quantitative and qualitative categories are included. Although qualitative categories are not amenable to objective, exact measurement, they are included since they are recognised to be integral aspects of rhythm and timing in performance events. This inclusion is supported by other researchers (Wallbott 1982; Stone 1981). However, the category 'time and energy use' which involves performer's 'inner attitude' may be considered a particularly problematic category (see p.131). Under 'Environment', 'response/participation of spectators' is included as a general category to remind observers of the potential importance of this in the overall rhythm and timing of an event. Clearly, more detail and a rating system is needed if these categories become a particular focus of study. Furthermore, in any development of a rating system, ambiguous and general terms such as 'frequent' should be avoided.

Researchers may prefer to make initial observations without recourse to the check-list of suggested elements of rhythm. But if its general validity is acknowledged, it could be used subsequently to ascertain whether any aspects have been overlooked which on reflection perhaps should be included. This manner of usage may also allow researchers to check their own bias and draw attention to their own preferred perspectives.

Although the listed order of elements of rhythm has a coherence, choice and order of elements may predetermine observations and findings in a counter-productive way. Therefore, it is advisable to change or rotate the order so as to jolt observers' perceptions and perhaps provoke their own, new discoveries. As Hollenbeck comments 'In observing behaviour, humans filter sensory information into scoring categories that have focused their attention to predefined responses. Reliability of observation is influenced by the observing unit, the behaviour observed, the scoring categories used, and the interaction between the observer and the scoring system' (1978, p.83).

Body and Space

Participants
number
gender
age

Body structure
natural, innate rhythm
parts engaged in the rhythm
left/right
extensions and accessories

Position in space
symmetrical/asymmetrical
standing, sitting, kneeling, lying ...
falling, lifting
stable, labile

Type of action
simultaneous
unison/complementary/contrasting
successive
adjacent/separate
discrete actions

Movement path
movement reach
in personal space
in the performance area
amplitude
quantity of movement
in personal space
in the performance area
gestures
shaping
starting and ending point
tracks
shaping
starting and ending place

Focus
projection inward
(*within the performer*)
projection outward
up, down
to the side ...
to fellow performers
to spectators

Development of Action

Accents
occurrence
single/multiple
frequent, dense/sporadic, sparse
recurrence
regular/irregular
location
in the body
in personal space
in general space
in the sequence, phrase
in group interaction

Pauses
duration
location
occurrence
frequent, dense/sporadic, sparse
recurrence
regular/irregular

Metricity
metric/non-metric
regular/irregular

Tempo
pulse, underlying beat
regular/irregular
constant/inconstant
pace
acceleration/deceleration

Time and energy
degree of emphasis
degree of urgency
restraint/spontaneity

Progression
duration of events
a beat
an action
motif or movement unit
phrase
phase
sequence
regularity of events
repetition of events
movement: time

Environment

Site, building
Size of performance area
Configuration of performance area
shape
height
levels: steps, stairs, gradients
floor or ground surface texture

Connections
entrances and exits
spatial disposition of spectators
spectators' response, participation

Setting
luminosity
visual effects
wind and weather
sound

9

An Application in Learning and Teaching

Rhythm and Timing in an Approach to T'ai Chi (Tai Ji)

Tai Ji: 'Like the sea it ebbs and flows ... it relaxes the mind as well as the body ... it keeps us in touch with nature ... arthritis pains me but Tai Ji makes me feel as if I am floating ... I feel so relaxed – from head to toe I've got that glowing feeling'. (comments from members of the classes referred to in this chapter)

This example describes my experience of rhythm and timing in the practice of two different forms of T'ai Chi Ch'uan – more commonly known as Tai Ji – in a western environment.[1] First, a brief introduction. There are many different forms of Tai Ji and all teachers and experienced practitioners develop their own approach. The practice is essentially an individual matter, and it can be interpreted and understood on many levels. My interest and gradual process of learning began in the 1970s; it is a continual process. I must state that I do not consider myself an expert. Furthermore, I make no claims for originality in the comments I make about rhythm and timing in Tai Ji. They are derived from observations of my own practice – chiefly of two forms or versions of Tai Ji, but also from the teaching I have received from inspirational teachers, and from reading, gathered from many sources over the years. One form I practise is a version of the traditional long Yang form which I have studied in England with Gerda Geddes.[2] Another is The Five

---

[1]   I have adopted the term and spelling 'Tai Ji' in this chapter since it is the best known Chinese Pinyin spelling and it encourages a pronunciation which is closer than 'Tai chi' to the Chinese original (see Huang 1987, p.vii). Also, *'ji'* avoids confusion with *'ch'i'* which has other particular meanings. In China the revised spelling for *'ch'i'* is *'qi'* and for *'Ch'uan' 'Quan'* which provides further clarification. These changes are in process of adoption in the West and used in the full title of *Tai Ji Quan (T'ai Chi Ch'uan)*.

Elements (and associated Circle forms) which I have studied in the USA and in Europe with Chungliang Al Huang.

As a result of an unexpected invitation from my teacher Gerda Geddes to introduce Tai Ji in a London Senior Citizens Day Care Centre, I began – with some hesitation – to share my experience of Tai Ji. Six years later this activity has extended to another such centre, and occasionally to sessions with other people. With Chungliang Al Huang's encouragement, in addition to an introduction to the long Yang form, my classes also include The Five Elements. This is the first in the series of progressively more complex Circle forms developed by Chungliang Al Huang from his deeply rooted knowledge of Tai Ji and traditional Chinese wisdom. He has described it as 'an organic choreography' (1989, p.55). During the process of moving through its fluid action sequences, participants visualise and learn to embody and integrate the changing energies and symbolic ideas inherent in the circle of elements or moving forces, identified in China as fire, water, wood-wind, precious metal and earth. The movements are derived from the essence of each of these, taking the ideas metaphorically (i.e. not mimetically). In the early stages The Five Elements is simpler to learn and more readily accessible to the western mind and body than a classic form may be for some people. Thus it is likely to provide more immediate experience of the beneficial harmony, balance and well-being which are generated through practice of Tai Ji.

Good teaching practice inevitably includes varied use of rhythm and timing, and teachers generally take this for granted.[3] Undue analysis or dissection of what we do intuitively as teachers could interfere with the process. However, the experience of leading sessions has necessitated a more intent focus for myself on movement ingredients in Tai Ji. Now, for the purposes of this chapter, a further step is to consider the elements of rhythm and timing in some detail as an example of an observation project in the context of practical movement teaching.

First, some comments about rhythm and timing in my experience of the long Yang form. In the version which I practise and share, the most obvious rhythm and timing features concern use of tempo, duration, specific body involvement, flow of energy, relationship with rhythms of nature, aspects of spatial rhythm and general style of the movement. The tempo is slow and sustained. This slow pace differs from an everyday use of 'slow'; it has a more lingering quality and a stronger sense of the present moment than we often allow ourselves in everyday life. The action is continuous and flowing, with a natural-seeming ease of timing. There are no held, static poses. Any named 'positions' are stages in the process,

---

2   Gerda Geddes, the first person to offer Tai Ji as a teacher in England in the 1950s, studied with Choy Hawk-pang and Choy Kam-man.
3   For example, I think all teachers are familiar with basic class timing-structures, which relate to phrasing: such as from energetic to calm (or vice versa) or a wave-like structure which grows from calm to energetic, calms again and then builds energy once more to end the session.

moved towards and through. This relates to the pattern of breathing which is regulated by the movement, in accordance with the action. 'Holding the circle' provides an example of this relationship. To refer solely to the arm movement, from a starting position with both arms down, as breath is gradually inhaled, the left arm rises to the side and the right moves out slightly, then both curve in towards the front – left remaining above, right below – with palms facing (as if carrying a sphere) and exhalation into 'holding the circle', with energies directed inward.

To consider duration – in the example above, inhalation and exhalation of breath is of approximately equal duration. But the timing of breaths is not repetitively the same throughout the form. Some of the movements take more time than others, and may require a longer inhalation – matched by an exhalation of breath. For instance 'the crane spreads out its wing' is a relatively expansive movement made on an inhalation, as one arm curves up sideways from low to high. This is balanced by the ensuing movement of the arm travelling down and across the body on the exhalation. There may be fractional pauses in the movement which are barely noticeable, as also occur between exhalation and inhalation. The subtle irregularity of the rhythm overall contributes an intriguing variety to the pattern, and may also help the practitioner to remain alert. There is no sense in which the rhythm is metric or counted numerically as in many other forms of movement training. There may be an underlying sense of one's pulse during the practice, but the varied breath and movement-action rhythms override this.

The entire form is in three parts, each of a different duration. The form consists of over one hundred movement motifs which are grouped into sequences, again of varied duration (no specific set time – in my practice it takes approximately 25 minutes). There is a degree of repetition: some of the movements introduced in parts one and two recur later.[4]

Practised in a standing position – upright but not stiff (with ease in the neck, 'open' across the chest, and with 'soft' shoulders, elbows, wrists, knees, ankles) – the rhythm and timing is carried in and through every part of the body. To help readers visualise the form a little more clearly I should mention that the starting position, and many subsequent positions of the feet in this traditional form of Tai Ji, is with the toes straight forward and the feet parallel. The knees are always aligned above the toes, including when they bend (sometimes called a 'riding horse' stance). This position has the result of releasing tension in the lower back, to healthful effect.

---

4   I do not lead the Day Care Centre groups through the whole of the long Yang form. The classes are specified as an *introduction* to Tai Ji and at the time of writing include Part One and a few motifs from Part Two.

The aim of the movement is that every part of the body be co-ordinated with economy of effort and without muscular force, to promote sustained, flowing, circular patterns. Tai Ji muscular action is sensed – allowed, rather than commanded to occur. The movement-rhythm and timing is essentially organic, and a ceaseless shifting between opposites – for instance, the arms may lift, then lower; weight may transfer forwards into one leg and then backwards into the other. There is focus on the way the body actually functions (e.g. in rotation, flexion, alignment). Indeed, through Tai Ji practice I have become increasingly aware of anatomical structure and of the location of inner organs and internal rhythms of the body.

Beginners frequently first notice the movement of the arms and may think that they initiate the timing. But before this occurs, action is sensed in the soles of the feet, which retain contact with the ground much of the time during practice of the form. The Chinese refer to *yong chuen* 'the bubbling well' point which is located just behind the ball of the foot, an apt description of an energy source. In fact when I practice, I imagine that I am drawing the energy up from below the feet, from a well of energy in the earth beneath. From the feet, the movement-energy, known as *ch'i* and associated with the breath, is thought to travel and be discharged throughout the body, if the channels are clear.

During practice of the long Yang form we pay close attention to the timing of action in the feet. For instance, in the action of taking a step, as in all the movement of the Tai Ji, the foot is easy and relaxed. But this is never a heavy relaxation; there is life and awareness in the action and care is taken over timing the placing of the foot. There is resilience in the feet and a sensation of gently 'rolling through' the foot as the weight is gradually transferred from the heel through to the whole foot and leg. Rooted in the ground but not stuck or remaining there, the action is much as if the foot were to be softly yet unmistakeably imprinted in sand or in a first fall of snow, only then to move on or shift to another soft imprint.

The knees are usually in a gentle *plié*, that is, in a slightly flexed position, or the legs are moving towards or away from such a position. The pattern of continually shifting weight, from one leg to the other, is sensed and described as changing between 'full' and 'empty'. This, with the gentle release of one foot when it is necessary to take a step, are key features of the rhythm.

The play or fluctuation of energy – a basis of rhythm as identified in Part I – is especially important in Tai Ji. Of several treatises now available in translation, Lun Chin in *Discourse on Intrinsic Energy* clarifies the distinction between intrinsic energy and force: 'force is visible, energy is invisible; force is linear, energy is circular; force is harsh, energy is smooth' (Olson 1994, p.37). Described as *ch'i* 'breath essence' (or energy) of Tai Ji, during Tai Ji practice the mind is trained to sense this travelling through legs, hips, waist, spine, upper body and head, as well as through the arms, hands – into palms and fingers.[5]

The lower *tant'ien* which is the mid-point of the body – the abdomen just below the navel – is sometimes described as a 'cauldron of energy'. This is considered as the centre of gravity for Tai Ji practice. As Chungliang Al Huang explains:

> [the *tant'ien*] is concerned to be both a reservoir for the ch'i, and the center from which our movement originates. Tan means the distilled vital essence, and also the rich, red color of blood. T'ien means field or place. So the tant'ien is the field of energy, the intrinsic energy, the reservoir of your vital force. (1987, p.23).

As we inhale we imagine our breath sinking down to the *tant'ien*. A sense of this place not only as the reservoir of vital force but also as the location of our centre of gravity is important. Essentially a moving centre, our sense of the *tant'ien* aids in the development of a mobile balance and of being stable and well grounded: all of which are inherent in the experience of Tai Ji.

Rhythm in the Tai Ji is generated by the contrasting actions that occur, and by the irregular alternations in the use of right and left sides and limbs of the body. The basis of this contrast, and of other aspects of the Tai Ji, is in the interchange of *yin/yang* vital energy, but 'within every yang some yin, within every yin some yang' (Crompton 1990, p.19). In Chinese thought, this energy is considered to exist not only in ourselves but also as the two great complementary opposite forces of the whole universe, symbolised by the Tai Ji inter-related *yin/yang* circle, in perpetual balancing motion. *Yin* – the passive principle, *yang* – the active principle, each containing the germ, embryo or vestige of the other. Indeed, the concept is the fundamental basis of Tai Ji. As Hua Ching Ni states:

> In doing *t'ai chi* movement, it is helpful to know the cosmic T'ai Chi Principle. [This] is rhythmic alternation or rhythmic movement: for example, inhale to exhale, or movement inward to collect energy in the center to movement outward from the center back to the limbs ... The cosmic *T'ai Chi* Principle is to follow the alternation of the two [*yin* and *yang*]. (quoted in Tsui-Po 1994, p.20)

For instance, in the arms these contrasting movements include actions of lifting (mainly *yang*) and lowering (mainly *yin*), of moving the arms apart then towards each other, of taking them around in a circling, horizontal movement or of gently 'pushing' hands forward. . The waxing and waning of the gestural shaping is

---

5   Chungliang Al Huang provides a fuller explanation of this (and other concepts). An extract: 'CHI or QI is the force of the Cosmos, between heaven and earth. It is the primal life energy that we receive from our parents ... It is the air we breathe, the food we eat and the enveloping atmosphere' (from Huang 1982).

predominantly curved and circular, and the arms appear slightly rounded since they are never fully extended.

There is a sensation of ebb and flow of energy in the rhythm as one moves through the form. This relates to rhythms in nature, such as the waves of the sea as they surge towards and draw back from the shore. Sometimes I am reminded of the effect of wind passing across a field of wheat or long grass, especially when the form is practised together with other people and the flow of movement travels through the whole group. Another image which frequently comes to me when I am moving my arms is of long fronds of water-weed being moved by the flow of current in a clear stream.

Figure 9.1 Flowing lines of rhythm from plant life.
Source: Wen Cheng-ming (1470–1559). Courtesy of the Victoria and Albert Museum.

Throughout the form there is an ordered sequence of named movements or images, most of which are derived from nature. These may be read as a series of symbols which connect with other aspects of ancient Chinese culture – art, religion, mythology (see Cooper 1978 and Geddes 1995 both of whom have made a particular study of this connection). This material enriches and extends understanding limited by a western viewpoint. As with the movement of the crane (or 'large bird') spreading its wing referred to above, the timing may relate to the image in some way. Each of the three main sections of the form begins and ends in a mood of calm tranquillity with the image of a mountain: energy within, stillness without. Each section also draws to an end with the image of a tiger – symbol of energy: 'Embrace' or 'carry tiger', a gently scooping action as arms cross in front of the chest, before the 'return to mountain'.

Next, some aspects of spatial rhythm. Tai Ji is traditionally oriented to north, south, east and west and to the diagonal directions in between. In our sessions we do not take this literally. In class we adopt the geometric directions of the form but we position ourselves at the outset in the most congenial, appropriate way in the given architecture.

Turns and changes of focus in the body, in the arm gestures and in the movement of the legs generate spatial rhythm. The co-ordination of the rhythm is subtle and quite complex. There is a multi-dimensional flow of energy in the action as parts of the body move in a complementary manner in different directions, both simultaneously and successively. Ease of movement in the waist area promotes an easy turning of the spine, as if around a vertical axis. When this occurs the motion then continues through arm and hand, into palm and fingers. Sometimes the backs of the arms lead the direction of the movement, sometimes other surfaces of the arms or the hands. The supposed origin and subsequent development of the form as a martial art lends a logic to the direction of the gestures and to the spatial rhythm, albeit in slow motion in the version of the form which I practise.

An interesting experiment is to attempt Tai Ji standing breast-high in water. Awareness of different aspects of the movement and of the timing can develop through this. The water resists movement and gestures have to be firmer to retain their correct pathway. It is almost as if one is participating in a martial arts version of the form and confronting an invisible opponent. The different surfaces of the arms and hands have to press or slice through the water. The challenge of holding one's ground and the details of physical co-ordination, spatial rhythm and timing, are heightened.

The effect of the spatial rhythm in Tai Ji has often been likened to that of unwinding or winding a skein of silk. It winds up and around the body and encircles the space within arm's reach; sometimes close to the body, sometimes further away. An eternal, mysteriously unending, invisible web. Chen Kung describes the mobilisation of energy as like reeling silk: 'when reeling long pieces of silk from a cocoon it must be done gradually, and softly, otherwise it will break and be of no use' (Olson 1994, p.167).

The preferred ground surface in a practice location is horizontal and the spatial rhythm has an even, horizontal emphasis. The predominating plié position and almost cat-like prowling action of the legs means that the head stays on one level, without bobbing up and down. With ease in the neck, the head is perceived as a continuation of the spine, with the crown (the *pai hui* point) sensed as if lifted or suspended from above by a thread. The back is felt to be rising while shoulders (and elbows when in use) relax downwards. There is a sense of a plumb-line from the top of the head through the spine and continuing down. This simultaneous, combined upwards and downwards sensation prevails throughout, together with the multi-dimensional flow referred to earlier.

The rhythmic flow, mood or quality in the general style of movement in the form is calm, sustained and tranquil; relaxed yet alert. It is thought that any unnecessary tension in the body, blocks or restricts the flow of *ch'i*. We aim to attain the sense of stillness in motion, of motion in stillness and of being 'present here, in the now' which Taoists describe. There is no intentional movement in the face. Eyes, mouth, jaw and even the tongue are quiescent. (It is specified that the tip of the tongue should rest, gently touching the back of the top teeth, and that breathing should be through the nose). As the stance settles, tension is released and tranquillity is brought about before any movement begins; this may be assisted by preliminary breathing or *chi gong* exercises. There is a sense of the space all around, and of the earth beneath, but the practitioner's focus is inward rather than outward. The eyes sometimes follow the movement of the hands, or look gently downward – aptly described as 'slantingly forward' by Gerda Geddes. The practice of Tai Ji is for oneself. Even if spectators are present it is not a performance to an audience. Perhaps it could be said that during practice of the form there is an inner sense of an outward focus to the universe.

The movement rhythm is clear, intentional and disciplined, but never accented or sharply marked. No one individual movement should be stressed. In the second part of the form there is a section in which there is a series of movements which are termed 'kicks'. Although energy is gathered to perform them, they are executed softly, with the economy of effort and lack of urgency or strain which is characteristic of Tai Ji. There is none of the hard attack or emphasis usually associated with the action of kicking.

The degree of restraint is an especially interesting feature of style in the movement rhythm to consider in relation to the practice of the form. From tradition, and as it is 'a form', there is the restraint of a pre-determined structure. It is practised with enormous respect for the tradition and for past Tai Ji masters. Students may be advised how to execute the various movements and how to consider the internal aspects of the form, such as the breathing pattern. There is discipline and control in the practice. However, the degree of physical mobility, ease of movement, continuity, and inner sense of flow – which are essential features of the style – offset, contradict and balance the formality of the learned structure. But, a certain restraint does remain in the outward manner of performance.

Some comments about rhythm and timing in my experience of The Five Elements version of Tai Ji now follow.[6] Given the shared traditional roots, some of the features of rhythm and timing in this form are similar to those already identified as characteristic of my experience in the long Yang form. One essential difference lies in an increase in the relative sense of freedom with which the movement is performed. There is an inner attitude of spontaneity in the movement, perhaps due to Chungliang Al Huang's reference to it as dance, for instance: 'Allow the sense of the movement to flow to you without worrying, and the dancing will come to you' (1987, p.122). The regeneration of energy and the sense of discovering the movement anew at each 'repetition' – as if for the first time – are important aspects of the experience. These features are also fundamentally inherent in practice of the long Yang form, and in my experience of both forms, we speak of 'playing' the Tai Ji. But it does take a considerable time and discipline to learn the long Yang form, and although this has not been true of my experience of Gerda Geddes' teaching, sometimes conventional modes of teaching may seem at odds with the development of a sense of freedom, spontaneity and life. Anyway, in The Five Elements, this developmental experience is brought to the fore, made explicit and evident in the beginner's experience from the outset.

The form is never rigidly fixed or set. In my experience of classes with Chungliang Al Huang, although the overall sequential order of The Five Elements has remained the same, details and movements are varied from time to time. With people who have had more experience, and in the later Circle sequences, there is focus on more precision and clarity in execution so that students may reach more understanding. However, since Chungliang Al Huang developed the form himself from the mastery and knowledge of his own traditions, he is able to introduce and develop it as he wishes, in different ways, at and for different times. This reinforces the realisation that any creative form is open to change, that any natural, living form is always changing, and that as we have seen in the comments about the long Yang form, change is at the heart-core of Tai Ji itself. Also, perhaps it is useful to remember this warning:

6   The Five Elements contains the essence of Tai Ji. The introduction of this version has not confused classes since it is compatible with my way of practising and teaching the long Yang form, yet it provides a beneficial and interesting contrast.

Unfortunately, when each master begins to teach, he may use *his* master's teaching method as he remembers it, instead of sharing with you out of his own experience now as a result of years of practice, instead of showing you a process that can gradually lead you to this. (Huang 1987, p.64)

Features of rhythm and timing in teaching style are prompted by the characteristics of a movement form to be taught. For instance, in The Five Elements, just as there is limited emphasis on absolute rhythmic precision in the performance, when introducing the form I do not rank this as of paramount importance in my teaching. Instead, the rhythmic flow and fluctuating patterns of energy which the form generates are emphasised.

During the sessions at the Day Care Centres, focus and concentration is excellent. But, in keeping with the spirit of change, free timing and spontaneity, if a new idea emerges unexpectedly, I may go with it and improvise. For example, one day a class member suddenly uttered the familiar phrase *'mens sana in corpore sano'* (a healthy mind in a healthy body). This apparently represented his understanding of Tai Ji at that moment. We all joined in and learnt the words. I found that the phrase fitted most satisfyingly with the movements of one of our

Figure 9.2 Earth. This Chinese character evokes a sense of vast expanse, broad stability and deeply rooted power. Sky above, earth below.
Source: Chungliang Al Huang

breathing exercises, which we then all repeated with much enjoyment – words and movement together – an unpremeditated rhythmic development.

As in practice of the long *Yang* form, we begin The Five Elements from a feeling of relaxation, ease of movement and a calm mind. The well-grounded stance and verticality of the torso is also similar. As a preliminary movement (and repeated at the end as a conclusion) it has become customary to sweep both arms up in a wide curve, as if to embrace the sky and to draw from the energy all around us in space, then to bring the arms down towards the earth. Next we generate a sense of drawing *ch'i*-energy up from the earth, coursing up through the body and out of the head, before we bring the arms round to 'Embrace tiger, return to mountain' in a way similar to the long Yang form. We are then ready to continue into an experience of the five elements and their changing, constantly circulating energies.

In group practice we synchronise our movements, as – with a sense of unity – we follow the recognised sequential pattern together. But there is no absolute uniformity. Details of rhythm are not timed to be in a precise unison. Chungliang Al Huang likens this to the movements of the branches of a tree: 'the different branches of the same tree do not move the same but they are moving in unity' (1987, p.15).

If we compare the general impression of my experience of tempo in the practice of The Five Elements with that of the long Yang form, although the tempo may vary and fluctuate, the overall impression in The Five Elements, as in the long Yang form, is that tempo is relatively slow. However, the ebb and flow of movement in the form is more marked, with clear upsurges of energy at times. As in the long Yang form, the action is continuous and flowing. This relates to the breathing, again as in the long Yang form, but the breath rhythms are not matched to movement in any specific way.

The Five Elements form consists of an extended, continuous sequence of movement motifs or phrases of different durations. There is no recurrence of these at later stages of the form as there is in the long Yang form.[7] As in the latter, there may be fractional pauses between sections or phrases, particularly when there is change or transformation from one element to another. For instance, there is a sequence when we visualise fire-energy (*yang*) changing into (or moderating) water-energy (*yin*) – each of which possess both powerful and soothing characteristics. We imagine that we embody and generate fire-energy outwards

---

7   There is recurrence in Chungliang Al Huang's later Circle form sequences.

Figure 9.3 Water. This Chinese character evokes a sense of the ever-streaming flow of rivers and the power of springs gushing from the earth's centre.
Source: Chungliang Al Huang

and upwards. It is then transformed into water-energy which we imagine receiving as it streams down from above, and through the body into the earth.[8] Here there is usually a moment of pause. This pausing occurs as we visualise the water fully sinking into the ground and then being drawn up and into the body as nourishment, like sap rising through the roots and into the growth of tree-wood.

Some understanding of the Chinese many-layered approach to the meaning of a language-symbol or 'word' helps us when we study Tai Ji. In his teaching Chungliang Al Huang introduces the rich symbolism of Chinese calligraphy, with its ancient, even primal roots. He draws attention to the full, detailed translation of each character and to the movement rhythm and energy of the brush strokes. For instance, the character for water 'means forever flowing constant: the oneness in the nature of the movement of water.' And he explains 'The brush stroke should

8   Chinese cosmological ideas are bound up with a system of classification and correspondence of everything in the cosmos. A basic idea is that there is movement of transformation between Five Phases (or the Five Elements) which applies to all categories of life. There is a cyclical order with correspondence to the seasons: Wood corresponds to Spring, Fire to Summer, Metal to Autumn, Water to Winter. In what is known as the productive cycle the Phases lead from one to the other: Water produces Wood; Wood, Fire; Fire, Earth; Earth, Metal; Metal, Water. The destructive cycle (or regenerative) is opposite: Water versus Fire; Fire versus Metal; Metal versus Wood; Wood versus Earth; Earth versus Water. (from Schipper 1993, pp.33–35). In the version of the Tai Ji described, the concept is taken metaphorically rather than realistically. Although the movement sequence does not appear to be designed to relate precisely to the cosmological ideas about the elements, we may note that the 'destructive cycle' is taken in reverse, beginning with Fire, then Water, Earth, Wood, Metal.

have the same sensitive contact with the paper that you feel between your feet and the ground in tai ji' (1987, pp.125–126). These ideas may be shared and incorporated in movement teaching even if the teacher is not a proficient calligrapher.

The duration of The Five Elements is roughly equivalent to the first part of the long Yang form. Choice and fluctuation of tempi, and the number of repetitions, determine the duration – which may be as long as desired.[9]

As in the long Yang form, the pattern of rhythm and timing is carried in and through every body part, the movements being co-ordinated in a flowing pattern. Since the process is essentially one of grounding and centering, there is again emphasis on the *tant'ien* as centre of gravity. The movement rhythm is balanced in the body since it is usual to practise with alternate sides leading the movement.

The images of the five elements follow from one to the next, and each generates a particular pattern of rhythm and timing. For instance, the fire-energy sequence begins with a sense of power in the *tant'ien*, and growing *yang* energy. This develops from the central 'lift' which precedes most steps, then continues in the legs with a strong surging step forward, while with arm gestures from low to mid-height the fire-energy travels up the body, and is finally released through the palms. From there, although a trace of fire energy remains, a softening of the movement and less urgency in the rhythm is sensed. This occurs with a transformation of energy into the *yin* energy of water, imagined as being received from above. A gentle, less obvious free rhythm follows, as with arm movements near to the body and fractional shifts in the head and torso, a sense of a cascade and flow of water streaming down and through the body and into the earth is experienced.

There is a transformation into the imagined element of wood (with traces of fire and water energies still present) as the flow of *ch'i* grows up and outwards again, coursing through the body. Energy is felt tingling in the spine, and there are gentle, rippling accents in the rhythm as the energy surges into and out of the arms. This movement and rhythm is combined with a pattern of repeated slow, circling steps, 'riding the energy round' in an even, regular pattern. This is like the natural rhythm of the growth and expansion of a tree, being rooted and branching out in all directions from the central core of the trunk. (In no sense is this akin to the well-known clichéd caricature of the worst kind of British 'music and movement' class of former days typified by the instruction 'Be a tree!').

Although the five elements are experienced in turn, a sense of the energies of each remains and accumulates through the form. Towards the end of the whole sequence, after the experience of gathering in the precious, shining energies of metal, there is a strong accent in the rhythm with a movement of the arms

9   From approximately 6 minutes for the first part of the long Yang form or The Five Elements.

relaxing, dropping down and outwards, and a sense of release through the entire body of all that has accumulated. This movement may be identified with the eventual return of everything to the element earth.

It can be seen from these illustrations which are characteristic of the whole, that – at least in my experience – there is more overt ebb and flow of energy in The Five Elements than there is in the long Yang form, and a use of accents in the movement rhythm which is foreign to that form.

Spatial rhythm in The Five Elements has more symmetrical balance and less of the complexity that exists in the long Yang form. The arms frequently move together into the same direction – up or down, forwards or outwards, for instance. Personal space is fully used as in the long Yang form. The arms may mirror one another simultaneously or with right and left moving alternately, in gestures of stretching out or gathering, for example.

A major difference in the execution of The Five Elements which affects the rhythm lies in the way we space ourselves for group practice. We adopt a circular formation, with a common focus towards the centre. This offers an experience which totally differs from that of traditional practice of the long Yang form. There, as already described, the group shares a focus towards the imagined compass directions, which necessitates positioning with everyone facing the same way, in a loose group formation or in rows. (However, I should mention that in group sessions with Gerda Geddes, when space permits, and with more experienced practitioners, we execute the long Yang form in a circular formation as well as opposite one another in pairs, mirroring or both retaining the original right/left action).

Given the circle formation of the group, it follows that in The Five Elements the spatial rhythm which is generated is one of the individuals within the group, continually curving outwards and inwards in relation to the shared centre. Arm gestures and the few steps involved in the form follow this pattern. There is one sequence of turning and stepping around and away to an outward focus, but with awareness of the common centre and returning to that shared focus. A perceptive member in one class with Chungliang Al Huang, likened a similar group movement-rhythm to the action of an ever-moving kaleidoscope, as our energies and movement rhythms were gathered, not only into ourselves individually, but in towards each other, and outwards again, in ever-widening circles as in our imagination we connected with the world and the whole universe. A free sense of energy streaming out and in, and of extension into space around one's body and beyond, is emphasised in The Five Elements.

The formation of the group in a circle encourages a sense of relating to other people and with the environment. Synchronicity of shared rhythm and timing develops. In the Tai Ji context, this is usually found to be a beneficial experience for a group. It can be extremely powerful, particularly when a large group practises together. Since the movement-action of The Five Elements is relatively simple to perform, not technically complex, attention can be given to group participation more easily than would otherwise be the case.

This is not to suggest that the form is practised in an extrovert manner. For many practitioners it may be an extremely 'inwardly' focused experience. Perhaps the inner attitude to the use of time throughout may be described as sustained in quality; this despite the fluctuations in the output of energy, and the use of accents. However, Chungliang Al Huang positively discourages anything which approaches a pompous or pious solemnity in the execution of the form. On one occasion an over-serious, downward-looking group provoked a general suggestion: 'Don't be like a frog asleep at the bottom of a well!'

Tai Ji is traditionally performed in silence, and another major contrast to practice of the classic long Yang form is in frequent use of music with The Five Elements. We may occasionally perform in silence, or indeed as we do in practice of the long Yang form, in the out-of-doors location preferred by all Tai Ji practitioners – to the accompaniment of birdsong, wind in the trees and other natural sounds. But Chungliang Al Huang encourages varied use of sound, anything from natural sounds to carefully selected, appropriate classical or jazz music, or sometimes fun surprises. On some courses, as opportunities present themselves, we may be joined by live musicians, or sometimes by the flute playing of Chungliang Al Huang himself.

Musical accompaniment can serve to promote the rhythmic flow of the movement, it encourages and stimulates more dance-like movement, and it also has the power to aid the release of tension. Although I have not known Gerda Geddes to use music actually in a class, herself a trained dancer, she has suggested it for individual experimentation. Music certainly affects and changes the mood of a group. It can of course dominate the tempo and also the phrasing. However, in Chungliang Al Huang's teaching of The Five Elements, students move 'with' rather than 'to' the music. Details of a metric pattern of the music are not intended to be imposed on the form, but an invigorating surge or pulse of music may be matched in the movement. As in practice of the long Yang form, there is no numerical counting of movements.

Despite the fluctuations in tempo and energy use which I have identified, there is a satisfying sense of balance about the timing and rhythm in the practice of The Five Elements. This, together with the enrichment of ideas, variety and contrasts in the movement experience which it provides, has made a most effective contribution to sessions, in particular at the day care centres. Furthermore, the relatively simple gestural patterns do not unduly alarm the beginner or become an insurmountable obstacle to hinder enjoyment. A section of our sessions takes place seated (on chairs) in a circle, and sometimes a class member may need to be chair-bound throughout. Indeed, the Five Elements is a form which can be adapted and usefully, enjoyably practised sitting on a chair.

The weekly sessions at the centres take place through the year, interspersed with a number of breaks. This is a limited time allowance, but members assure me they go through some of the movement from our class daily. Both general and specific physical and mental benefits of Tai Ji practice are now widely documented; improvement in the physical condition of centre participants has certainly been most apparent. Together we experience Tai Ji as movement practice which brings well-being to mind and body, a means of harmonising with nature and of bringing mind and body together as one organic process, occurring through each present moment.

Primary aims of the sessions are enjoyment and a re-awakening of the senses – which of course includes the kinaesthetic sense – as well as relaxation and a time away from anxieties, urban rush and competitive attitudes. 'If your mind becomes calm, you can think in front of a tiger' (Mencius quoted in Geddes 1995, p.33). Our general orientation is open and alive to possibilities and to new and deepening experience. There is a varied rhythm to the sequence of events in each session. Tai Ji masters' demonstrations on video are occasionally shown in class, and material from Chinese arts, poetry, journals and current newspaper articles is frequently shared.

I do not theorise about movement elements in class or even necessarily refer to features of rhythm and timing directly (and certainly not in the words of the check-list). But I have found that if I myself pay attention to different features of rhythm and timing, and include these in various ways in the class, an enjoyable, physically beneficial, manageable challenge is presented which interests and stimulates the group. The wealth of features which there are to consider provides variety (quite apart from other aspects of Tai Ji practice, of course).[10]

Each week, from the oldest student of 93 to the youngest – a mere 65 – the groups share an experience of continuous rhythm from recharged energy – 'plugging-in' – and discharge – release, letting go. The session brings renewed vitality and a sense of having achieved something different or in a fresh way, however simply. Together we gradually discover more about Tai Ji and about the flow and pattern of rhythm and timing it contains. 'The form is a process that serves you, not an adornment like a beautiful art work you buy and bring back to hang on your wall' (Huang 1987, p.65); it is a process of transformation.[11] And as one of the over 90s frequently tells me: 'It keeps me young!'

10 Just as I was completing this chapter, I was interested to read that in the opinion of Robert Parry, a
    well respected teacher: 'Rhythm and tempo are, in fact, the keys to fluent tai chi technique' (1997,
    p.9).
11 Also, since my Tai Ji experience is a continuing process, the contents of any future chapter would
    inevitably differ from this one.

PART III

Performance Events
Time Elements, Rhythm and Timing in Action

10

Easter in Arizona and Mexico

An Experience of Yaqui Ceremonies

A Yoeme (Yaqui)[1] greeting:

Lios em chonia wyla (God be with you).

Ketcha ma leia (And with you too).

Prologue

It is one night in Easter week, and I am recalling my first visit to a Yaqui Indian community in Tucson, Arizona, at this time.[2] I remember stumbling across an expanse of rough ground to reach a dazzlingly lit, totally open-fronted small church in the wide expanse of a plaza. Under the dark desert sky, stalls are selling hot food, cooked on the spot; while dimly visible round the edges of the plaza are reminders of everyday life – parked cars and trucks, and children playing about.

Then, all of a sudden, for no apparent reason, a phalanx of menacing, black-clothed marching figures, with drum, flute and flag-bearers, are firmly trudging the length of the plaza, filing around and back, and up again; then departing, to be heard tramping in the darkness around us as they encircle the plaza at some distance. Then they are getting nearer, returning once more, ever-present like the evil and persecution I later found out they represented (until their decisive defeat on Easter Saturday, and the joyous triumph of good).

Many things seem to be going on simultaneously, so that while watching the marching it is easy to miss the slow, gentle figures of women in the church,

---

1   The Yaqui Indian people call themselves *Yeomem* (The People), but they are more familiarly known as the Yaqui, the term used throughout this chapter.
2   From work in progress, this account is based on my experience and observation during three visits to each of four areas of Yaqui settlement in Southern Arizona, and one visit to six of the Pueblos (villages) in the earlier Yaqui homelands area of Sonora, north west Mexico 1990 to 1994. (See Acknowledgements). I have obtained clarification and supplementary information in particular from Painter (1971, 1986), Spicer, E. (1980, 1984 (orig. 1940)), Spicer, R. (1939), Evers and Molina (1987), and from archival material. For further information about Yaqui history, life and ceremonies, readers are referred to these sources.

attending to the altar, extinguishing or lighting candles in the brightly coloured tall glass containers of pink, scarlet, magenta, puce, or a man quietly brushing the church floor. How did that fire by the church suddenly become larger? I hadn't seen the Caballeros, responsible for some of the heavy tasks, throwing on more logs. Although there is no 'on-stage/off-stage', there is a sense of things going on behind the scenes, such as the activities of the women who are busy cooking for participants in the kitchen adjacent to the plaza – smoke rising from their makeshift oil-drum stoves, the hiss and splutter of fat, the soft flap of deftly turned tortillas.

Another memory is of times when nothing seems to be going on anywhere. This is equally mysterious, inexplicable, yet strangely compelling. Bright daylight this time. The dusty, wind-swept plaza looks quite different under a hot sun, brilliant in a deep blue sky. Men lounge against walls or spread out on benches. A group of Caballeros drag a huge swathe of green-leafed branches across the plaza. Where did they come from? They disappear. Where are they going? Time for reflection. Waiting. A masked Chapayeka trots by. (Remember not to stare, laugh at his antics – never gesticulate or point). It is an experience of clumsily learning how to behave in a different world, with its unfamiliar rhythms and timings, and where we are not totally sure of our welcome. Waiting. Being in the present moment.

Introduction

Fifty years of resistance and warfare in Mexico brought the reputably fierce Yaqui armies to eventual defeat in 1887, and the Yaquis who arrived in the USA in the early 1890s were refugees from these battles and from the long struggle for existence on their native land. After living in the USA quietly for some years, in fear of deportation, they began to observe their customs openly once again – never truly defeated.[3]

> Welcome to Pascua Pueblo. This is the most joyous sacred time in the life of all Yaqui Indians. (from Yeomem Tekia Foundation Easter leaflet)

Although the events of the Yaqui Easter are not 'put on' as a show and are certainly not intended as an entertaining spectacle, non-Yaqui visitors are allowed to be present at most of the ceremonies, and are welcome – provided that certain rules of attendance are followed. Apart from a bank of raised seating at one location of the ten I have visited, there may be some chairs or benches around, but there is no official seating provided for any spectators who might be present. The Yaqui are sensitive about exploitation of their culture and to intrusive behaviour from outsiders. For instance, no one should enter the church without permission.

---

3   There were 30,000 Yaquis when the Jesuits came to them in 1617, and 20,000 in 1970 (the census figure quoted by Spicer).

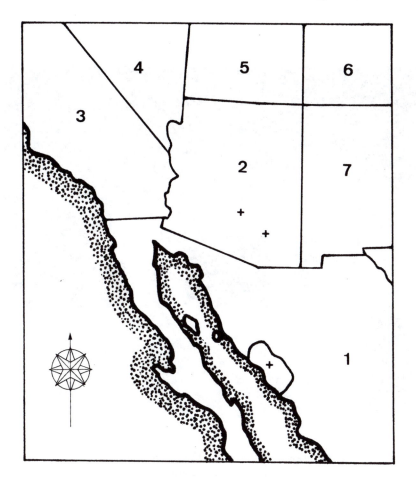

Key:
Yaqui areas visited = + (ten settlements in total, six in Sonor, Mexico, four in Arizona)
Mexico = 1; Arizona = 2; California = 3; Nevada = 4; Utah = 5; Colorado = 6;
New Mexico = 7

Figure 10.1 Map of the area.
Source: Liane Payne

Rules are displayed for the benefit of visitors, and should be taken seriously. Cameras, tape-recorders are banned. The Yaqui do not wish photographs of their ceremonies to be taken or reproduced and this wish is respected in these pages. (Photographs may be seen in cited publications, dated before this rule was enforced. See references in note 2). On one occasion a Yaqui official near me, seeing someone with a camera, pulled the film out and threw it on a nearby fire. It is not possible to make notes or sketches at the time of observation.

Figure 10.2 The church on the plaza at Old Pascua, after the Easter ceremonies. Security grilles were in position at this time. Yaqui churches vary in appearance from place to place, but the bell tower, crosses and open frontage are common features. (Photograph taken with permission from a member of the community.)

We are glad you have come to share this time with us. Please respect our holy areas and the few rules we have that govern our behaviour as well as that of visitors.

There are no cameras, tape recorders or video recorders allowed in or around the cultural area! Leave these things in your car – come and experience with your eyes and your heart. You will remember this time and we hope you will come to Yaqui Easter again. Thank you. (Anselmo Valencia Toni, Spiritual Leader, Pascua Yaqui Pueblo, from a Yoemem Tekia Foundation Easter leaflet)

However, despite the understandably ambivalent attitude to non-Yaqui visitors, the supportive presence of sympathetic observers is valued, as adding power to the event. Local Yaquis throng the church for the Easter ceremonies, but sometimes it is as if it is enough for them to know the ceremonies are taking place – much of the time it seems as if few are watching outside, but hundreds, both Yaqui and non-Yaqui, may attend on Easter Saturday, while contributions to funds made by visitors are gratefully received. At the end of the Easter Sunday events one year, I was formally thanked for my presence by a local Yaqui woman who was standing near me.

The Easter ceremonies and their significance in Yaqui life

The traditional Lenten (*Waehma*) to Easter (*Pascua*) cycle of ceremonies is held in all Yaqui settlements. It is carried out in the area of the central plaza with its church, open to the east (the favoured Yaqui direction, towards the dawn), and ramada,[4] taking place in much the same way as it did far back in Yaqui history. The ceremonies originate not only in traditional Yaqui, pre-Christian beliefs but also in European Christianity, accepted and absorbed into their own beliefs when it was brought to the Yaqui. The two Jesuit missionaries who arrived in 1617 are particularly credited with bringing liturgical drama to the area.[5]

A collective expression of Yaqui solidarity and renewal of spiritual belief: this cycle of Easter ceremonies has particular importance in Yaqui life, reaffirming the Yaquis' sense of identity, and celebrating their survival. The cycle includes ceremonies during Lent as well as the intensive phase in Holy Week, and finally on 3 May the *Kusim Taewa* (Day of the Crosses).

Charged with social, cultural and spiritual significance and meaning, the period is a time of serious endeavour termed 'our work' by the Yaquis. As Muriel Painter, who experienced and observed Yaqui life and ceremonies through four decades tells us, it is 'a time of consecrated community enterprise' (1971, p.8). The main participants fulfil their duties for the entire seven-week period. During Holy Week itself, they may have little sleep; with prayers to start each day, day and night they live at the plaza.

The ceremonies are organised through the Yaqui system of membership of ceremonial societies and sponsorship of individuals through life. Each person has a number of godparents. This is a relationship which involves mutual bonds and obligations related to the societies who are responsible for the organisation and performance of ceremonial events through the year. Membership of the societies results from a *manda* or vow.

The vow is usually made during serious illness, when the aid of Jesus or Mary is sought for help in curing, in return for which a promise is generally made on

4   The plaza and church were brought by the Spanish missionaries; the ramada: an open-fronted shelter on the plaza, also to be found at Yaqui homes, thought to have been of earlier history and used in fiestas and ceremonies, with an altar at one side.
5   That is, the development of tropes (sung dialogues in the church liturgy) and dramatisation of Biblical texts, as part of religious teaching and practice.

behalf of a child by the parents. But it may be made by an adult for himself. The term of service is generally for life, but it may be for a shorter time… When he is confirmed, the child is sponsored by godparents whom he retains for life. It is thought that if an individual does not carry out his ceremonial obligations he will be punished by illness, by accident, or even by death. Almost all the participants in the Easter Ceremony are under such religious *manda* to carry out their parts. (Painter 1971, p.9)

The social organisation, the continuing use of the Yaqui language and knowledge of customs keep the traditions alive.

There is an inter-locking, multi-layered mix of many rhythms and timing patterns to consider in the Yaqui Easter week. In all Yaqui settlements or villages the same sequential cycle is being enacted during that period. The timing of the arrival of visitors from near and far, including family members, who traditionally gather at this season, is one important feature of the rhythm. There is a time-depth aspect too, when memories are shared of ancestors who enacted the self-same sequence. I was made particularly aware of this during an interview with Rosamond Spicer when she showed me a short film made in the early 1940s during fieldwork with her husband, the anthropologist Edward Spicer. The rural environment seen in the film differs from the urban one of today (local roads nothing but dusty tracks, hardly any buildings in the vicinity of the plaza, and very few non-Yaqui visitors). But although the environment and some details are different, the action, appearance and behaviour of participants seem almost identical to that of today, some sixty years later.

Spicer wondered how the Yaqui had managed to remember and revive their ceremonies so effectively, despite the hiatus of more than twenty years when such public expressions had been suppressed in Mexico, and further years when the people had dispersed or been driven into hiding, and many had died. She conjectured that the Yaquis probably thought through the ceremonies at the specified times, and recalled the action quietly among themselves. Apparently, this was just as she had done the year we met, when she had been unable to attend the Easter ceremonies. During years of absence, I have found myself doing the same.

Rhythms through time: components and participants

Today, at the ceremonies, rhythms ancient and modern are juxtaposed. In one of the Yaqui settlements in the Arizona area, traffic on an elevated freeway (motorway) thunders by, only just beyond the edge of the plaza; in another, a fairground is adjacent. In the performance arena (the church, the plaza and surrounding area) everyday activities take place, including cooking, eating and sleeping as well as selling food and other items such as the traditional Yaqui-made *cascarones*.[6] All these activities contribute a strand of rhythm and timing.

In fact, after my first visit to the Yaqui Easter I began to realise that the ceremonies, organised and enacted by different societies and groups within Yaqui society, may be thought of as an amalgam of various strands, derived from a range of sources and equal in importance. Each has its own significance and patterns of rhythm and timing, and the drama lies in the action of the various groups involved. There is no attempt at theatrical embellishment as there would be in a west European context, but readers familiar with Christian liturgy, medieval European drama and folk dance, are likely to be as intrigued as I am to discover some echoes and parallels. One strand in the ceremonies is the Yaqui interpretation of the Catholic Easter liturgy. This is performed by members of the church group, 'Mary's army' (wearing cassocks over normal clothes) led by the Maestros[7] with sacristans (assistants) and women singers. These are joined at times by women who tend the church altar, girl flag-bearers and small boy and girl-angels, dressed in white dresses, each accompanied by a female 'godparent'.

Simultaneously, another strand – a version of the Christian Easter story – is symbolically enacted. In this, other members of the church organisation symbolise followers of Mary and Jesus and carry images of the three Marys and of Jesus in procession.[8] Further removed from anything I have seen in European Easter traditions, Pilate and those who persecuted Christ are symbolised by the Fariseo and Caballero societies who, known as the *Kohtumbre* (Lenten/Easter customs authority) are in charge of the Lenten and Easter events, and are readily recognised by the black hats they wear, Fariseos' black clothing and other distinguishing features. In the role of *Kohtumbre* they effectively 'police' the plaza and endeavour to see rules of behaviour are followed. For instance, on one occasion at the beginning of the procession to Christ's crucifixion I was asked to remove a small headscarf (which I was wearing as protection from the intense mid-day sun, having taken off a hat; but even though it was black *all* women's head-coverings are expected to be removed as a sign of respect). A threatening force with their repeated marching up and down the plaza in front of the church,

---

6   Of Mexican origin, these are blown eggshells filled with confetti, decorated with paint and sometimes with sequins, feathers, glitter-dust. They often seem too beautiful to destroy but are designed to be broken over people's heads at fiestas or celebrations.

7   Leaders of the Yaqui church which has been independent of the established Catholic Church since 1767 when the Jesuits were expelled from Mexico.

8   A number of Holy figures and crosses are displayed on the church altar and carried in the Easter processions; the three Marys are three figures of the Virgin.

and even surrounding the whole area when they march round the Way of the Cross,[9] they are organised like battalions of infantry, with officers and soldiers – of mixed ages, including young boys. Some of the Fariseos are dedicated by vow to be the people of Pilate (known as the Pilates).[10]

The Caballeros are cavalry officers and soldiers (traditionally mounted on horseback in Mexico, and where I did see them, suddenly looming up in the dark during the ceremonies one night, urging their horses on with star-shaped spurs). Two of the soldiers give various signals with drum and flute during the ceremonies, such as for starting, halting the marching or changing the rhythm, and officers (with flags) lead the ceremonies with signals at different times. The Caballeros march and are associated with the Fariseos until Good Friday afternoon when they withdraw their support.

The marching may be described as a determined trudge: with knees slightly bent, the feet are thrust into the ground with a flat step, and a forward impetus. The leaders and more experienced participants lead the lines, and the intention is for a synchronised unison, not always easy to achieve in the long lines, though those near each other are usually in step and the general impression is one of unison and a shared beat. As the men and boys tramp over the rough terrain, marking the ground with intent, these frequent periods of marching seem to represent a reiteration of purpose, a re-dedication, perhaps in memory of Christ's sufferings.

Christian European preconceptions about Easter ceremonies are further challenged by the appearance of the Fariseos' soldiers – the masked Chapayekas.[11] Of uncertain ancestry, but akin to some other native mask traditions, they seem to come from a realm which is alien, even to Yaquis. Although they recognise and sometimes mock or appear afraid of the words and activities of the church group, the Chapayekas play about and often behave as if they don't quite understand all that is going on. They wear an old coat or a blanket folded and pinned as a coat,

9   Stations of the Cross: the 14 places marked with crosses for devotional halts along the way associated with Christ's journey to Calvary – the Way of the Cross; a traditional route and practice familiar to pilgrims to Jerusalem, a number of whom from the early fifteenth century created symbolic representations in their home countries in order to foster the devotion of those who could not make the pilgrimage. To this day the Stations are represented with crosses or pictures around the walls of Catholic churches. All the Yaqui Easter church group processions travel in an anti-clockwise direction – but occasionally the Fariseos and Chapayekas reverse this.

10   Participants may not all be immediately visible: wives of the Kohtumbre provide food in the community kitchen on the plaza during Easter week.

11   Chapayekas from *chapa* (narrow) *yeka* (nose) – many of the masks made of hide or cardboard have narrow pointed noses. With his mask on, the man becomes a different being, and there are rules associated with this. For instance, he must not speak while wearing the mask, and to sneeze or cough is held to be a sin. The small holes in the mask provide limited ventilation. If a Chapayeka needs to cough or feels unwell during his arduous, taxing participation in the ceremonies (which includes various heavy jobs as well as the ceremonial sequences), he lies down on his left side and is immediately surrounded and hidden by others while he recovers, briefly removing and replacing the mask. Beneath the mask and costume each man wears a rosary, with the cross held in his mouth as protection against the evil inherent in the mask and role, and in case the man dies during the ceremonies.

and traditional Yaqui thong sandals. Their masks, helmet-like, cover the entire head and are considered sacred. They may represent caricatures of non-Yaquis such as a Mexican soldier, pink-faced 'white' man or a cowboy, as well as birds, animals and the occasional comic-book character. Although the Chapayekas frequently seem amusing, it is said to be dangerous to look directly at them or show enjoyment of their antics; their behaviour can be menacing and they do frighten children at times.

Immediately recognised by their appearance and distinctive behaviour, the Chapayekas perform tasks left-handed or backwards. They march with the Fariseos but sometimes improvise movement en route; they walk in a special way with trotting-like steps, cocoon rattles rustling round their ankles, and may adopt some movement characteristics appropriate for their masks, such as the stance of a bull or of a superior government official, or the scratching feet of a flighty chicken. They communicate in their own language of signs, even at some distance from each other, with shakes of their deer-hoof rattle belts and raps of their wooden daggers on their wooden stick-swords (which they also tap jauntily to accompany the marching which they join). When there is news to impart or exchange, it is relayed and spreads in waves of a continuing rhythm of communication through the group.

The Chapayekas improvise much by-play with their daggers, pretending these are everyday items of various kinds – such as combs or drinking vessels. A favourite game is to catch imaginary fleas on dagger-points. Each year, the making of the masks, sticks or swords and daggers is the responsibility of the individual concerned. The Chapayekas consider Judas their chief, and all the objects made are burned on Judas' pyre on Easter Saturday.[12]

Allied to the church group, the activities of the Matachin society,[13] dedicated to the Virgin Mary (as soldiers in her army to fight evil), generate another strand in the ceremonial, with distinctive, bright rhythms reminiscent of European folk dance, and accompaniment from violin and guitar musicians. This society is in charge of other ceremonies, and the change of authority, which dominates the pattern of the Yaqui year, is transferred to it in the course of the Easter events – an important strand of community rhythm. With their devotional dances which bless the ground where they dance, the Matachinis do not enter the proceedings of Easter week until Saturday, to aid the destruction of evil. Their dances, closely structured in three parallel lines and rectangular formation, are performed with

12   Except for two masks which are retained to be buried with any who may die during the year.
13   As the name 'Matachin' suggests, the dance figures resemble European folk dance (including English Morris), performed with a slight lean forward and a downward focus and emphasis. It has been suggested that dances of this kind were introduced by the Jesuits (Spicer 1980, p.101). Boys who dance behind the lead dancer in the middle line are known as Malinchim; said to be dressed like the Virgin Mary to honour her, they wear a white blouse and long skirt over their trousers. Malinchim are 'promised' and in training as future dance leaders. (Other American Indian groups in New Mexico and Mexico perform Matachin dances also.)

downward, forward emphasis, well centred in the body, and repetitive patterns of steps which include low kicks, crossing feet, turns and sometimes figure-of-eight chains or files, up and down the set.

There is usually a minimum of nine men and boys in the dance group and a non-performing leader who stands outside the dance. Dressed in shirts, trousers and ordinary shoes, the Matachinis wear special regalia which is treated with respect, including prayers, before they put it on: brightly coloured crown head-dresses decorated with paper flowers, shining discs and streamers. They carry gourd rattles in their right hands, which are rotated clockwise during the dance – stressing the beat and with a sound said to frighten devils and witches. The dance-leader sets the tempo, performs the first step and the rest join in. In their left hands they carry trident-shaped wands, bedecked with flowers and feathers, which are waved and used in a sweeping action during the dance as a form of blessing, and also used by the leader, together with a particular swaying of his body, to signal changes in the dance patterns.[14]

A further strand in the ceremonies is drawn from earlier Yaqui life and legend, from Yaqui spiritual belief, before the influence of Christianity and Spain. It encompasses the complementary domains of nature, wilderness, night-time, dreams, visions and enchantment. This is the realm of the Pascolas[15] and the Deer Dancer (*Maso*) who are on the side of good against evil, but they do not make formal vows in the manner of other participants. There should be three Pascolas present, who, with the Deer Dancer, make their first appearance at the ceremonies during Easter week on Easter Saturday. Unlike the group of Matachinis, they dance as individuals. Bare-footed, with bare torsos, they wear a light-coloured blanket wrapped around the waist, tied to the legs, and a leather belt hung with bells; traditional beads and a shell cross are worn around the neck. In their right hand they have a wooden rattle with metal jangles (a *sonasum*) which they beat against their left, while a long string of cocoon rattles is wound around their lower legs. These, with a sound similar to that of a rattlesnake, are said to represent the snake, and rustle vigorously during the shuffling, juddering heel beats and low jig-like steps of their dances – performed with a downward focus, torso bent towards the ground. With his hair in a top-knot tied with a red *pahko sewa wikia*

14   Flowers, known as *sewam*, which decorate the Matachinis' regalia and confetti – *sewam ilichi*, (little flowers), figure prominently at Easter and elsewhere in Yaqui ceremonial life. (In everyday life too, e.g. decoration on clothing or scarves). In Yaqui culture flowers not only symbolise blessings, holy acts and duties but are also thought of as weapons against evil. The concept is incorporated into Yaqui Catholic beliefs with the legend that Christ's blood falling to earth from the cross was transformed into flowers.

15   *Pascola* from *pahko* (fiesta) and *o'ola* (old man). Despite their pre-Christian origins, Pascolas and deer dancers are dedicated to Jesus. This is not seen as contradictory since Christianity was absorbed into Yaqui beliefs, and Jesus, with his love of animals, people and gift of healing, is thought to be a Yaqui. Also as Spicer states, to explain the historical origin of the Pascola 'there are a number of obviously post-Christian myths ... which suggest that his role has been much reinterpreted since the Jesuits began teaching in the 1600s' (1974, p.326).

(fiesta flower string), the Pascola wears a small black wooden human or goat-featured mask with a long white horse-hair beard and eyebrow tufts, which, when not over the face, is worn on the side or back of the head. Of the Pascola musicians (who wear everyday clothes and hats) two or three play the violin and harp and when the Pascola dances with the mask over his face, one man, the *tampaleo* plays a combination of flute with drum (music said to have been learnt from wild birds and animals).

The Deer Dancer (who always appears with the Pascolas) is accompanied by his own musicians: singers with songs which refer to the flower forest world, and playing wooden rasps – said to imitate the sound of antlers against bushes – and a gourd water-drum.[16]

Quite distinct and different in behaviour from the Pascolas (although he is always in their vicinity) the Deer Dancer does not generally interact with them, and appears remote from the audience.[17] Closely associated with the wild deer and its environment, his head-dress is a real small stuffed deer head, with glass eyes and antlers. This is worn, tied over a white cloth wound round his head and folded low just above his eyes. Like the Pascolas, the Deer Dancer is bare-foot, with bare torso, and wearing bead necklaces and a cross. Over rolled up trousers, he wears a *rebozo* (cloth) round the waist to below the knees; he also wears a deer-hoof rattle belt, cocoon leg rattles and holds a gourd rattle in each hand. While he waits to dance he stands impassively by, then when the time is right, he ties on his deer head-dress, adopts a position of alert readiness, and bending forward suddenly begins to shake his rattles rapidly towards the ground. He plays patterns of some complexity with his rattles (the accented rhythms are varied individually by the dancer, contrasting patterns in each hand).[18] Retaining a well centred forward-downward focus, he makes deer-like, sharp turns of his head, and as the tempo increases, he treads the ground and takes rapid steps with changes of direction – all performed within a limited radius, which generates intensity. After passages of both metric and non-metric movement, the dance comes to an abrupt end; the dancer immediately turns away and removes his head-dress.[19]

16   The water in the resonator of the drum, symbolic of the streams of the deer's habitat, is considered to be enchanted or sacred after the songs have been sung over it, and, as is customary after the ceremonies, I have seen the singer make a cross on the ground with it before sprinkling the remains over any spectators nearby.

17   Not only a source of food and skins in the life of early Yaquis, the deer was the most sacred, respected wild animal in their environment.

18   For example, with clockwise circling action in the right hand and up–down action in the left.

19   It is thought that there used to be dancers who represented other animals, and at one period there was a military society, the Coyotes, which took part in Easter ceremonies. I saw them during the Yaqui Easter ceremonies in Mexico and their Coyote dance was being revived when I was last present in Arizona, and I was very fortunate to catch sight of it. Three young dancers, with the distinctive narrow animal pelt hanging down their backs, travelled forward and backward in a line, galloping sideways a few steps and stopping, or sometimes crawling along. Occasionally one dropped a small stick and picked it up in his mouth. These were accompanied by a drummer who also sang into a hole in the side of his drum.

The number of participants in each group depends on who is available in the community and who is socially qualified to take part – on one occasion I counted 158 people in the circle at the end of the ceremonies – but there could be considerably fewer or more than this. As Kealiinohomoku pointed out to me, certain elements, such as the number of people taking part, are fluid, while others, such as the order of sequences and number of repetitions, are essential.

The participants are not assuming roles or performing as actors do on a stage. Except for the Chapayekas there is none of the characterisation, facial expression or use of rhythm and timing which we would expect to see in a stage performance. Also, the only relationship with an audience I noted was during interchange with the Pascolas in the ramada during the Saturday all-night fiesta; occasional, limited by-play with the Chapayekas at one or two moments, and during three informal collections from some spectators for monetary contributions. However, there is full expression of real feeling, particularly noticeable at certain times. Surely this, the people's feeling for the significance of the Easter ceremonies, forms the most important strand of all.

Sequences of action

Again, the events are not defined or clearly set out as they would be with a theatre audience in mind; timings are uncertain, or at best approximate, but the following extracts from the whole event, taken from the last days of Holy week, may provide a general impression of the timing and mode of sequential patterning during the ceremonies.[20]

Let us imagine that it is about 8.00 p.m. on a warm night in southern Arizona, the Wednesday of Easter week. Picture arriving at a plaza similar in outline orientation to the sketch-plan. The ten different Yaqui communities I visited each had the plaza with church, barracks (*guardia*), kitchen, ramada, and a wooden cross on the plaza. There was a path or *Loria Vo'o* (Glory Road) the width of the church entrance from the church down the plaza, marked with cottonwood twigs stuck in the ground and which visitors are forbidden to cross. But environments, terrain and size of the enactment area varied considerably (I have walked down one Yaqui plaza for 150 paces, another was smaller, but some have been considerably larger than this).

With just a few other bystanders, there is a relaxed, calm atmosphere. We are standing on dusty ground, the well-trodden sandy earth of the plaza, near the wide entrance to the open-fronted church.

Inside the church, the Holy figures on the altar have been wrapped in purple. Leafy branches which represent the forest, the Yaquis' own country and legends of Jesus' wanderings, decorate the building. A sacristan is lighting the 15 candles on

20   The extracts following are drawn from observations made at different Easter visits between 1990 and
      1994, with some reference for clarification to library sources.

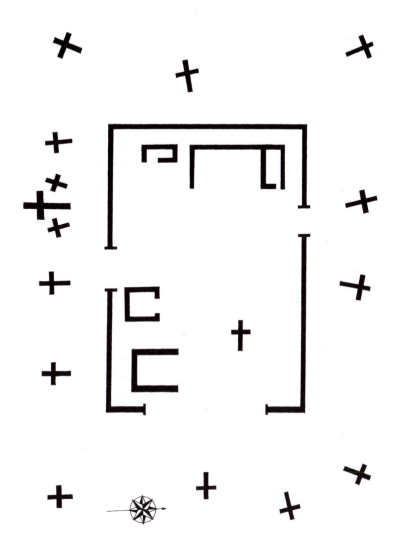

Figure 10.3 Schematic plan of a Yaqui plaza (not drawn to scale – the church may be much smaller and the plaza much bigger than this implies). Included are the east-facing open-fronted church, ramada at the opposite end of the plaza, other community buildings and approximate positions of the Stations of the Cross.
Source: Liane Payne

a triangular candelabrum in front of altar, while members of the church group are singing the office of *Tenebrae*. During this time, outside the church we are suddenly aware of a large group of black-clothed men and boys resolutely marching in unison towards us – our first sight of the Fariseos and Caballeros, accompanied by the masked, bulkily-clad figures of the Chapayekas, their belt-rattles clattering. They march to the east end of the plaza and halt.

Caballeros	Fariseos	Fariseos	Caballeros
Officer + flag	Officer + flag	Officer + flag	Captain
Corporal	Pilate	Pilate	Corporal
	Captain	Sergeant	
	Soldier + drum	Soldier + flute	

Chapayekas	Chapayekas
(Fariseos' soldiers)	(Fariseos' soldiers)
"	"
"	"
"	"
"	"
"	"
"	"
Corporals	Corporals
"	"

Imagine the ominous effect of this unexpected appearance in the dark plaza, a strong contrast to the calm, candle-lit interior of the church where the candles are being extinguished one by one. The Fariseos make a gradual, ritualised approach towards the church, advancing three steps as each flame is extinguished. Also, during this period of time, about ten successive pairs of Chapayckas set out to approach the church. Most of them seem to be using their swords like hobby horses and, without any vestige of theatrical exaggeration, gallop and trot along quite naturally, in a variety of ways – some mounts appearing to be more recalcitrant than others. Each pair has a Caballero-guide who indicates the path to the church, which the Chapayekas enter. They crawl up to the altar – as spies 'searching for Jesus', then report back to the officers outside. This all takes some time – at least 30 minutes or more.

When only two candles are left alight, two Chapayekas enter the church and crawl under the altar, howling like animals. This is said to express fear of the increasing dark, and perhaps a sense of evil in the darkness. Along with other visitors we leave the church, but we may be able to glimpse what is going on from the church entrance. The last lighted candle (which represents Jesus – 'Light of the World') is then carried into the sacristy and the church is in almost complete darkness while the *Miserere* is chanted.

Next, the Fariseos rapidly enter the church for a ritually enacted whipping ceremony. The officers kneel, the Chapayekas lie down and the Fariseo corporals lash them.[21] A recurrent time-pattern of three repetitions is apparent in the

21   There are various explanations of this procedure such as that the whipping is in memory of the lashes received by Jesus, it is a penance and is in mutual blessing and forgiveness.

ceremonial and sometimes actions are repeated three times into four directions, which I particularly noticed in the action of the flag-bearers. The pattern of three repetitions was evident when the Fariseos approached the church, and again here as the Fariseo corporals make the sign of the cross on a Chapayekas' back three times (symbolic of the Trinity), then whip it three times. The procedure is repeated with the officers being whipped, and the whole whipping sequence is repeated three times. The Chapayekas once more howl like animals. The whipping ritual is taken up in socially determined pairs by most of the congregation to request *hiokoe* (forgiveness and blessing) for which thanks are given. This whole procedure takes a considerable time. There is no sense of urgency or doing things 'to time' during the ceremonies.

The church service continues while the Chapayekas may improvise a few dance steps and deride the church people, but seem to react in fear when they hear Holy names; and then the service ends. The night air is cold now. The church group prepares to sleep in the church, while the Fariseos and Caballeros retire to the barracks or round the fire outside. We leave the plaza.

Thursday, early afternoon. Various ceremonies have taken place in our absence, and a wooden clapper has replaced the church bell which remains silent until the *Gloria* on Saturday, when dramatically it rings again. The plaza seems deserted. This is one of the times when obvious watching or being anywhere near the activity is positively discouraged. In the distance we may notice some Chapayekas carrying out a sequence in which they pursue one of their number who represents Jesus, portrayed as an old man – *El Viejito* – who stumbles about and appears a pathetic figure. In what seems a preview of Christ's sufferings on the Way of the Cross, captured by a small group of other Chapayekas he journeys round the Stations on a rope. He is teased – and although at each Station he lightly whips his tormentors he becomes more and more exhausted until eventually the Chapayekas carry him to the plaza cross. From there he is led by the Chapayekas to approach visitors for money, contributions towards the cost of the ceremonies.

Later in the day, towards the east end of the plaza, the Chapayekas make a bower from cottonwood branches to represent the Garden of Gethsemane, and the figure of the Nazarene[22] is taken in procession from the church to the Garden by members of the church group. It is noticeable that the more clustered formation of the church group's processions differs markedly from straight-lined spatial rhythms of the Fariseos.

During the evening, the church group processes to the Garden with lit candles, and mounts a vigil. I have always experienced this, and what follows, as one of the most solemn, moving and profound sections of the ceremonies. After about an hour, the Fariseos and Caballeros march to the church. Two Chapayekas go to

---

22   The Nazarene figure carried in the Easter processions is a standing figure of Christ wearing a red robe and carrying a cross.

look for Jesus and return to the Fariseo officers with the news that He has gone. This causes the captain to command the capture of Jesus. The Fariseos and Caballeros then march away from the church to the east end of the plaza where the captain orders three Chapayekas in turn to act as a spy. Using his sword like a hobby-horse, each Chapayeka goes round the Garden, and reports back that Jesus is there. The Fariseos and Caballeros (with the Chapayekas) march towards, file back and march again towards the Garden (getting ominously closer each time).

When the last of the three Chapayekas returns with a twig as proof that Jesus is there, the Captain orders the troops to advance and seize Jesus, and all march again in the direction of the Garden. Tension builds; members of the church group are chanting prayers. The Fariseo who is the head of the Pilates approaches the Garden and strikes the ground three times. He speaks with the sacristan who is inside. As bystanders, we cannot hear the exchange (which is true of all the dialogue in the ceremonial; not only is it in the Yaqui language but not intended for spectators' ears). It has been reported that the speeches usually proceed in a manner similar to the following: The Sacristan: '*A quien buscais?*' (Whom do ye seek?). The Pilate: '*A Jesu Nazareno*' (Jesus of Nazareth). The Sacristan: '*Yo soy*' (I am He). The Pilate retreats. The Fariseos and Caballeros march closer to the Garden. This approach, dialogue and marching is repeated three times. The third time the Pilate asks the question, the sacristan replies '*Os dicho que yo soy. Si me buscais a mi, dejad ir a estos, para se cumplan*' (I have told you that I am He. If ye seek me, let them go, so that it will be fulfilled.) (Painter 1986, p.445).[23] The Fariseos and Caballeros in two lines march in opposite directions to surround the Garden – an implacable, intimidating, encircling force. The Chapayekas lie down and howl (once more representing wild animals) then the tempo accelerates as they leap up, pull down the branches and destroy the Garden. The captain of the Caballeros ropes the Nazarene and four Chapayekas carry the figure to the church. The church group, singing in mourning, follow. The Chapayekas place the figure of the Nazarene in front of the altar, and a Chapayeka stands on guard in the church.

A procession takes place round the Stations of the Cross, which symbolises Mary searching for Jesus. The Maestros lead a closing service with the church group, mocked by the Chapayeka guard (who also appears nervous – for instance, he reacts fearfully when he hears Holy names). Chapayekas take it in turns to be on guard in the church throughout the night (they act with bravado but also continue to behave as if they are afraid). The Arizona nights are chilly. As at other times, hot coals are brought from the large log fire outside to warm the church. Two by two, the Caballeros and Fariseos say their rosaries in front of the Nazarene through the night.

---

23   This exchange is reminiscent of the exchanges in early European liturgical drama which developed from the *Quem quaeritis* trope (a verse in the church Mass).

Good Friday: perhaps we are returning to the plaza around noon. Various activities will have taken place in our absence – a curtain has been hung across the front of the church, and now unseen by us, the figures of the Marys and other figures on the altar have been covered with black cloth.

Women of the community arrive in dark clothing. The general mood appears sombre; Fariseos in black shirts, the Pilates in black capes. The long processional march outside the plaza around the Stations of the Cross to Calvary now takes place, with the community dividing into two groups after prayers together at the First Station. In brief, the women who carry the figures of the three Marys, accompanied by two lines of the Kohtumbre proceed in an anti-clockwise direction, the Chapayekas with the figure of the Nazarene and other men with the Way Cross, clockwise.[24] The Chapayekas indulge in mockery of the Maestros and much by-play en route.

When the two groups meet eventually at the Eleventh Station – Calvary – where three crosses have been erected, the Way Cross is put down on the ground, showered with confetti (*sewam ilichi* see note 14) and a ritual is enacted which symbolises the crucifixion. There is more by-play from the Chapayekas who joke and pretend to hammer nails into the Way Cross (reminiscent of soldiers in medieval European Passion plays). The Way Cross is lifted and carried in procession round the final three Stations and to the church for the closing services. A sacristan places the Way Cross in front of the altar and binds the figure of the Nazarene to it, as the crucified Christ.

Various activities follow through the next hour or more, during which the bier for Christ is collected from nearby in the local community, where it has been decorated. Traditionally made of an arched bamboo framework covered in gauze, it is trimmed with lace, ribbons, artificial flowers and a paper dove. The Fariseos and Caballeros (in their role of *Kohtumbre*) march to fetch the bier. The church group meets the Fariseos and Caballeros at the First Station of the Cross, and all proceed to the church where the bier is placed on a table. Further processions and other ceremonies take place later in the afternoon, the Fariseos' faces now forebodingly covered with black scarves. The church group processes in the following order, but in a less regimented manner than the Fariseos:

The Way Cross with the men accompanying it
Boy angels with godmothers
Bier of Christ carried by four men
Girl flag-bearers
Girl angels with godmothers
The figures of three Marys carried by the women

24   The Way Cross, about 6 feet high, carried in the Easter processions, is kept behind the altar in the church at other times.

Maestro and singers
Other people of the community

Towards evening the church is packed for the full group veneration. This is another of the many passages of the ceremonies which for me is imbued with the powerful, heartfelt feeling of the community. In a solemn silence men place the figure of Christ (which has been taken from the Way Cross) at the entrance to the church, the women scatter confetti over it, and the girl flag-bearers ritually wave their flags over the figure (in four directions), then kneel. All come forward to venerate the figure of Christ while the Maestros chant. Offerings are made of flowers, candles and money. The mass of lit candles clustered on the ground, fills the church with warm, flickering light. Reverently, four men lift the figure into the bier and cover it. The bier is now taken in procession around the Way of the Cross and returned to the church (which symbolises taking Jesus to the tomb). The Chapayekas take turns to guard the bier while the Maestros and church singers keep vigil. Further veneration from members of the community takes place during this time, and later in the evening a procession takes place round the Stations of the Cross, which represents Mary looking for Jesus.

Around midnight, women remove the black cloth from the three Marys and the mauve flags are replaced with red. A sacristan takes the black cloth from a figure of the Infant Jesus which has been on the altar and which becomes the focus of the ceremonies from this time. There are now further sequences of action, including a procession with the figure of the infant Jesus round the Stations of the Cross, said to symbolise the Resurrection and Jesus born again as a baby. Meanwhile a sacristan in the undemonstrative, practical way of all the action, secretly takes the figure of Christ from the bier and substitutes a small toy (often one of the Chapayekas' playthings). This is a seemingly small happening, done so quietly we may easily miss it, but in fact it is the trigger for the massive climax tomorrow when the Fariseos have discovered the frame of Christ is no longer in the bier, in their possession.[25]

At some time after midnight, there is another distinct change of pace and resulting mood. The Fariseos march again, with the bier, in quick time round the Stations of the Cross with a Chapayeka mock Mexican-style band – the Chapayekas appear self-satisfied and braggartly. The bier is placed on a table at the front of the church, with a Chapayeka on guard. The Chapayekas (who behave more confidently and aggressively as the week progresses) now have a private party, a mock fiesta, with much clowning: for instance, they pretend their daggers are bottles and drink from them, then act as if inebriated. They try to dance in different styles and generally fool about with spontaneous and imaginative by-play.

---

25   In theatre terms, this is a key turning point in the action, and could be seen as most 'dramatic' – here performed in untheatrical manner and context.

Easter Saturday dawns. Activities now include tidying the church, sweeping and dampening down the dusty surface of the plaza and marking the pathway from the church to the east end of the plaza with fresh cottonwood twigs. A line of ash is made across the main church path about 50 feet from the church, to designate holy ground: this is the day 'when the church and the holy ground in front of it are identified with heaven itself' (Painter 1986, p.477). A pole for Judas' pyre is put in place at the far east end of the plaza. During the morning, a lively extended sequence takes place when, marching in procession and playing their own version of Mexican tunes (a further rhythmic element), the Chapayekas carry a straw figure of Judas which they subsequently fasten to the pyre. They dance, embrace and honour him as their chief. Members of the community also bring small items to burn on the pyre.[26] About this time, the Pascolas appear at the plaza and the Ramada is prepared for events which follow later.

After a further church ceremony (blessing the New Fire) preparations for the *Gloria* are under way as the Pascolas prepare a special large sheet onto which people put flowers and confetti – which is used later as ammunition to 'kill' the Fariseos. The Deer Dancer stands and waits nearby, his head-dress at his side. In the church, women, altar girls and child-angels in fresh, white dresses and flower crowns assemble by the altar preparing to defend it. Meanwhile, outside, the Matachinis have arrived. Entering the church to pray they dedicate themselves at the altar and return to the plaza where their musicians are seated and starting to play a little. The excitement of anticipation gradually begins to gather as spectators arrive in their hundreds, it seems, for this special day, and line the route from the church all the way down the plaza.

At about midday, the Fariseos assemble at the barracks. They are still clothed in black and with the black scarves over their faces, a black cloth covering the drum. By now they have discovered that the figure of Jesus is missing and is with the church people, so they prepare for attack and further pursuit of Jesus. To a sharp beat from the accompanying Chapayekas' weapons they march in strict unison away from the church down the plaza then back towards the ash-line several times, and again back to the end of the plaza. The Caballeros march with the Fariseos at first, then leave them and march to stand inside the ash-line, which signifies their change to neutrality and separation from the Fariseos. Godmothers run out to tie scarves round Chapayekas' arms.[27]

26 One explanation is that these items (such as small toys) may be contributed in the name of sick children – as if to have their illness burnt away. (There is also a connection with Judas as a saint, which I have yet to understand.)

27 I had thought of the scarves here as 'flowers' and as symbols of protection until I found an authority stating they are mainly for ready identification of godsons in the later rush (Painter 1986, p.477). Action with a practical purpose, a salutary example.

Surrounded by the inexplicable, unknowable, it is easy to jump to the wrong conclusions. In addition, in a personal communication, Kealiinohomoku contributed 'It is my experience that many metaphysical reasons also have practical reasons as well'. The action with the scarves again seems 'dramatic' but is totally without theatrical intention.

The head Maestro sends a written message to the chief Fariseo warning him to surrender: he tears it up and gives a piece to each Chapayeka. They pretend to read with much irrelevant by-play and then stamp the papers scornfully into the ground. The Fariseos again march determinedly towards the ash-line and back several times. Chapayekas sharpen and flourish their swords, threatening the defenders of the church; the Pascolas call to the Chapayekas to surrender and show them the array of flowers (their 'weapons'). Tense anticipation now, with on-going threats from the Pascolas, as two further warnings are sent; each time to be met with scorn, Chapayekas' bravado and repeated, defiant marching back and forth several times to the ash-line.

When the Maestro begins to recite the Litany, the Fariseos' marching continues but the step-rhythm alters to a pattern with step and stamps, (which I remember as something like R RR R L LL L). Then, as the church group's *Kyrie* begins, the marching rhythm changes again – back to the usual RL pattern but with a heel scuff inserted before each step, and an increase in tempo. Tension gathers and next, as the Maestro begins the *Gloria,* there follows the most exciting, stirring sequence of group rhythm I have ever witnessed – a torrent of colour, sound and movement, initiated by the Fariseos' final attack.

There is sudden action from everywhere as many rhythms occur simultaneously: with voices from the church raised loud in the *Gloria,* sounds of the church bell fill the air, Pascolas throw flowers at the Fariseos as they dash past to the ash-line, the Deer, Pascolas and Matachinis dance (with their three separate groups of musicians each playing or singing their different music full out), the church curtain is swished open and the wide-eyed child angels – urged by their godmothers and ranged with the church women at the front of the church – hit out with their switches at the fast-approaching headlong rush of Fariseos; behind the angels (many of whom look increasingly alarmed) the flag girls ritually wave their flags, the church women throw flowers, the Caballeros kneel and cross themselves; spectators throw confetti and flowers – many spontaneously, irrepressibly calling out against the forces of evil represented by the Fariseos as they pass.

Then, repulsed by the flowers, confetti, energy and multiplicity of rhythms, the Fariseos stop suddenly, turn back at the ash-line and quickly withdraw to the other end of the plaza where they and the Chapayekas hastily begin to take off accoutrements – godparents hurry to collect them before the lines re-form and the marching begins once more.

As the church group sings the *Gloria* again, with gathering intensity the entire sequence of action is repeated, each group of musicians with different specific tunes or songs. Again the Fariseos march. Finally, the *Gloria* is sung for a third time, and with even more noise, different tunes, songs, and energetic action, the whole sequence is repeated. There is uproar as the Fariseos begin to rush right up to the church entrance; the enemy now at terrifyingly close range, the little angels (some really frightened now, one or two sobbing) bravely thrash out still more vehemently with their switches (backed up fiercely by their godmothers); I'm aware of a heightened tension all around me as a great cry goes up – the Fariseos are successfully repulsed – they tear away to their waiting godparents at the end of the plaza.

Rapid action now: as if the Chapayekas realise Judas has betrayed them, they rush to the pyre, and throw onto it their swords, daggers and masks.[28] The pyre is lit – fireworks hidden in the bonfire explode and flames leap high. Good has triumphed over evil: the power of God, Jesus and the Virgin has saved us once more. The Fariseos have been defeated and 'killed' by the dancing of the Matachins and the Deer, by the thrown flowers (that is, by everything which they represent) and by spiritual powers. Now, again simultaneously: godparents throw a blanket or coat over the Chapayekas in their charge to hide and protect them, and rush them up to the church altar for re-dedication and blessing (the evil of the role has been shed as the accoutrements were shed). The Caballeros too dash to the altar, kneel, cross themselves and then stand outside the church. Godparents take the angels to the altar for prayers. The pyre continues to burn, carefully tended, until nothing but a rough scatter of ash remains. There is a sense of relief from anxiety now, and the Pascolas, Deer Dancer and Matachinis dance in celebration in front of the church. Finally, with the figure of the Infant Jesus, there is a procession of all participants to the fiesta ramada.

> The Yaqui believe that the blood and tears of Christ which fell to ground grew flowers of eternal life. Therefore, the flower is stronger than the sword. The confetti and flowers will eventually conquer evil spirits. (from a Yeomem Tekia Foundation Easter leaflet)

Activities continue through the rest of the day. Around sunset, and to my great surprise the first time I saw it, the Matachinis perform a maypole dance in front of the church, winding over and under ribbons (the maypole surmounted by a crown and dove in honour of the Virgin). (Surprising to me, since it, at least from a distance, matches the dance I know from England.) Then they dance their other usual dance figures all night. In some places I have witnessed the Matachinis actually dancing in the church at this time, to honour the Virgin Mary, and with no other spectators present. Members of the church group, Fariseos and Caballeros, spend the night at the ramada where the Pascolas go on performing in secular manner until day break, with dance, songs, jokes, stories and ribaldry, interspersed with more serious, intense dances from the Deer.

---

28   That is, except for the two masks which are retained for the burial at ta Chapayeka's funeral, should this occur in the year following.

Easter Sunday activities usually include, near dawn, the Matachinis' maypole unwinding dance, and perhaps we may see a sequence of Pascolas pretending to hunt the Deer. Later, the head Pascola gives a sermon in the ramada, and there is a collection for funds from bystanders.

The news of the Resurrection is brought to the plaza by two girl flag-bearers in flower crowns – *Alleluia* and the final surrender of the Fariseos is fully recognised. As Spicer has pointed out: 'the major rhythm of the Yaqui ceremonial year is marked by the substitution of one kind of dance for another kind' (1974, p.321), and from this time the Matachinis with their dancing rhythms are officially in charge of ceremonies until next Lent, when the Fariseos' marching patterns take over once again.

As we near the end of our shared Yaqui Easter, the Matachinis followed by the Pascolas and Deer Dancer lead a procession to the church, and continue round the plaza; the Holy figures are returned to the altar. The Fariseos are taken into the church by their godparents for a final blessing and re-dedication.

To conclude, all the participants move into a large circle in the plaza (traditionally known as the 'Farewell' or 'Thank You' circle). The Maestros and Matachin leader stand in the centre. The head Maestro delivers a sermon (which I have been told includes reference to the meaning of the Easter ceremonial, the blessing (flower) received, completion of vows, new vows, report of money collected). The final ritual: the *Kohtumbre* officials (the Fariseos and Caballeros) go round the circle three times in traditional manner, touching hands and saying farewell. There are then general farewells as people disperse and leave the plaza.

> Even though we are a poor nation, we still talk for the whole earth through our songs, prayers and dances ... We constantly ask for world-wide peace. Yes, this is what we do here in our poor villages. (Jean Leon Naehto, Potam Village, 1989)

Epilogue

A multiplicity of rhythm and timing patterns, both seen and unseen, contribute to an experience of Yaqui Easter ceremonies, together with a release from the pressure or need for precisely measured timing. A sense of performance in real time (unlike theatre time) with variations in tempo and intensity, duration of pauses and periods of waiting for the more noticeable events to occur, combine with details of the rhythms of the different sequences and dances, variations in processions and marching patterns, and contrasts of timing in movement behaviour. Presence at the event is to witness a many-layered mix of rhythms and timing patterns. These, derived from a range of sources (through traditional knowledge and the distinctive Yaqui system of cueing and signalling), contribute to meaningful, highly expressive action. It is an extensive, intensive enactment which has so far survived remarkably through history.

There is a wealth of traditional knowledge embedded in the Easter ceremonies, and I have only been able to offer a glimpse of this. There are various, sometimes conflicting, explanations of the events. Much will never be understood by non-Yaquis. Even many Yaquis themselves are not able to explain everything, or do not wish to do so. They are known to smile quietly when they see visitors checking the explanatory leaflets which are sometimes available, in efforts to sort out meaning, order and timing of events. Perhaps it is preferable simply to allow the events themselves to speak.

This series of summarised, fragmentary extracts described by one observer from work in progress, cannot do full justice to the actual experience, to the privilege of being present at the Yaqui Easter. It is difficult to convey the transformative power of the events, the sense of a dedication which is truly lived through the period of Easter, and beyond.

Dominant memories of my experience of the ceremonies are many: an ever-present sense of ignorance, of having entered a new world peopled by a blur of mysterious happenings, a sense of wonder, and certainly an abiding respect for the Yaqui. This is an extract from a Yaqui deer song:

> *Sewa yotume sewa yotume*
> *sewa yo machi hekamake sika*
> *Machi hekamake hekawapo chasime*
> *yo yo machi hekamake sikaaa*

> (Growing flower, growing flower,
> flower with the enchanted dawn wind, went.
> With the dawn wind's air, you are flying,
> with the enchanted, enchanted dawn wind you went)
> (Evers and Molina 1987, p.106)

11

Papua New Guinea
Rhythm and Timing in Traditional Maring Life

With this account, which is an approach to the study of rhythm and timing from ethnography and film, we are looking at an example from one of the last regions of the world to be explored. Ethnographers who were writing at the period of the film which I viewed (early 1960s) tell us that the Maring were approximately 7000 people, organised into more than 20 named territorial and political groups, living in scattered hamlets in the densely forested Bismarck mountains (Madang District) of Papua New Guinea. The term 'Maring' is recognised as the name by which they are known to outsiders but it is not used by the people themselves. They feel 'no corporate identity beyond speaking the same language (*menga*) and sharing certain other cultural traits – traits similar to those found in the broader Highlands area' (Healey 1990, p.28).

Daily activities of the people were those which arose from social, domestic and ritual obligations. These included gardening, pig-rearing, hunting and trapping animals, and gathering plants for food and other purposes in the forest. The gardens, planted in forest clearings, provided the staple crops of taro, yam, sweet potato, manioc and bananas. (For further details *see* Rappaport 1968.)

Contact with non-indigenous people even in the 1960s was extremely limited. As film footage of an earlier time vividly records, the first sight of white men in the 1930s confused and frightened the New Guinea Highlanders (Connolly and Anderson *First Contact* (1987). Visitors to the remoter parts were still rare in the 1960s when Rappaport and Jablonko first went there.[1]

---

[1] Since that time there has been much change in the area (which it is beyond my scope to describe fully). In order to avoid giving a false impression I have therefore adopted a generalised past tense except for the film description. Some aspects of traditional Maring life, beliefs and customs do remain, but there are no longer the large-scale ceremonies of the kind referred to in this chapter. It is probable that the last of these occurred in the 1980s, to be replaced by the *pati* (party) where people gather together for dancing and other activities. Other events are hosted by the mission at Christmas, and by the government e.g. to celebrate new buildings or roads. 'Fundamentalist missions have had wide influence in suppressing pig festivals ... branding them as satanic and also by persuading the people

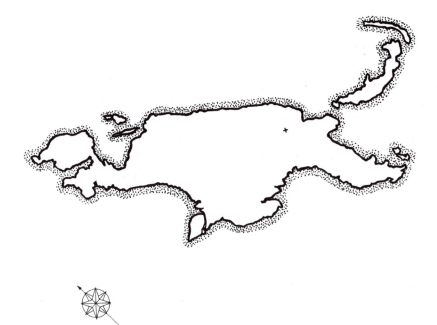

+ = *approximate location of the Tsembaga Maring*

Figure 11.1 Papua New Guinea.
Source: Liane Payne

Our focus is a traditional Maring ritual event – the *konj kaiko* (pig festival), as celebrated by the Tsembaga group or 'clan-cluster'.[2] Each clan-cluster had its own 10- to 20-year ritual cycle. The *konj kaiko* was the final part of the culminating year-long ritual period (known as *kaiko*) during which friendly groups were

to keep fewer pigs so that they do not have the capacity to hold festivals' (Healey 1990, pp.253, 260). Modern dress is preferred by young Maring men, and increasingly worn by the younger women. I understand that on the ceremonial occasions remaining, they still decorate themselves traditionally along with the older men.

2   'Clan-cluster' is a term which Rappaport and Vayda adopted from Ryan (1959) to describe two or more neighbouring clans, approximately 130 to 200 persons, living in clearly defined territories of approximately 3 to 10 square miles in area.

entertained; it was the largest Maring gathering – Rappaport estimated that 1000 were present at the *konj kaiko* he describes in *Pigs for the Ancestors* (1968).[3] The event included dancing, ceremonial presentation of salted pork, feasting, socialising and trading. It took place principally during two days although final preparations started before this, and relatives began to arrive from several days beforehand.

The *kaiko* was of fundamental importance in Maring life. It influenced or facilitated growth and dispersal of the population, food accumulation and sharing, as well as trade among groups. Moreover, as Healey writes in a recent study 'The number of allies present as helpers could, in the past, serve as an indication of military strength' (1990, p.74). According to Rappaport, the *kaiko* regulated the frequency of inter-group fighting and mitigated its severity. Groups who were prepared to support each other in fights were established through it: 'to join a group in dancing is the symbolic expression of willingness to join them in fighting' (1968, p.196). There is something of a paradox here, since those present may also have been potential enemies. Mounting the *kaiko* was a demanding, expensive and time-consuming affair. The ability to do so indicated the viability of the local population as a working unit, as well as its effectiveness in the exchange network vital to Maring life.[4]

This chapter demonstrates how through study of ethnography and film it was possible to gain some understanding of ways in which time elements functioned in the life of a vigorously ritual-based society during the period when they were visited by the expeditionary team.

The preferred procedure for the study of events is of course to undertake fieldwork if circumstances permit. Participating in life with the people concerned is the ideal. No written account or film can replace the experience of being present at a live event. However, in the case of remote locations it may not be realistic or helpful to advocate foreign trips. Even if finance is available, it takes a considerable amount of time to establish the relationship of trust needed for satisfactory fieldwork. Local or intermediary contacts are needed and not always easy to get. Also, however sensitive we may strive to be, the outsider's presence is not always welcome. It inevitably affects the people and not always to their advantage. Thus I suggest we should take full advantage of both written and film ethnographies for study purposes.

3   Although each clan-cluster celebrated a *kaiko* on average perhaps once every 12 to 15 years, it was possible for an individual Maring to participate in *kaiko* events somewhere every year, due to cross-cutting clan-cluster relationships (see Jablonko 1968, p.44).
4   The term '*kaiko*' was used in more than one context. For instance, it described both the year-long festival which ended the 10- to 20-year-long ritual cycle, and the occasions on which friendly groups were entertained, as well as the dancing which took place on these occasions.

However, with film we must take note of any limitations of the medium. Ethnographic film, like any written ethnography, has the status of a historical document which cannot provide an accurate picture of life as it is now. We are witnessing an event from the film-maker and editor's perspective. In relation to movement or dance study, footage with adequate views of moving figures and what we would like to see may be limited. Lomax wrote of his team's frustrations during their massive study of ethnographic films (see p.104). In relation to rhythm and timing, for example:

> One of our most common experiences in screening filmed footage is to see movements cut off in mid-phrase or interactions sliced in two as they are unfolding. The length and ... spatial dimensions of movement phrases and segments of interaction vary profoundly among cultures... The placement of accents, whether they come at the beginning or the end of actions, whether they produce an effect of follow-through or sustained energy, gives human behaviour all sorts of different rhythms. (1971, p.29)

But with adequate footage, the opportunity for repeated viewing is an advantage for observation practice, and in order to focus on different aspects of rhythm or use of time elements in detail.

A chance remark, a magazine article or TV documentary may provide the spark which stimulates interest in a particular ceremony or ritual. The ensuing study process can be like a treasure hunt – as it was in this instance. After initial interest has been roused by whatever means, ethnographic studies are a source of further information; travel books may provide useful ancillary material while cultural departments of embassies can sometimes offer helpful advice and further references.

Sometimes the professional jargon and style of theoretical anthropological writing can be somewhat daunting, and may seem too far removed from actual events to be useful for a study of rhythm and timing 'on the ground'. However in this case I had access to two fine ethnographies about the Maring which provided insights, stimulating description, and considerable background information: Rappaport's *Pigs for the Ancestors* (1968), and Jablonko's doctoral dissertation 'Dance and daily activities among the Maring people of New Guinea', (1968). The latter was a real find since the focus was on Maring movement.[5]

Jablonko's emphasis on movement as signature behaviour and interest in synchrony coincided with my own. However, she had not commented extensively

---

5   These ethnographers took part in anthropological expeditionary team work (led by Andrew Vayda, from Columbia University, New York) during 1962 to 1964. The basic assumption of Jablonko's study was derived from the Lomax and Bartenieff choreometric studies (see p.104). Her aim was to examine the hypothesis that Maring dance was a formalised and repetitious use of movement patterns that were frequent and important in their everyday life.

on a full range of rhythm and timing elements. I was able to study extensive footage with this topic in mind, footage which recorded daily activities and rituals among the Maring clans, shot by Marek Jablonko (62,000 feet of research film and an edited film *Maring in Motion*). I was immediately captivated by the energy and vitality in scenes of dancing and ritual action, and intrigued by the rhythm and timing palette on display in traditional Maring life. The head-dresses, resplendent with plumes from forest birds, attracted attention straight away with their flamboyant colours and varied rhythms.[6] Purposeful engagement in the dance was evident. The men's apparent enjoyment of the synchronised, regularly repetitive bouncing steps in small clustered groups contrasted with an exhilarating free-time, full-tilt rush when visiting groups descended on the dance ground, and at the climax of the dancing. The proceedings were enlivened by unexpected explosions from burning bamboo canes (which I later learnt had ritual significance).

The performance time-frame and timing of the ritual cycle[7]

Traditional Maring life and ritual seems complex to an outsider. It involves relationships with various groups of people and with different sets of spirits, as well as use of specific animals and plants, fire, stone objects, particular songs, food, spells and taboos; all with accompanying action and ritual procedures. Much remains mysterious. A brief introduction with reference to a few features is all that can be provided here.

As illustrated in other examples included in Chapter 3, traditional Maring events did not follow what native west Europeans might think of as a regular calendar dating system. Traditionally, towards the end of one of the long ritual cycles, sporadic fighting led to a decisive rout or a truce. If there was a truce, *rumbim* (a small tree – *Cordyline frulicosa*) was ritually planted as a boundary marker. This signified that the particular host group should not initiate axe fights or beat drums (which were used to incite warfare), and that preparations for the *konj kaiko*, the culmination of the ritual cycle, were to be undertaken. This principally involved nurturing pigs, growing crops and performing associated rituals. Also, members of the host group transferred their homesteads near to the ritual dance ground for the *kaiko* year.

There appeared to be nothing more decisive than a general consensus as to when the *kaiko* should take place. Days were appointed, but temporal arrangements remained uncertain. The feather plumes and other decorations

---

6   Other western highlanders such as the Melpa have even more elaborate decorations – more skins and plumes.

7   For background information I have drawn principally from Rappaport (1968), Jablonko (1968), Strathern andStrathern (1971), O'Hanlon (1983, 1989, 1993) and Healey (1990) and from personal communication with Strathern, Jablonko and O'Hanlon.

worn for the event had to be gathered together and new ones acquired through hunting or trading. Particular crops had to be grown and sufficient pigs had to be reared and accumulated. Clearly time duration was crucial here. It was associated with Tsembagas' judgment of 'good' or 'bad' places – in a 'good' place pigs were accumulated more quickly (see Rappaport 1968, p.155). Anthropologist Michael O'Hanlon points out that the shifts of political rivalry and jockeying for position which occurred at this time, may have given an impression of indecision to an outsider, but the process was not intrinsically vague (1989).[8]

Other groups influenced when the *konj kaiko* took place, or frequently caused delays. For example, Rappaport states that during his visit the Tsembaga could have staged a *konj kaiko* several weeks earlier, but had to wait until their most important allies and closest neighbours had conducted the ritual which allowed them to eat the pork which was to be presented to them (1968, p.201). During the year, it was customary for Tsembaga youths to visit neighbouring settlements to announce a forthcoming *kaiko*, and later to check on any need for postponement if visiting groups were delayed. The process of making arrangements and travelling to meet, dance, share ritual and feasting and then to depart in different directions, was the basis of the overall macro-structure of this impressive event.

Preparation for the *konj kaiko*

The considerable period of preparation for the *konj kaiko* was an essential component in the rhythm and timing. Nurture of pigs, crop-growing, collection and preparation of body decorations took some time. New paths had to be cut, special arches, ritual dance ground fence and visitors' shelters constructed. Various rituals were enacted which included meetings with allies and processions to establish territorial boundaries to protect the men's *min* ('life-stuff' or spirit), and to prevent enemies' spirits from entering the enclosure – defined by ritually planted stakes. During the year, groups of allies visited the host group to dance through an afternoon and night, with trade the following morning. The Tsembaga entertained 13 such groups on 15 occasions during a year observed by Rappaport. Sometimes two or more groups were entertained at the same time and three groups attended more than once.

The basis of traditional Maring life was belief about their ancestor spirit-world (believed to be on the mountain tops). The *konj kaiko* was an occasion for fulfilling obligations to the spirits as well as to the living, and pigs were sacrificed to the

8   I have been concerned about lack of direct contact with the Maring throughout this study. Independent feedback was sought at an early stage, and again more recently, from anthropologist Michael O'Hanlon, who is well known for his studies of another Papua New Guinea Highlands group, the Wahgi. This group has a way of life and ceremonials which share characteristics with the Maring (O'Hanlon 1983, 1989, 1993). Hence the references to his comments in the course of this chapter.

Figure 11.2 A group of Maring men bedecked for dancing. The young man in the centre who is playing his drum, wears the decorated mamp gunc *hairstyle.*
Source: Roy Rappaport

spirits during the many other ritual preparations. According to the Tsembaga, the purpose of communicating with the ancestors at this time was to induce them to look benignly upon the dance ground. This was so that all might dance strongly and the drums sound 'rich'. It was also in the hope that the *min* (as above) of the local girls be kept inside the fence during the *kaiko*: 'The men often express the fear that some of the unmarried girls might elope with visitors whose strong dancing and finery have captured their fancies' (Rappaport 1968, p.174). Apparently a number of men maintained that their wives were first attracted to them because of the admirable figures they cut in the dance.

The last preparations for the *konj kaiko* continued for two or three days during which visitors who were to be honoured with ritual presentation of pork arrived to assist. The tempo of preparations built up through this period. Apart from the slaughter of pigs (a total of 96 were killed for the event filmed), ovens had to be built, and firewood, ferns, and greens (to cook) were gathered. Finally, on the day when all the visitors were expected, the dance ground was ritually prepared.

The decorations of men and some young unmarried girls took several hours to complete. The young men's head-dresses were particularly flamboyant. These were of vertical black, white, green or yellow feathers set around red feather crowns mounted on a basket base. The bird of paradise plumes and the eagle and parrot feathers commonly used in a head-dress were among the most valuable Maring items, and usually worn only at the *kaiko*.[9] Head decorations of some of the young men also included *mamp gunc* – a crown-like decorated hairstyle (constructed on 6-in.-high frames) – ritually created by 'fight-magic' men, dedicated to the spirits and associated with strength and empowerment. Also shells were worn by men through the pierced nose bone (septum). Other decorations included bead and shell necklaces, and for the men, large bunches of several kinds of leaves which hung from their waists at the back, and loin-cloths trimmed with glossy fur.[10]

During repeated viewing of the film material I tried to identify the order of events and the nature and purpose of activities, as sketched in the account following. After initial general impressions of the use of rhythm and timing elements I later referred to the categories described and listed in Chapters 7 and 8 in order to consider the rhythm, timing and dance elements in more detail, and in relation to traditional Maring life.

The sequence of events and use of rhythm and timing in Maring dance as viewed in the film material[11]

At the dance ground, morning. This ritual ground is a sloping area of approximately 150-200 feet. A 15-ft-high fence (*pave*) made of saplings and

9   The head was considered to be the seat of the red spirits, *Rauamugi*, who possessed the warrior and enabled him to fight.

10   Highlands' groups continue to use traditional decoration at certain times, with imported items and material which have long been incorporated in decorations and used as gifts. For instance, a photograph in O'Hanlon (1993, plate 16) shows a young Wahgi girl whose decorations for the presentation of her bridewealth include traditional shell necklaces, fur, pelt, luxuriant feather head-dress (with a tinsel ball among the fronds), Papua New Guinea paper currency tucked into her arm bands and ring-pulls from beer cans as earrings. Healey refers to the Kundagai Maring preference for the bright colours and range of store-bought paints (1990, p.199). Bridewealth presentations of valuables in the area now include 'money trees' – tall bamboo poles to which paper money is attached. Writing in 1990 Healey states that most younger men are familiar with the use of money as currency too, but that many older people are not (1990, p.201).

11   In order to retain something of the film's immediacy, I adopt the present tense for this part of the chapter. As anthropologist Kirsten Hastrup has pointed out, the 'ethnographic present' is frequently adopted in fieldwork reports. Although criticised by some, it 'reflects the reality of fieldwork' and 'the instance of the discourse' (1995, pp.20–21).

Figure 11.3 A group of visitors charge onto the Maring Tsembaga dance ground.
Source: Roy Rappaport

foliage encloses three sides of the upper part of the ground (which slopes at approximately 20 degrees). The term '*pavé*' refers to the fence and to the area behind it, which is concealed from the dance ground. This incorporates the principal men's ceremonial house where the chief host men assemble, hidden from visitors' view. Separation from potential enemies outside and the strength of the group seems emphasised by this containment within a fenced enclosure.

Before any visitors arrive, men and girls of the host group begin some dancing. Then visitors can be heard singing as they approach, and contingents, fully decorated, come into view. (Rappaport describes similarities between dance and battle behaviour. The visitors approach the gate: 'silently, led by men carrying fight packages, swinging their axes as they run back and forth in front of their procession' (1968, p.187)). Followed by their women and children who join the other spectators, the men from each of the visiting groups charge onto the dance ground (again with movement like an attack in battle). The fight packages which the men carry are magically endowed, containing ritually prepared leaves and other items. It is said that if pressed to heart and head they will bring courage and improve the chances of killing an enemy. A further link with warfare is obvious here, especially since the men also carry weapons.

The host groups of men continue to dance. The feathered head-dresses which add at least 2 feet to their height and the prominent bunches of leaves hanging from their belts at the back add 'presence' and make the men appear bigger than they are in everyday life, more conspicuous.[12] Appearances differ, with no two men identical, but there is a similarity between the style of the head-dresses and other decorations worn by each group. The dance ground is edged by local married women, children and some older and undecorated men. (According to Rappaport, there would have been men from other places who had come to watch and join the trading which followed the other activities). Thus, the ceremonial and dance action is framed by the *pave* round the three upper sides and spectators round the rest of the periphery.

As people continue to arrive, small groups of girls gradually start to dance, singing amongst themselves. At times, local men meet the visitors and greetings are exchanged.[13]

I estimated that each of the visiting groups observed consisted of approximately 30 people. There were about 7 to 8 persons in each of the dancing groups, which circled around the general area of the ground, using the whole space. I could not make a clear distinction between hosts' and visitors' use of rhythm and timing.[14]

Next, concerning body position and action: individually, the movement could be described as 'contained'. The reach of gestures was limited (and included use of

12   Rappaport judged the approximate height of a Maring man to be 4ft 10in. at most.
13   Rappaport provides further details of *kaiko* events. For instance, he writes how 'fight magic' men apply magic to the feet of the local dance contingent. This enables them to 'dance strongly' and empowers 'the beauty of the feathers' to attract the visiting girls, while local girls remain 'unmoved' by the visitors. He also describes the speeches of presentations and encounters including trade transactions (1968, pp.187–188).
14   Most of the dancing was done by the men, and all or most of the young men and those older men who had direct kinship or trading connections with members of the visiting groups, danced. Some other older men also danced or assisted the dancers with decoration repairs or in other ways. Women and girls danced some of the time; Jablonko confirmed that it was only unmarried women who danced. The other women and girls clustered in small bunches round the edge of the dance ground. In his study of the Kundagai Maring clan-cluster, Healey states that some married women danced, in decorations provided by their husbands, but that the women dancers appeared before the massed groups of male dancers and on the periphery of the dance ground (1990, p.78). (In the Lomax analysis of Maring movement, which made use of the Jablonko films, it was implied that men and women dance separately (1968, pp.254, 124f). Although this is the emphasis, men and girls are shown dancing together in the film *A Kaiko Entertainment*.)

drums near the body, see also p.251). I particularly noticed that the men's torsos were held in a steady, balanced and controlled manner.[15] The movement of the men's feather head-dresses and bunches of leaves hanging over their buttocks added considerably to the rhythm. The dancers remained on their feet throughout and the stamps or steps down into the ground were emphasised. There was little change of body position except for the vertical shift as knees flexed with each dance beat.

The groups adopted various formations, with varying degrees of precision. There were groups in which a number of dancers were roughly oriented towards the middle of the group with varied distance between them, at no more than an arm's reach apart, rarely touching – described as 'clumps' by Jablonko. Sometimes a group of dancers adopted a single file formation, moving counter-clockwise in a circle, once more with individuals fairly close together and with the distance between them varied. A block was formed when several rows of dancers lined up, one behind the other (with two to four dancers in each row and spacing as before). Spacing was again close but inexact. Just once I observed another formation when two lines faced each other and moved sideways in synchrony. Individual men sometimes danced ahead of a formation or occasionally in the middle of a 'clump' group. People did not necessarily retain position in any of these formations, none of which were regimented or strictly precise.

I have described certain group formations but the positioning of men in the space seemed more like a flock of birds than a group of people in a choreographed dance pattern. This impression was of course emphasised by the bird feather head-dresses. Reference to identification with birds was also voiced by a local inhabitant: 'and when we dance we dance like the bird' (BBC TV programme *World About Us: New Guinea*, 25 October 1981).[16]

Dancers' focus was generally within-group, except for a bank of dancers who moved directly towards and away from the *pave*, with focus on it. However, the projection of energy and group rhythm seemed directed forward and outward to the space in general. Structured use of rhythm in dancing tends to generate

---

15 I have discovered from Healey that it was the Kundagai Maring custom to attach the waving birds of paradise plumes to a flexible stick which projected above a dancer's head and extended down through the base of the head-dress to the nape of the neck. The neck was held against the stick so that 'the head and torso move as a rigid unit'. I do not know if this was a Tsembaga custom also. With this impediment, 'to achieve the admired undulating, beckoning movement of the plume, the dancer is obliged to master a difficult undulation of the whole body through movement of hips and knees'. Healey goes on to remark, as indeed I had observed with the Maring: 'The effect is almost as if the plume is waving the man' (1990, p.78).

16 Healey emphasises an association between the Maring plume bearing birds and virility 'signalled in the act of display by both birds and men'. Also, 'to dream of plume-bearing birds is a sign of future good health' and 'soul consciousness' (*miny-nomani*) may be manifest as birds (Healey 1990, p.80). During discussion O'Hanlon emphasised the competitive nature of the display during dance at a similar Wahgi pig festival which he witnessed.

energy: here it seemed that rhythm activated the release of dancers' energy into the environment, although contained within the performance area for the benefit of all present, and perhaps symbolic of a wider meaning: O'Hanlon was told that by dancing you will be building a protective fence around your land' (1983, p.324 and see 1989).

I was able to observe two main dance steps and a variation performed in the groups, which Jablonko (1968) has described in some detail. A bouncing step with transference of weight from one foot to the other was the principal step used. All these steps were characterised by synchrony, predominance of leg motion, repetitive continuity of movement, and durationally short movement segments. The dancers also used a walking step, marked by synchrony within the group, and a variation with more angular directional changes.

Some men had bows and arrows or an axe or spear in their right hands. The use of drums strengthened the sense of cohesion in each group: many men held a small one in the left hand, beating it with the right. It was noticeable that the men synchronised their steps and drum beats only within their own group. However, although there was match of feet contacting the ground, there was not a total unison since each dancer appeared to have an individual, complementary pattern of body movement.

The overall tempo of the dancing varied from medium to medium-fast and accelerated to a faster rate at the breaching of the *pave*. The beat was regular and the dance stress was on metricity and repetition. Patterns of rhythm were seen chiefly in the steps (feet and legs), in the movable body decorations, and in the spatial rhythms created from use of formation and direction. Accents in the body movement generally occurred in a simultaneous complementary manner – successively only in the ever-dominant feather head-dresses. The steps themselves were not rhythmically complex if one assessed the action of a single dancer, but the overall effect was polyrhythmic. In fact, there was a multiplicity of patterning which included not only the different individual bodies, but also the feathers and leaves which were fastened at the waist and bounced on their buttocks as the men moved. O'Hanlon told me that for the Wahgi, keeping the plumes and leaves moving at maximum display was 'the most important thing' (see O'Hanlon 1989, for more detailed local assessment of displays). Indeed, the long feathers of the men's head-dresses were in constant movement.

The spatial rhythm generated by the groups' dance routes consisted predominantly of wide curves and occasional angular changes of direction, together with some straight pathways. As noted above, there were some individuals dancing on their own, in advance of a group, and others who danced among the rest of the people. These tended to traverse more complex, cross-looping pathways. The various dancing groups moved back and forth, between and around each other, rarely retracing the same pathway. Little use was made of 360° turns.

The ratio of movement to duration was high in the sequence viewed, with no pausing within the movement phrases. Phrases were extended and of an even character without strongly marked accents. At the end of a sequence of dancing, the groups and individuals in them did not stop at precisely the same moment; likewise they did not start at precisely the same moment when dancing recommenced. There seemed not to be any one leader. When a group was standing together in preparation, the first sign of dance beginning was the long head-dress feathers starting to wave; once they were all in motion the group would begin. The feathers and plumes never seemed to drop off or get entangled. O'Hanlon comments that the Wahgi in their dancing consider it a bad omen if they do (1989, p.114). The movement was moderately energetic yet controlled (but in a relaxed manner) – again with the exception of the swaying head-dresses, nose quills and buttock leaves which provided a lively, unrestrained counterpoint.

To return to the film of the event: by mid-afternoon it seems that all the visiting contingents have arrived. A host man climbs a pole behind the *pave* and shouts to the crowd. An older man raises his arm in a gesture to silence the people, but groups of men continue to drum, sing and dance. Eventually, the dancing subsides, and the groups of dancing men draw closer to the lower edges of the dance ground. The host men behind the *pave* have been busily preparing the salted pork fat for the ritual distribution, unseen by the visitors.

As this important ceremony begins, the movement rhythm begins to build with an increase in tempo. Behind the *pave* another man from the host group climbs up a stake beside the first, and calls by name the men honoured to receive gifts of salt pork. (The honoured men are any who have been wounded in battle, sons of those killed, as well as kin and trade relatives from visiting groups.) Summoned in order of honour, each individual runs up to a small window in the *pave* with members of their household shouting – battle cries are included in the shouts. Some are brandishing axes. (There were 28 of these men who were followed by their dance contingents.) When the honoured man reaches the window of the *pave* he removes the shell from his septum. A large chunk of salted pork fat is pushed through the window into the honoured man's mouth. Salt is rubbed into his shoulders and then bundles of pork are handed through the window. The man then dances back to join his dance contingent. Local girls continue to dance inside the *pave* throughout the pork presentation, while older women and children continue to stand on the fringes beyond, watching. Grouped along the edges, these spectators contribute to the rhythm and timing chiefly by defining the performance time-frame and the ritual dance area, and by their general focus on the action. (They did not appear to be concentrating directly on the action all of the time, but when the presentation of pork began, attention was immediately drawn to that.) Use of rhythm had built to this prolonged first climax of the event when the pork was presented to the allies as described, one by one, through the window.

Late afternoon, 5.45 p.m. approximately, and the presentation has finished. The men come down from the stakes, and all the Tsembaga men remain within the *pave* enclosure. The visiting dance groups spread over the dance ground and sing and dance with great vigour and excitement. In traditional Maring ritual a time-marker is the cracking sound made by bamboo tubes burning, which is thought to attract the attention, protection and assistance of ancestors. On this occasion, after about half-an-hour, the last phase of the ritual cycle is initiated when men of the Tsembaga clans gather round a small fire in the *pave*. Bamboo tubes that had been heated and burned there begin to explode. As each length explodes, a man holds it up above his head, talking loudly and vociferously, while a young man dances and drums. (These bamboo explosions acted as a signal. The sounds contributed strong accents as non-metric punctuation, and generated excitement and a sense of building to a climax. Although an important signal, they were not produced at precise moments since they were the result of the burning process and thus exploded at random, without any overall control. This was consistent with other observed aspects of the Maring handling of time (see pp.256–257).)

Both men and women greet each bamboo explosion with enthusiastic shouting. After several explosions the host men rush down to a corner of the *pave* which others have begun to break down. Then with the girls following, the men in the *pave* form a column, and one of them holds a split bamboo over his head. He leads the column of leaping men out through the breach, followed by the girls. There is a strong climactic impetus as men rush across the dance ground and regroup at the lower edge of the slope. First, they dance together and then all groups dance in the area, seemingly as equals, with no one group appearing to be the centre of attention.

The whole group dances several times round the ground, and then gathers at the lower gate. While the women, children and visitors watch in a close crowd, one of the host men digs out the *rumbim* which had been ritually buried by the gate to the dance ground to indicate territory boundary and a time of truce (see p.244). The *rumbim* roots are carried among the crowd by two host men, who then lead the column of dancing men and the whole group once more around the dance ground. As this formation disintegrates the dancers leave the dance ground, and go along a narrow path, a few men singing and drumming. Rappaport describes how the men carrying the *rumbim* walked to a distant bluff and performed the last act of the ritual cycle – the roots were thrown over the bluff towards the enemy territory. Names of enemy men were called out with 'We have finished our *kaiko*; we are here' (1968, p.218).[17] There was further distribution and consumption of food on the dance ground later (not recorded in the film, but reported by Rappaport and Jablonko) and hosts' speech-making. The speeches apparently recalled obligations, exchanges and assistance given in fights.

There was some film footage which showed that the dancing continued and went on spasmodically through the night with a mix of group members. During this, men would drop out of the dance groups and go into shelters to eat snacks – such as sugar cane, roasted tubers or bananas. Eventually many local women returned to the gender-defined houses. Others stayed round fires.

The next morning, according to Rappaport, there was 'a massive trading session' (1968, p.218). The final section of film starts when it is about 7.00 a.m. that morning. The dance ground is only about one-third full, and the dancing has ceased. A little trading is going on. (For example, I noticed that one man traded a £1 note for a green sea-snail shell – a highly valued item.) Relatives and acquaintances meet and acknowledge each other, shaking hands. People are milling freely on to the dance ground and the young men are drumming a little. The decorations are being taken off and these and other items are being offered for trade, with women and children again standing watching on the perimeter.

People from distant territories had been leaving since the early morning. Men carried their gifts over their shoulders – sides of pork and bundles of sugar cane. Women's string bags were full of smaller pieces of pork and tubers (often with a small child riding on the top). They carried these bags in the characteristic manner of the region's women, suspended from the handle over their heads. According to Jablonko, people continued to leave throughout the day – an attenuated, gradual ending to the event, which marked a truce (although in former times, warfare broke out within a few months of ending a *kaiko*). Through the *kaiko*, obligations to the living and the spirits were met, exchange of goods and marriage of women facilitated and new debts generated – the next ritual cycle was beginning.

General observations

Observations of the use of time elements and rhythm in the film material brought out several features related to traditional Tsembaga Maring life. It seemed that the impression the men made in their dancing had a direct bearing on the effectiveness of the all-important alliances. The richness of their decorations which was fully displayed in dancing signalled the relative wealth and economic standing of a group (see also Healey 1990, p.74). The more assertive and

---

17   Jablonko told me that at this stage the young men with the ritualistic *mamp gunc* hair style cut it off.

impressive the dancers were, the more effective they may have been in securing or strengthening alliances (and the stronger the alliance, perhaps the more confident the dancing). Counting and securing marriage partners was an important part of the proceedings. As Rappaport discovered, a *yu wundi* (good man) who will attract women is one who 'dances strongly, whose plume waves bravely, and whose adornment is rich' (1968, p.189). Appreciation of strength of legs and feet in dancing is shared by other Papua New Guinea societies such as the Wahgi (O'Hanlon 1989, p.114). Impressive, 'strong' dancing, with plumes waving 'bravely' clearly arises from effective use of time elements, the more especially here since body position, gesture and other spatial design elements were limited. In his studies O'Hanlon stresses that to the Highlanders themselves, the adornment and display (such as the use of feathers and bunches of leaves in the Maring dance action) are not the 'natural and rather passive adjuncts', as usually viewed by anthropologists (1983, p.317). 'Plumes should participate in the vigorous and lively bearing of warriors' (1989, p.114). I certainly saw the body movement, with use of the body extensions, as intrinsic to the display.

With its opportunities for display, show and trade, the *konj kaiko* was both an expression of solidarity between allies and of a wary truce between past or potential enemies. The demonstration of solidarity, vigour and size of groups – the number of people in the host group and number of allies – was mentioned by Rappaport as significant. O'Hanlon supports this view. A local Wahgi man told him:

'Generally we don't really know whether ... other groups have many men or not. But when they do *gol* or displays associated with food prestations all their component groups take part. We look at one and say "Ah! They've got a lot of men", and at another and say "Ah! They've got a lot of men (too)", and so we assess them. We look closely at their appearance, at their arms and legs, we see whether they are well built men or not. So we carry on assessing them and then we come home and tell of what we've seen...' The challenge '*Nim ye owol ma*' (you are not many men) is a particularly provocative one leading to heated arguments and violence. (1983, p.323)

It can readily be seen that displays such as those undertaken by the Maring during the *konj kaiko* had similar communicative functions – they asserted power, emphasised relationships and deterred actual and potential enemies.

Group solidarity was particularly evident in the use of complementary rhythm and timing in the dancing, especially that which occurred after the *pave* was breached. As previously noted, some of the dance movement and distinctive use of rhythm and timing was similar to that of battle action. For example, the men leaping and rushing across the dancing ground was like a battle charge, reminding us of an ambiguous Tsembaga saying 'those who come to our *kaiko* will also come to our fights' (Rappaport 1968, p.195). The *pave,* until breached, represented a barrier between the hosts behind it and the visitors. They stood in an ambivalent relationship to one another, both friendly and hostile.

Time elements in other aspects of traditional Maring life

In addition to the relationship of both the *konj kaiko,* and the dance movement within it, to fighting, there were characteristics in the use of rhythm and timing in the dance movement which seemed to relate to other aspects of traditional Maring life.

Although clearly articulated steps and group patterns featured in the dancing, randomicity and lack of regimentation emerged from my observation as predominant characteristics of rhythm and timing in Maring dance style. Jablonko was surprised by this evaluation:

> In [my] dissertation, this randomness of movement was passed over with scant mention... The astonishing new perspective which suddenly burst on our vision was that this randomness is a crucial 'glue' for the Maring 'world'. Previously, seeing through my own cultural blinders, I had perceived randomness as an 'undesirable' or 'non-optimal' quality. I had unconsciously construed it as at the low end of a hierarchy (randomicity to complex precision). Therefore, I virtually dismissed it and went on to analyze in painstaking detail movement activities and phrases that were more recognisable to my own culturally trained eye/mind. (Jablonko, personal communication, 13 February 1978)

From the film it was also possible to note a degree of randomicity in Maring use of landscape. With unpredictable weather and no clear-cut seasonal variations it is necessary to be prepared to vary the timing of planned activities. Some film footage (in *Maring in Motion*) showed a lack of precise, geometric order in the way dwellings and garden plots were laid out. Indeterminate pathways predominated. The placing of the dwelling settlements and the mixed planting layout in the gardening areas was far from uniform. Gardens were at many stages at any one time. In addition to visual randomicity, a complex rhythm and time action pattern was generated. As Jablonko had noted:

> it is clear that a variegated movement pattern is used to cope with this rich plant-space pattern. She [the woman working] has taros, then she picks a handful of *kem* which she holds in her elbow-bent left hand (at shoulder height) while picking pit-pit with right hand. (Notes for *Planting Stakes at Gai*)

In some sequences of the *konj kaiko,* it was relatively easy to identify ritual leaders who could be observed initiating phases of the ritual action. On the other hand, it was not easy to identify dance leaders. Now and then someone would emerge as an initiator or apparent co-ordinator of rhythm, but different people led each group off around the dancing ground. To the outsider, inexactness and apparent randomness were thus striking in both the formations and in formation-leadership. These characteristics of leading or cueing changes of rhythm in the dancing appeared matched by the way in which authority in daily life appeared to shift from one person to another. In relation to this, it is interesting to note that the Maring had no hereditary or formally elected chiefs. Some men were recognised as 'big', that is, they are more important than others, but they did not command obedience from others. Older men with traditional ritual knowledge were respected but even they were not leaders in the usual sense. Where headmen had been appointed by government officials, some managed to adjust and cope with this, others not. Rappaport reported 'loose' discipline and organisation – in fights 'discipline was not tight nor control close' (1968, p.138). Persuasiveness and rapport, rather than authority or position, appeared to cause or result in action. On at least one occasion I noted lack of immediate response to an older man's signal.

Rappaport commented that Maring processes of decision-making were 'as amorphous as the structure within which they take place' (1968, p.30). When I was studying the film I noticed that meetings had the appearances of being more for discussion than for decision-making. Groups of men were shown standing or sitting and talking among themselves; a few men would move from group to group and occasionally one man would address the whole group. Also there was no apparent or definite end to meetings. It seemed that the purpose was to reach a consensus, and when any one man thought that had been achieved, or that there had been enough discussion, he would initiate what he considered was the appropriate course of action.[18]

The film material gave me the impression that everyone present pursued their own course of action in an individual, personal manner. In daily life in general I observed that people typically moved about separately. For the few activities which required concerted action, those available gathered together but drifted apart at the end of the activity.

In conclusion, use of the suggested mode of observation with identification of rhythm and timing features, brought out aspects of traditional Maring dance movement and behavioural style not previously evident to anthropologist Jablonko. It stimulated a less preconceived, judgmental approach and drew attention to the significance of use of these features in the life of the Maring. Jablonko had described Maring social organisation as exhibiting 'looseness'. The

---

18   O'Hanlon emphasised during discussion that this is classic New Guinea Highlands behaviour. There is no coercion. He suggested that for these autonomous individuals to come together for group action as in the *kaiko* – despite internal factions, problems of communication and necessary preparation – is a triumph of consensus and of organisation. He also made a further interesting point that competitiveness lies at the root of any apparent lack of order.

lack of precise synchrony and clear group focus in the movement rhythm and timing appeared to reflect this characteristic. Jablonko admitted:

> It is hard for us, either in the field or looking at film, to even be able to *see* this looseness – our eye is immediately caught by 'discrete bits' which have the character that we have been trained to find important within our own cultural context. The theoretical base that I used for my dissertation, Lomax' Choreometrics, also used a model of a 'vertical scale of complexity'. So, it was all too easy for me to fall into judging the Maring movement style as an all too simple and vague version of 'the human movement style'. Now I perceive Maring style as a totally different style, exactly right for the total situation binding people to people and people to environment. (Personal communication, 13 February 1978)

Jablonko wrote later of further awareness which developed during our period of film observation. She had been studying synchrony in Maring dance:

> Suddenly I realised, to my horror, that I had always been perceiving this as a 'second rate sense of synchrony'... I suddenly saw that it is not a matter of some sort of laxity, of falling short, but that it is a sense of timing in its own right and is a crucial part of the whole cultural system... the loose synchrony observable in Maring dance is the precise parallel, though condensed in time, of inter-personal relationships in daily life with their extreme flexibility in timing and the dependence of each person on his own decision and timing. (1979, p.51).

Judging from this study of film and ethnographic material, we can see that features of rhythm and timing may be considered a significant component of cultural identity, of distinctive dance style and movement signature. Furthermore, this observation project showed that it was possible to extend perception of stylistic, cultural, and societal features through focus on movement-rhythm and timing.

12

For Queen and Country
A British Event: Trooping the Colour

Now we travel from distant lands back to London, in June. A blue sky and just enough wind to lift and display the flags: these are the ideal conditions for the staging of perhaps the best-known British royal annual event, both here and abroad – the ceremony of Trooping the Colour. If we observe this ceremony where it's held on Horse Guards Parade in the centre of London, on the occasion of the Queen's official birthday, or as one of the millions world-wide who watch it on television, we have an opportunity to notice links and differences between ritual, ceremony and theatre performance, the influences of 'natural' and culturally determined timing, as well as the function of rhythm and timing in the structure of an event. My purpose here is to present not only a contrasting location and context, one closer to home and readily available for viewing through television, but also a simpler, more limited introductory approach than in the previous two chapters.

A visitor is immediately struck by the sheer size of the Horse Guards Parade ground, an area of approximately 174 x 120 metres. A sense of history is gained from the quietly impressive government buildings of Whitehall, the statues and the Guards' Memorial. These, together with the trees of former royal hunting territory – St James's Park – and tiered banks of spectators, frame the performance space – once the tiltyard of Tudor kings. Visitors line The Mall and are packed into the seating on the parade ground. The ceremony begins and the excitement builds.

The Queen arrives attended by the Royal Procession and escorted by the Sovereign's Escort of the Household Cavalry. The imperturbable proud-looking figures of the Guards impress in the vibrant colour of their full dress uniforms – red, white, dark blue, shining gold and gleaming black – all emotion withheld, faces partially masked by thick bearskin cap or fearsome helmet. Attention is caught by the grandly caparisoned, high-stepping horses; the Guards' traditional stoic fortitude is displayed as man and horse submit to the demands of the

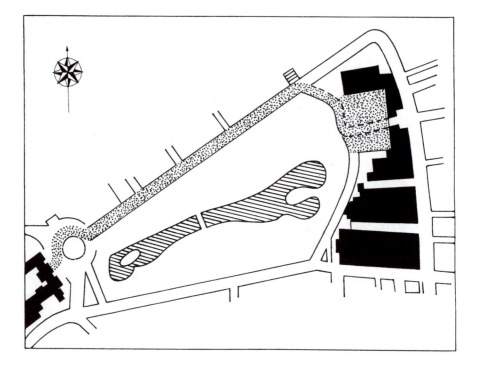

Key:
blocked areas = buildings – Buckingham Palace, Whitehall
dotted areas = route of processions along The Mall and Horse Guards Parade
slashed lines = lakes in St James' Park

Figure 12.1 Plan of the area.
Source: Liane Payne

occasion – they, like us, buoyed up by the stirring music of the bands. Spectators wonder at the precision, the seamless exactitude of the drill and the well-schooled discipline. The most important figure – the Sovereign – is tiny in that vast space, honoured by row upon row of highly skilled fighting men, albeit disguised today in the grand panoply of ceremony. The basic elements of early Guard-mounting ceremonies of the eighteenth century have changed little but they have developed into the elaborate occasions of today (see Bland 1759). We are witnessing a time-honoured tradition which brings diverse memories of a nation's past.

Colours are carried by regiments of many nations today to display past battle honours and to stand for the reputation, existence and prowess of the unit. The

Figure 12.2 The wide expanse of Horse Guards Parade and grandeur of adjacent buildings: saluting base and Royal family's view from the window above are situated on the left of the picture; other spectators are in tiered seating on three sides. Stillness of men and horses at attention contrasts with the movement-rhythm of other horses, accoutrements and helmet-plumes.
Source: Courtesy of the Guards Museum

Colours of a regiment were first used as flags for a readily recognised rallying point and to help maintain order in battle. Respect is always shown to the Colours. An order of HRH The Duke of Cumberland, 15 May 1755 refers to occasions when the Guard parades with Colours: '[each of the men] are to pay the proper respect to the Colours by pulling off their hats as they pass.' (quoted in Gow 1988, p.17). The first reference to the Sovereign's birthday being marked with Trooping the Colour is in 1748. It is seen as a personal tribute of the Guards to their Sovereign and Colonel-in-Chief. The parade when the Queen's Colour of a guards regiment is trooped is a symbolic representation of the values embedded in the traditional power of the monarchy protected and effected by the army.

The ceremony takes place on a specific day in time, yet it is set apart in a traditional time-world of its own. Provided the reigning monarch is there (or, as happened once, a fit representative) with members of the Royal family,

Figure 12.3 Pike drill: one position of many from a book of instruction which records the patterns of movement and timing for troops' drill in seventeenth century Europe.
Source: Seventeenth-century drill manual. Courtesy of the Guards Museum.

high-ranking government officials (and ideally, heads of state from overseas), the event would take place whether or not other spectators were present. It is the official birthday, rather than the actual date, partly to allow for the vagaries of the British weather. There is a degree of flexibility in the timing in that the date varies from year to year, but it is always on a Saturday, selected as being the most suitable day for organising the large public function the event has now become (and to avoid week-day traffic). Complete cancellation is rare. Gow (1988) lists all parades since 1895 and notes 19 years since then when the parade was not mounted. Nature sometimes overcomes culture, bringing frustration to those whose job and preference is to be in control. Cancellations have been due to weather (1905, 1906, 1909, 1948); to human frailty and death – court mourning (1910), world wars (1915–1918, 1940–1946); to human action – the general strike (1926), the national rail strike (1955). The coronation of George V (1911) also caused a cancellation.

Apart from the human element and the uncertainties of the weather, the other obvious 'natural' rhythm present with influence on the timing of the event is the horse. A trained horse may look sedate and disciplined, but there is always the chance it may shy. One notices how the eyes shift and ears twitch. Like all hoofed animals, the horse is designed by nature for flight. The riders have to be ready for any changes in tempo. When the trumpeter sounds 'trot' for the Household Cavalry, the horses know the signal and if their riders aren't prepared for it, are likely to respond before the band strikes up. Also, observant spectators may notice that when there is an acceleration in the band's tempo, the horses tend to surge forward and have to be judiciously held back by the riders.

During the ceremony, the horse's walking pace gives an impression of dignity. The trotting of the Household Cavalry generates energy and enlivens the proceedings. Occasionally the true nature of the animal comes through and dominates the rhythm. In 1932 a spectator reported that HRH The Duke of Gloucester's charger 'entered a rather active protest against the noise made by the bands and the fact that it was made to wear a crupper'. The duke left the parade to re-appear on a 'better behaved' mount (Gow 1988, pp.60–61). There are anecdotes from 'The Empty Saddle Club' about member officers who have 'had the misfortune to dismount involuntarily'. One tale in particular has entered Guards' folklore about a battalion adjutant whose horse persisted in going backwards the entire length of The Mall from Buckingham Palace to Admiralty Arch. One horse in living memory is known to have bolted in the wrong direction. But these are exceptions.

Dominance and control of time is a long and well-established feature of official British life and planning, not least in the pattern of events and ceremonies which mark the royal year. Attention to timing is an important feature of British army life and discipline. Regiments and battalions of The Household Division have to be ready to leave England for operational duty at any time. As fighting men they are trained to be capable of organised speed and precision in action. Furthermore, a soldier's training and schedule is strictly timed in terms of minutes, hours, days, weeks, months, years.

The punctilious attention given to the use of time elements during the Trooping the Colour ceremony and throughout its preparation period is essential for its successful organisation. In this the aim of the Household Division is assuredly achieved: 'in their Service to the Sovereign, the aim of all members of the Household Division is never to accept second best; but always to strive for perfection' (Langley, 1981). This is evident also in the appearance of the almost motionless guards on duty throughout the year at Buckingham Palace, Windsor Castle, in Whitehall or during the Birthday Parade. Bystanders seem unfailingly impressed by the fine example of the stereotypically British 'stiff upper lip' and by the unflinching, held position of the men whatever the weather – on foot or on horseback. Gow quotes *The Times* report of the bitterly cold 1920 ceremony which refers to the gratitude and relief of the stoic men when the arrival of the Queen and Princess Mary 'gave an opportunity for brisk movements of rifle' (1988). The stillness at attention, and the timed precision of action when the Guards move individually or in ranks are notable features of the ceremony. These are particular elements of the rhythm which attract favourable comment and are valued. For instance, Major-General Sir George Jeffreys remarked with reference to the 1924 occasion: 'The two sentries of the Colour were particularly good, moving and handling their arms perfectly together, and with absolute precision' (*Guards Magazine* 1924).

The parade is carried out in accordance with the procedure set out in the Standing Orders of the Household Division. The timing of the event which is, of course, crucial, is measured precisely, and based on a 'physical' feature, the 30-in. pace of those marching on foot at 116 paces per minute in quick time, and 65 paces per minute in slow time. This quick time rate is a distinguishing mark of the Guards – it differs from the infantry's 120 steps to the minute. (When troops from different regiments are massed, they march at 116 steps to the minute.) The distances between points for lining the route and between individuals participating in the parade are also based on pace lengths. For example, the two soldiers who act as double sentries standing on each side of the Colour, are stationed precisely 3 paces from it and they are ordered to patrol 7 paces from the Colour. Positions of other men and officers are similarly all determined by various pace lengths.

When lining the route, the interval between soldiers is measured from the centre of the heels of one soldier to the centre of the heels of the next, at the position of attention. Distances between mounted soldiers are measured in horse lengths. For example, throughout the royal procession it is stipulated that one horse length is to be kept between ranks of horses. The travelling rate of the horse is controlled by the rider who adjusts to the pace of those marching on foot.

There is no flexibility of timing within the event. The movement of the various individuals and groups of people involved in the ceremony is co-ordinated to the minute with all watches synchronised. A staff officer initiates the departure of Her Majesty the Queen from Buckingham Palace, using a stop watch: at the correct second he salutes and addresses Her Majesty: '*Now ride out, Ma'am.*' Specific timing for all concerned is given in the *Standing Orders of the Household Division* (1972) which provides the guidelines.

The order of events (with some time references to indicate degree of detail taken from the Standing Orders) briefly summarised:

1. From 9.20 hours the Foot Guards prepare to take up position.
   10.13 hours: Left markers of all Guards report to the Adjutant of the parade on Horse Guards parade, 8 Colour Sergeants likewise at points

identified along the Mall.

10.20 hours: Her Majesty the Queen Mother leaves Clarence House for Buckingham Palace.

10.21 hours: Troops lining the route are to be in position.

2. The Queen Mother arrives at Buckingham Palace and the Queen's procession forms up.

   10.25 hours: The 8 troopers report (4 to the Brigade Major, north side Queen Victoria Memorial, 4 to the Deputy Assistant Adjutant-General, Guard Room, Buckingham Palace). Assembly in forecourt, Buckingham palace. (A veterinary aid post is established at Foreign Office Green by 10.25 hours.)

   10.35 hours: Into formation.

   10.36 hours: Bands are lined up on Horse Guards Parade.

   10.40 hours: Household Cavalry, Sovereign's Escort, is in position in Queen's Gardens west of the Queen Victoria Memorial, facing north.

3. Departure of the Queen Mother from Buckingham Palace, procession down The Mall, arrival at Horse Guards Parade and into a room in Admiralty House which overlooks the Parade.

4. 10.45 hours: Departure of the Queen from Buckingham Palace. Household Cavalry, Sovereign's Escort, leaves with her Majesty. The Royal procession and mounted band proceed down The Mall and arrive at Horse Guards Parade

5. 11.00 hours: The Queen at the saluting base, and at the same time precisely, the first gun of the 41-Gun Royal Salute in Green Park.

6. The Queen inspects the parade.

7. Trooping the Colour. Manoeuvres of the Guards.

8. The march past of the Guards and of the Household Cavalry.

   11.55 hours: The old Guard, accompanied by the Corps of Drums, leaves St James's Palace.

   12.00 hours: 5 Colour Sergeants mark the points in front of Buckingham Palace and report to the Deputy Adjutant General in front of the Guard Room of Buckingham Palace.

9. Departure of the Queen, procession up The Mall and arrival at Buckingham Palace saluting base.

10. The Guards march past, followed by the King's troop of the Royal Horse Artillery and the Sovereign's Escort of the Household Cavalry.

11. The Queen enters the Palace.

12. Preceded by a row of police at a walk, the crowd moves up The Mall to arrive in front of the Palace.

13. 13.00 hours: appearance of the Queen and Royal family on the balcony. RAF fly past.

In Major Sir Henry Legge-Bourke's account, he refers to the actual Trooping the Colour section of the ceremony as 'the most solemn part of the parade' (1965, p.143). Readers will note that it is timed to take place in the central part of the ceremony. The details of the drill and reclinical Guards' terms are complicated to explain, but an outline summary of the action from the trooping to the march past is as follows.

When the entire parade is called to attention the Field Officer orders 'troop'. The Senior Drum Major commands the massed bands, pipes and drums to advance in slow time towards the Colour; four paces from the Colour they counter-march and halt. Then as they march back to their original position in quick time, one drummer leaves the corps of drums and marches towards the escort for the Colour. The band counter-marches, halts and stops playing. As the single drummer begins to beat 'Drummers' Call', the Captain and Lieutenant of the escort and the Regimental Sergeant-Major take up position. The drummer rejoins the corps. The Field Officer orders the Escort to come to attention and shoulder arms. The band strikes up a quick march, the Escort manoeuvres into position and marches to halt 20 paces from the Colour, the band turns away, halts and stops playing. The Sergeant-Major marches round the Escort and the Ensign moves with the Sergeant-Major to halt in front of the Colour. The Sergeant-Major salutes the Colour, takes it from the Sergeant who then shoulders arms.

The Sergeant-Major brings the Colour to the Ensign who salutes it, returns his sword, receives the Colour and faces the Escort. The Lieutenant orders the Escort to present arms. The four non-commissioned officers at the flanks of the front and rear ranks of the Escort, turn and lift their rifles high to bar the way to the Colour from all directions. The Sergeant-Major salutes (with drawn sword) and the band plays six bars of the national anthem. On 'Shoulder arms' the Ensign, the Sergeant-Major and the Sergeant who formerly held the Colour move into position, while the band turns about.

A series of impressive manoeuvres with the Colour follows, including the famous massed 'spin wheel', with the band and Guards in slow time. Individuals have to make careful adjustments in timing and pace length during the changes of direction (known as 'forming') which are a notable feature of the group movement. Next, the march past begins, first in slow time. The Colour is lowered in salute as the Ensign passes the Queen. The march past continues in quick time; then the Household Cavalry walk and trot past; to conclude, the band plays the national anthem.

The progress of the whole event is maintained through the accumulative effect of repetition and through contrasts in the use of tempo. This is of course emphasised by the music of the band which considerably enlivens the proceedings and expands the ceremony in sound, filling the wide expanse of the parade ground. The unremitting, repetitive, precise metric beat of the marching steps and the advancing movement of the mounted troops make an awesome impression. But this repetition could be dauntingly relentless and tedious were it not for the contrasts and variation in tempo. The major contrast is from slow to quick paced marching. At the slow march the Guards' toes press forward in a sustained movement, crushing the gravel with a distinctive crunch (a sound which considerably aids retention of the unison movement), and heels sharply strike down on the beat for the quick march, which is an easier unison to achieve. A further, different contrast in tempo is produced by the Household Cavalry horses at the walk and at the trot. Both three-beat waltz and two-beat march tunes are played, and so there is variation in the metric patterning of sound. There is sometimes swift change from one metre to another, and sudden stops, even in mid-phrase if the action demands it – to surprising and enlivening rhythmic effect. This alerts spectators to new phases of the ceremony. There is also variation in the duration of different phases of action. Times of stillness and pauses contrast with the massed on-going patterns of movement. In addition, the orchestration of the action provides variety. For instance, at times the single figure of the Queen, the lone drummer or a Guard (e.g. sentry and officers of the Escort) contrasts with the large groups on parade.

For spectators, the well-drilled, sharp attacking action of the presentation of arms and salutes, emerge as predominant in the movement rhythm of the ceremony. A significant gesture, the traditional Guards' salute shows the weapon-free, open hand and is a sign of respect. Rhythmically, salutes provide accents which mark and identify honoured people and important moments. There are salutes as the Queen Mother leaves Buckingham Palace, when the Queen comes out of Buckingham Palace, again as she leaves the palace and as she passes the Colour on arrival at Horse Guards Parade. During the proceedings on Horse Guards Parade, the Queen salutes as she passes below the Queen Mother at the window of Admiralty House. There are salutes once more when the Queen passes the Colour on inspection of the line and again when she passes the standard on the inspection of the Sovereign's Escort. When the Escort takes over the Colour, when the Colour passes (during the march past of the Guards) and when the standard passes during the Household Cavalry rank past at the walk and the trot, there are further salutes.

The movement of spectators rising (and sitting) also provides accents in the time structure and marks the salute to greet the Queen Mother, to honour the Queen at the Royal Salute, honour the Colour at the march past and during the national anthem. The Guards halting and coming to attention at important moments contrast with the lively variability of horses hooves and plumes. To summarise, the predominant features of rhythm and timing are: use of varied phases of duration; contrasting slow/fast tempi; accents and pauses (with stillness) in actions of the drill and salutes; extreme metricity in the marching formations. Individual idiosyncratic use of rhythm and timing is markedly limited; rhythmic accents are restricted to legs, arms and occasionally heads; there is extensive group unison action and patterning in the large space. The action of the horses and presence of spectators bring a degree of unpredictability and spontaneity to the overall rhythm of the event.

Traditional pageantry with its spatial ordering and evidence of man's endurance and control (which includes mastery of the horse) are key features in the ceremony. The contribution and central importance of rhythm and timing aspects is evident, with precision about time-keeping seen culturally as a form of excellence and way of honouring the monarch.

Conclusion

All the leaps into the air, thought of together, leave room for more. (Eli Siegel and Chaim Koppelman, title of an art work, New York 1972)

In conclusion, some ideas about possible directions for further research and practical work. My focus on rhythm and timing in performance has included examples from a wide range of sources with an international, cross-cultural perspective – appreciating and celebrating difference and variety in human action. To adopt a cross-cultural perspective provides an uncontested, continuing basis for future studies. Also, many authors have been summoned both in support of ideas or as innovators. I suggest that further study, to investigate their work and to honour neglected early pioneers in the field of movement and performance, is warranted. As contemporary director Peter Sellars remarks, 'not to hear the voices of your ancestors is a deafness that is not helpful ... I think it's really important to constantly test our own lives against the greatest wisdom that we're inheriting' (Delgado and Heritage (eds) 1996, p.238).

Study visits to the USA have been a particular inspiration over the years. In acknowledgment of this, I include reference to several current developments principally from the USA, which may also stimulate ideas for future research. (This is of course not intended to deny the existence of interesting developments in other countries too.)

In 1993, dance pioneers of the 1930s new dance era were the subject of a notable New York conference (with performance), and during more recent visits I have been interested to discover that my concern about neglect of the valuable work of early pioneers was shared by others in the USA. For instance, Martha Davis (who continues to be in the forefront of present-day developments in movement research) told me that she thought important pioneers in the field of non-verbal communication are in danger of being forgotten. I refer to some of these in the first chapters of the book: people such as Scheflen and Birdwhistell who, as Davis commented, explored uncharted new territory and made radical discoveries (see reference to Davis' earlier work, pp.28–29). Much has been done since on how judgments are formed from observing aspects of an individual's movement, but these earlier researchers had a different approach and purpose, they observed movement in more detail, and set about the labour-intensive task of describing, analysing and investigating its significance in human interaction: 'If lost, it would have to be discovered again, and probably not done as well' (Davis, interview June 1997). Davis has found, as I have done, that contemporary researchers are sometimes ignorant of the pioneers in their chosen field, or may not give them due credit.

Pioneers in the field of performance include not only those to whom I have referred in Part I, but many others as well. Also, there is much to learn from dance and drama-in-education pioneers, such as Barbara Mettler (about dance in the USA) or Peter Slade (drama in the UK), whose ideas about the use of rhythm and timing could not be included since work in education as such was not the focus. Perhaps this omission is particularly regrettable at a time when there has been considerable change in UK education, with some discrediting not only of teachers, but also of ideas from the past which did so much to stimulate creativity, both in and outside the classroom (and which, contrary to current belief, included reading and writing, often lots of it). Some of my North American friends relate to this too; as New York-based choreographer Nancy Zendora remarked, 'these days it's like a subversive act to be purely expressive' (interview, June 1997). Perhaps there is an opportunity for further investigation and research here.

In this, my last chance to offer advice to readers, I recommend oral history resources, for vivid accounts of early work – pioneers were not necessarily adept at writing and can often be misunderstood from the printed page. For instance, material in Birdwhistell's books was compiled from his lectures, by students, and we know that the translations and sundry interpretations of Laban's work (not least my own) cannot do full justice to his ideas. Hearing Doris Humphrey voice her ideas in audio recordings did as much as anything to set me going on this track (at the New York Public Library Dance Collection). It is worth hunting not only for the voices of pioneers, but of people who worked closely with them, or knew them.

Suggestions for further research and for practical application of ideas about rhythm and timing in the arts (that is, in drama and dance, as well as in ceremony or ritual), have been made or implied in various chapters. For instance, reference was made to the potential of historical research into our ancestors' use of rhythm and attitudes to time for insights about performance style in past centuries. In the present, use of computers is at the forefront of new directions, especially in dance, as mentioned with reference to the latest work of Merce Cunningham. The production of CD-ROMs is an important development – with potential for rhythm and timing studies. In the USA, at Ohio State University's Dance Department (Columbus), a pioneering five-person faculty team has developed a *Multimedia Dance Prototype*. This is a computerised 'content concept and software shell' for creating CD-ROMs which may be applied to dance study projects. As an example, the team has recently produced an interactive CD-ROM which profiles the work of choreographer Victoria Uris through the perspectives of dance history, criticism, video dance extracts, analysis and documentation. This provides an impressive demonstration of the medium's possibilities for movement study – not least in relation to aspects of rhythm and timing.

Computer-assisted dance score analysis has also been explored recently. Again at Ohio State University, Maletic and Maxwell have undertaken a pilot project, as a preliminary to designing a computerised search for salient features in Labanotation scores of contemporary choreography. As they acknowledge in a paper which describes the project (1995), it was inspired by Fügedi's computer search method for Labanotation signs to support the analysis of Hungarian folk dance (1992).

Indeed, studies of various dance styles continue to be an interesting research area in relation to use of rhythm and timing. As another example of work in dance style, I refer again to van Zile's work particularly since it relates to aspects of the approach adopted in this book (see earlier reference p.105). Van Zile's latest research is resulting in a detailed study of the dances of Korea. During work-in-progress presentations on the history, anthropology and styles of Korean dance (1996–1997), she has made intriguing comments about characteristic use of breath and other aspects of rhythm and timing in the dances.

The idea that perhaps various kinds of movement events, performance genres and styles can be distinguished, partly through their contrasting use of time elements and rhythm, was put forward in Chapter 2. Their role and significance in the structure and process of ceremonial and ritual events are topics to pursue. As I have indicated, levels of intensity, complexity and the use of repetition, punctuation (including stillness) and tempo (with acceleration and deceleration) seem of particular interest in this context (Cole 1975; Leach 1966, p.408; Reyman 1978; Turner 1981, pp.1–24).

Opportunities in teaching, in movement experience and in theatre performance seem endless, not least in relation to performers' perception of time and rhythm. An example of one obvious application which has not been my focus is in the area of sound, movement with sound, contemporary music and music therapy. To see an orchestral conductor such as the late Sir Georg Solti, or a fine musician such as the London-based Japanese master percussionist Joji Hirota, in action, is to witness a totally centred, inspiring display of all the factors and elements of rhythm and timing, with sound and motion inextricably linked. Sound in the theatre too – as former Meyerhold pupil, theatre director Radlov noted, an actor can create temporal effects through sound: 'not only by the sound of the voice, but also by the tread of the feet, by the clatter of objects in the actor's hands, he lets us listen to the passing of time. A thing is not just seen, but also sounds under the magic touch of his hand' (1975, p.121). Another obvious further application is in relation to the co-ordination of an actor's speech and movement, and in study of audience response, as Davis' and Dulicai's paper on Hitler's movement signature testifies: 'The exquisitely co-ordinated interaction between audience and speaker, the way in which applause and shouted approvals match changes in his energy level and timing are striking' (1992, p.156).

I am not advocating a return to the turn of the century when, as American dance critic John Martin tells us, 'rhythm became the catchword; it cured disease, restored prosperity and worked every conceivable type of wonder' (1965b, pp.28–29). However, as another potential study topic, may I remind readers of the importance of the sensitive use of rhythm and timing in the healing arts to which various examples in the book have referred – for instance Donna Williams' remarks in relation to autism in the Introduction, and some comments in the chapter on Tai Ji. Certainly there is considerable opportunity for further work in this field, both theoretical and practical, especially if we take the problems of present-day stress on board. Coupled with this, we can consider how experience of rhythm and timing in movement sessions may help people who need to re-discover their capacity for movement and a prozac-free zest for life, possibly during recovery from pressures of work or from the physically limiting effects of over-exposure to computer or TV screen.

Perhaps reference may also be made to a renewal and upsurge of interest in a related topic – the significance of movement-rhythm and timing in relation to mother–baby interaction in the early years of a baby's development, which is currently leading to more research. The importance of this subject has long been acknowledged by experts (see references to Stern and Beebe in Chapter 1). Due to the recent evidence of brain atrophy in cases of inadequate interactive stimulation during the first months and years of life, large-scale attention, with conferences and wide media coverage, has now been given to the subject, particularly in the USA.

Other current developments in the USA in the area of movement observation suggest possibilities for further research. As an example, I here again refer to Davis' work, and without apology, since it is particularly relevant in relation to my own approach to movement observation and study. (For instance, her approach, like mine, is influenced by Laban and includes adoption of the notion of an individual's movement signature, as in some of my work on rhythm and timing. Also, as indicated in Chapter 1, *Interaction Rhythms* (Davis 1982) was an important influential discovery at the beginning of my study.) Additionally, the progress of Davis' career interestingly illustrates how principles of rhythm and timing may be seen operating in our lives, not only on a daily basis, but also through a longer time span, as we persevere through phases, adopt changing patterns and respond to surprises and possibilities for switching direction.

Davis' early work in non-verbal communication and therapy is well known: she has been drawing attention to the significance of body movement in therapy sessions for many years, which provides, as she states, 'a rich source of information about fluctuations in involvement, rapport, stress, and effective quality and intensity' (1994, p.394). With influence primarily from Efron, Scheflen and Laban Movement Analysis (LMA), Davis has developed several complementary observation methods for the analysis of non-verbal behaviour in conversational contexts, with coding systems. In recent years she has been increasingly involved in identifying movement signature behaviour, through application of her system of Movement Signature Analysis (MSA), such as in a comparison of Hitler's movement signature with that of Saddam Hussein, cited above (Davis and Dulicai 1992). Her studies include fascinating work on presidential body politics, with a focus on the performance nature of staged debates and press conferences (1995).

One turning point and change of rhythm in Davis' research, which marked a transition from her previous preoccupation with therapy and non-verbal communication, was an invitation to teach in New York University's Performing Arts Department. A later change was initiated from an even more surprising quarter, with unexpected interest shown in her work by a member of the New York Police Department (NYPD) who is responsible for detectives' training. This led to the inclusion of Davis' system of interview analysis in NYPD detectives' training courses, and now to Government State Department interest and support for her project on non-verbal communication in high-level international negotiation. I am delighted to learn that this involves a return to the work of the pioneers (such as Ekman, Chapple, Birdwhistell, Scheflen, Lowen, Hall et al).

After some thirty years of research and an uncertain future for her work and for the subject area, Davis told me: 'This year has been a ship coming in.' There has been a leap forward with the aid of computer-video recording technology – a generic event recorder (a pioneer development from Holland). With this equipment it is possible to record and note multiple categories for movement observation and analysis, and to study their significance in events. Perhaps we can dream of studying rhythm and timing elements and other features in performance events – drama, dance and ceremony – with the aid of this advance in technology in the future, even in the UK.

Davis has not referred to rhythm and timing as such in her coding system, or included more than a relatively limited reference to aspects of rhythm and timing (in the terms I have described). However, a number of interesting movement categories are included. Those which coincide with or relate to some of those suggested in this book are namely: duration; frequency; onset; dynamic intensity – use of weight, flow, time; spatial direction and gestural exaggeration; complexity; immobility; and disorganised, fragmentary, 'out-of-sync' movement.

These, together with other elements of rhythm and timing to which I have referred, warrant further attention.

Following Davis' lead, having discussed the subject in a general way and having provided some specific suggestions about particular factors and elements of rhythm and timing and how we may observe these, one direction for future research could well lie more firmly in the area of identity, meaning and significance. Although mentioned, these topics have not been thoroughly considered in the book. We could consider how our use of rhythm and timing contributes to the notion of body movement as a form of intelligence, having regard at the same time for Howard Gardner's warning:

> A description of use of the body as a form of intelligence may at first jar. There has been a radical disjunction in our recent cultural tradition between the activities of reasoning, on the one hand, and the activities of the manifestly physical part of our nature, as epitomized by our bodies, on the other. This divorce between the mental and the physical has not infrequently been coupled with the notion that what we do with our bodies is somehow less privileged, less special, than those problem-solving routines carried out chiefly through the use of language, logic, or some other relatively abstract system. (1984, p.208)

Finally, to pursue this theme a little, when it became known that I was writing about movement rhythm and timing, reactions ranged from enthusiasm to dismay, from a dance enthusiast who exclaimed 'Great! Sounds as if you'll lead us into the whole world of movement!' to an immediate 'Oh, how awful!' from a well-respected former High Court Judge and peer of the realm, to whom movement, let alone rhythm, is far from being a worthy or interesting topic for a book. This, after a moment of initial shock, was my favourite reaction. First, it was such a delightfully spontaneous, honest and lively response, and it was also a salutary reminder of some attitudes still current, well over a century since Morgan, writing of American Indian dance and music informed us: 'These amusements of our primitive inhabitants are not, in themselves, devoid of interest, although they indicate a tendency of mind unbefitting rational men.' (1850, pp.289–290).

Although I have taken a broad approach, and rhythm is all-pervasive, there are many areas of movement not directly relevant in a study of rhythm. Thus the reaction of my dancer friend, although well meaning, in fact was not so useful, at least at that early stage when I was busy defining the field of study and taking care to observe boundaries. However, as I write in conclusion and consider possibilities for further research and practical work, the comment is apt, since I find now that the focus on rhythm and timing has led me to renewed interest in a wider perspective; indeed, into 'the whole world of movement'. My hope is that this book not only provides a richer understanding of the captivating energies of movement rhythm and timing in performance, but that it will also lead readers towards the abundant riches of that whole world of movement.

We must remember that the form of movement is not one line only; it is not an arabesque or a curve, and also not a single broken or curved surface as we may see on a crystallised mineral, but a cataract of forms, as if a heap of jewels or precious stones would be poured out vehemently, glistening, jumping, breaking. And more than this: it is as if single forms would grow and shrink, swallow each other or give birth to new ones, changing their shape in a continuous transformation. (Laban, unpublished manuscript, date unknown)

References

Writings

Acton, M. (1996) 'Essentials in the practice of taijiquan.' *Tai Chi Chuan* Autumn–Winter, 9–10.

Alkire, H.P. (1961) 'Resource material in modern dance for high school teachers of physical education.' Paper presented at Horizons of Physical Education Workshop, New York.

Alter, J.B. (1987) 'A critical analysis of Susanne K. Langer's dance theory.' *Congress on Research in Dance Annual XVI.*

Andrews, E.D. (1963) *The People Called Shakers.* New York: Dover Publications, Inc.

Arbeau, T. (1588) *Orchésographie* (trans. C.W. Beaumont). New York: Dance Horizons.

Aristotle (1934) *Poetics* (trans. T. Twining). London: J.M. Dent.

Aristoxenus (1959) (orig. c.370 B.C.) *Elementa Rhythmica* (ed. and trans. G.B. Pighi). Bologna: R. Patron.

Arnshtam, L. (1974) 'Meierkol'd i muzika.' *Sovetskaya Muzika* 3.

Artaud, A. (1958) *The Theatre and its Double* (trans. M.C. Richards). New York: Grove Press.

Aurobindo, S. (1948) *The Synthesis of Yoga.* Pondicherry, India.

Baensh, O. (1923) 'Art and feeling.' *Logos* 7, 1–28. Reprinted (1961) as 'Art and feeling.' In S.K. Langer (ed) *Reflections in Art.* Oxford: Oxford University Press.

Baker, P. (1972) *Integration of Abilities.* San Antonio, Texas: Trinity University Press.

Bambra, A. (1966) 'The art and science of human movement.' In J.E. Kane (ed) *Readings in Physical Education.* London: Physical Education Association of Great Britain and Northern Ireland.

Barba, E. and Savarese, N. (1991) *A Dictionary of Theatre Anthropology. The Secret Art of the Performer.* London: Routledge.

Bartenieff, I., Davis, M. and Pauley, F. (eds) (1970) *Four Adaptations of Effort Shape Theory in Research and Teaching.* New York: Dance Notation Bureau.

Bartenieff, I. and Davis, M. (1965) 'Effort-shape analysis of movement.' Unpublished monograph at Dance Notation Bureau, New York.

Bartenieff, I. and Lewis, D. (1980) *Body Movement: Coping with the Environment.* New York: Gordon & Breach.

Bartenieff, I. *et al.* (1984) 'The potential of movement analysis as a research tool: a preliminary analysis.' *Dance Research Journal* 16, 1, 3–26.

Basso, K. (1970) 'To give upon words: silence in Western Apache culture.' *South Western Journal of Anthropology* 26, 213–230.

Bates, B. (1832) *Peculiarities of the Shakers.* New York.

Bauman, R. (1992) 'Performance.' In R. Bauman (ed) *Folklore, Cultural Performances, and Popular Entertainments.* New York: Oxford University Press.

Bayer, R. (1953) 'The essence of rhythm.' In S.K. Langer (ed) *Reflections on Art.* Oxford: Oxford University Press, 1961. Originally published in *Revue d'Esthetique* 6, 4, 369–385.

Beckett, S. (1967) 'Act without words II.' In *Eh Joe and Other Writings.* London: Faber.

Beckett, S. (1972) *'Not I Breath' and Other Short Plays.* London: Faber.

Beebe, B. (1982) 'Rhythmic communication in the mother–infant dyad.' In M. Davis (ed) *Interaction Rhythms*. New York: Human Resources Press.

Behnke, E. (1977) 'Description of integral atonality.' Conference on Jean Gebser and comparative civilizations. Athens, Ohio: Center for Jean Gebser Studies.

Behnke, E. (1978) 'Cross cultural phenomenology and world hermeneutics.' Paper presented at the International Society for the Comparative Study of Civilizations, Milwaukee.

Benedict, D. (1824) *A History of All Religions*. Providence.

Benesh, R. and J. (1956) *An Introduction to Benesh Notation*. London: A & C. Black.

Berendt, J.E. (1988) *Nada Brahma The World is Sound*. (trans. H. Bredigkeit). London and The Hague: East West Publications.

Birdwhistell, R.G. (1952) *Introduction to Kinesics: An Annotated System for Analysis of Body Motion and Gesture*. Kentucky: University of Louisville Press.

Birdwhistell, R.G. (1970) *Kinesics and Context*. Philadelphia: University of Pennsylvania Press (Penguin Books, 1971).

Blacking, J. (1971) 'Structuralism in Venda music.' *Yearbook of the International Folk Music Council*, 90–108.

Blacking, J. (1973) *How Musical Is Man?* Seattle: University of Washington Press (republished by Faber, 1976).

Blacking, J. (1977a) 'Towards an anthropology of the body.' In J. Blacking (ed) *The Anthropology of the Body*. London: Academic.

Blacking, J. (1977b) 'An introduction to Venda traditional dances.' In R. Lange (ed) *Dance Studies* Vol. 2, 34–56. Centre for Dance Studies: Channel Islands.

Bland, H. (1759) *Military Discipline*. London.

Blum, O. (1973) *Dance in Ghana*. New York: Dance Perspectives No. 56.

Blum, O. (1987) 'An initial investigation into Ghanaian dance in order to ascertain aspects of style by the analysis and notation of the dynamic phrase.' *Dance Research Annual XVI*. Congress on Research in Dance.

Boas, F. (1972) (orig. 1944) 'Dance and music in the life of the northwest coast Indians of North America.' In F. Boas, (ed) *The Function of Dance in Human Society*. New York: Dance Horizons.

Branley, S. (1977) *Macumba: The Teachings of Maria Jose, Mother of the Gods* (trans. Meg Bogin). New York: St Martin's Press.

Brink, J. (1977) 'Bamana Kote-Tlon theatre.' *African Arts* 10, 36–37, 61–65.

Brink, J. (1979) 'Invocation of the theatrical frame in Bamana drama performance.' *Central Issues in Anthropology* 1.

Brink, J. (1980) 'Organising satirical comedy in Kote-Hon: drama as communication strategy among the Bamana of Mali.' Ph.D. dissertation, Indiana University.

Brock, J.C. (1992) *Horse Power*. Washington, DC: Howard University Press.

Brodzinsky, D.M. (1977a) 'Conceptual tempo as an individual difference variable in children's humour development.' In A.J. Chapman and H.C. Foot (eds) *It's a Funny Thing Humour*. Oxford: Pergamon.

Brodzinsky, D.M. (1977b'Individual difference variable in children's humour development.' In A.J. Chapman and H.C. Foot (eds) *It's a Funny Thing Humour*. Oxford: Pergamon.

Brook, P. (1968) *The Empty Space*. London: MacGibbon & Kee (reissued Penguin, 1972).

Brook, P. (1993) *There are No Secrets*. London: Methuen.

Browning, B. (1991) 'The body articulate: radical identification in the samba.' *Proceedings 1–29*, Society of Dance History Scholars 14th Annual Conference.

Burns, E. (1972) *Theatricality.* New York: Harper & Row.

Byers, P. (1972) 'From biological rhythm to cultural pattern: a study in minimal units.' Ph.D. dissertation, Columbia University.

Canetti, E. (1962) (trans. C. Stewart) *Crowds and Power.* London: Victor Gollanz.

Capra, F. (1991) *The Tao of Physics..* (first published 1975, London: Wildwood House) New York: Harper Collins.

Capra, F. (1996) *The Web of Life.* London: Harper Collins.

Carducci, A. (1661) *Balleto a cavallo.* Firenze: Il Mondo.

Carlo, P. (1978) *Nulato: An Indian Life on the Yukon.* Fairbanks, Alaska.

Caroso, F. (1581) *Il ballarino.* Venice: Appresso Francesco Ziletti.

Chaillet, N. (1982) 'Tender reunion of Beckett and Whitelaw.' *The Times,* 10 December.

Chambers, E.K. (1948) *The Medieval Stage,* Vols I and II. Oxford: Oxford University Press (1903 orig.).

Chapple, E.D. (1970) *Culture and Biological Man: Explorations in Behavioural Anthropology.* New York: Holt, Rinehart & Winston.

Chapple E.D. (1982) 'Movement and Sound: The musical language of body rhythms in interaction.' In M. Davis (ed) *Interaction Rhythms.* New York: Human Resources Press.

Chapple, E.D. and Coon, C.S. (1942) *Principles of Anthropology.* (Revised 1978) New York: Henry Holt.

Chapple, E.D. and Coon, C.S. (1978) *Principles of Anthropology.* Huntingdon, New York: Robert E. Krieger Publishing Co.

Chernoff, J.M. (1979) *African Rhythm and African Sensibility.* Chicago: University of Chicago Press.

Chopra, D. (1996) *The Seven Spiritual Laws of Success.* London: Bantam Press.

Clarke, M. (1987) 'The master of energy.' *The Guardian,* 27 July.

Cohen, S.J. (1972) *Doris Humphrey: An Artist First.* Middletown, Conn: Wesleyan University Press.

Cohen, S.J. (1982) *Next Week, Swan Lake.* Middletown, Conn: Wesleyan University Press.

Cole, H. (1974) *Sounds and Signs: Aspects of Musical Notation.* Oxford: Oxford University Press.

Cole, H. (1975) 'The art of festival in Ghana.' *African Arts* 8, 3, 12–90.

Collin, M. (1997) *Altered State.* London: Serpent's Tail.

Common Prayer of the Church of England, The Book of. London: Society for the Promotion of Christian Knowledge.

Condon, W.S. (1968) 'Linguistic-kinesic research and dance therapy.' Proceedings, Third Annual Conference, American Dance Therapy Association, 21–44.

Condon, W.S. (1978) 'An analysis of behavioural organisation.' *Sign Language Studies* 3.

Condon, W.S. (1982) 'Cultural micro-rhythms.' In M. Davis (ed) *Interaction Rhythms.* New York: Human Sciences Press, 53–57.

Condon, W.S. and Ogston, W.D. (1971) 'Speech and body motion synchrony of the speaker-hearer.' In D.L. Horton and J.L. Jenkins (eds) *The Perception of Language.* Columbus, Ohio: Charles E. Merrill.

Cooper, J.C. (1978) *An Illustrated Encyclopaedia of Traditional Symbols.* London: Thames & Hudson.

Copeland, R. and Cohen, M. (eds) (1983) *What Is Dance?* New York: Oxford University Press.

Cox, M. and Theilgaard, A. (1994) *Shakespeare as Prompter.* London: Jessica Kingsley Publishers.

Croce, A. (1968) Merce Cunningham. Dance Perspectives, 34.

Croce, A. (1977) Merce Cunningham. *New Yorker*, 7 February.

Crompton, P. (1990) *The Elements of Tai Chi.* Shaftesbury, Dorset: Element Books.

Csikszentmihalyi, M. (1975) *Beyond Boredom and Anxiety: the Experience in Work and Games.* San Francisco: Jossey-Bass.

Cunningham, M. (1952) 'Space time and dance.' Trans/formation. 1, 3.

Cunningham, M. (1955) 'The impermanent art.' *7 Arts*, No. 3. Indian Hills, Colorado: Falcon's Wing Press.

Cunningham, M. (1979) [Interviewed by Maggie Lewis]. *Christian Science Monitor*, 9 May.

Cunningham, M. (1980) [Interviewed by Dick Witts, 10 May]. *Programme Notes.* Merce Cunningham and Dance Co. Everyman Theatre, Liverpool (Hope Street Festival, 25–28 June).

Dalcroze, E.J. (1921) *Rhythm, Music and Education* (trans. H.H. Rubinstein). London: Dalcroze Society.

Davie, M. (1976) 'Le Grand Sam, plays it again.' *The Observer*, 2 May.

Davis, M. (1973) 'The potential of non-verbal communication research for research in dance.' Congress on Research in Dance. *News* 6, 1, 10–28.

Davis, M. (1977) *Methods of Perceiving Patterns of Small Group Behaviour.* New York: Dance Notation Bureau.

Davis, M. (ed) (1982) *Interaction Rhythms.* New York: Human Sciences Press.

Davis, M. (1982) 'Nonverbal behaviour research and psychotherapy.' In G. Stricker and R.H. Keisner (eds) *From Research to Clinical Practice.* New York: Plemina.

Davis, M. (1995) 'Presidential body politics: movement analyses of debates and press conferences.' *Semiotica* 106, 3/4, 205–244.

Davis, M. and Dulicai, D. (1992) 'Hitler's movement signature.' *The Drama Review* 36, 2 (T 134), 152–171.

Davis, M. and Hadiks, D. (1994) 'Nonverbal aspects of therapist allurement.' *Journal of Clinical Psychology* 50, 3.

De Mille, A. (1962) *The Book of the Dance.* New York: Golden Press.

Dean, A. (revised L. Carra) (1966) *Fundamentals of Play Directing.* New York: Holt, Rinehart and Winston.

Delgado, M. and Heritage, P. (eds) (1996) *In Contact with the Gods?* Manchester: Manchester University Press.

Denby, E. (1960) *Looking at the Dance.* New York: Horizon Press.

Denby, E. (1965) *Dancers, Buildings and People in the Street.* New York: Horizon Press.

Devi, R. (1972) *Dance Dialects of India.* Delhi: Vikas.

Dewey, J. (1958) (orig. 1934) *Art as Experience.* New York: Capricorn Books.

Douglas, M. (1973) (orig. 1970) *Natural Symbols.* (London: Cresset) Penguin.

Duncan, I. (1927) *My Life.* New York: Boni & Liveright.

Duncan, I. (1969) *The Art of the Dance* (ed. S. Cheney). New York: Theater Arts Books.

Duncan, I. (1977-78) Articles in *Ballet Review* 6, 4.

Durkheim, É. (1915) *The Elementary Forms of the Religious Life* (trans. J.W. Swain). London: Allen & Unwin.

Eliade, M. (1959) (orig. 1957) *The sacred and the profane* (trans. W.R. Trask). New York: Harcourt Brace & World.

Eliade, M. (1991) (orig. 1952) *Images and Symbols.* Princeton: Princeton University Press.

Embree, J.F. (1946) *A Japanese Village.* London: Kegan Paul.

Enders, G.L. (1941) 'The place of Dalcroze Eurhythmics in physical education.' In F.R. Rogers (ed) *A Basic Educational Technique.* London: Macmillan.

Eshkol, N. and Wachmann, A. (1958) *Movement Notation.* London: Weidenfeld & Nicolson.

Evans, B. and M. G. (1937) *American Indian Dance Steps.* New York: A.S. Barnes.

Evans-Pritchard, E.E. (1928) 'The dance.' *Africa* 1, 436–462.

Evans-Pritchard, E.E. (1940) *The Nuer.* Oxford: Clarendon.

Evans-Pritchard, E.E. (1965) *Theories of Primitive Religion.* Oxford: Clarendon.

Evers, L. and Molina, F. (1987) *Yaqui Deer Songs: Mabo Bwikam.* Tucson: Sun Tracks and University of Arizona Press.

Feuillet, R.A. (1701) *Choregraphie ou l'art de decrire la danse.* Paris.

Firth, R. (1973) *Symbols.* London: George Allen & Unwin Ltd.

Foerstel, L.S. (1977) 'Cultural influence on perception.' *Studies in the Anthropology of Visual Communication 4,* 1, 7–50.

Forti, S. (1974) *Handbook in Motion.* New York: New York University Press.

Foster, S.L. (1986) *Reading Dancing.* Berkeley, Cal.: University of California Press.

Fox Strangways, A.J. (1914) *The Music of Hindustan.* Oxford: Clarendon.

Frake, C. (1964) 'A structural description of Subanum religious behaviour.' In W. Goodenough (ed) *Explorations in Cultural Anthropology.* New York: McGraw-Hill.

Franko, M. (1987) 'The notion of "fantasmata" in fifteenth century Italian dance treatises.' *A Spectrum of World Dance* 68–86. Dance Research Annual 16th Congress on Research in Dance.

Frye, N. (1957) *Anatomy of Criticism: Four Essays.* New Jersey: Princeton University Press.

Fugedi, J. (1992) 'On the way to computer-aided dance analysis.' Proceedings of the first annual conference, *Dance and Technology 1: Moving toward the Future.* University of Wisconsin, Madison.

Fuller, L. (1913) *Fifteen Years of a Dancer's Life.* Boston: Small, Maynard. Reprinted NY Dance Horizons, n.d.

Furnival, F.J. (ed) (1969) *The Babees Book.* Vol. 1. New York: Greenwood Press.

Gardner, H. (1984) *Frames of Mind: The Theory of Multiple Intelligences.* London: Heinemann.

Geddes, G. (1995) (revised edition) *Looking for the Golden Needle.* Plymouth: Mannamedia.

Geertz, C. (1975) *The Interpretation of Cultures: Selected Essays.* London: Hutchinson.

Gell, A. (1992) *The Anthropology of Time.* Oxford/Providence: Berg.

Gellerman, J. (1978) 'The *Mayim* pattern as an indicator of cultural attitudes in three American Hasidic communities: a comparative approach based on Labanalysis.' *Dance Research Annual* 9, 111–144.

George, K. (1980) *Rhythm in Drama.* Pittsburgh: University of Pittsburgh Press.

Gluckman, M. (ed) (1962) *Essays on the Ritual of Social Relations.* Manchester: University of Manchester Press.

Goffman, E. (1974) *Frame Analysis.* New York: Harper and Row.

Goldberg, R.L. (1982) 'The art of notation.' In E. Schwarz (ed) *Tracking, Tracing, Marking, Pacing.* New York: Pratt Institute.

Goffman, E. (1974) *Frame Analysis.* New York: Harper and Row.

Goodridge, J. (1970) *Drama in the Primary School.* Oxford: Heinemann Educational Books. (In USA: *Creative Drama and Improvised Movement for Children.* Boston: Plays. Inc.).

Goodwin, N. (1973) *Programme Notes.* Royal Opera House, Covent Garden, 14 March.

Gorchaikov, N. *The Vakhtangov School of Stage Art.* Moscow: Foreign Languages Publishing House.

Gore, C. (1998) 'Shrine configuration in Benin City, Nigeria.' In F. Hughes-Freeland (ed) *Ritual Performance, Media.* London and New York: Routledge.

Gow, M. (1988) *Trooping the Colour.* London: Souvenir Press.

Greeley, H. (1838) 'A Sabbath with the Shakers.' *The Knickerbocker* or *New York Monthly Magazine* 11, 537, New York.

Green, C. Ms in the library of the Western Reserve Historical Society.

Griaule, M. (1938) *Masques Dogons.* Paris: Institut d'Ethnologie.

Grimes, R.L. (1982) 'The lifeblood of public ritual.' In V. Turner (ed) *Celebration.* Washington, DC: Smithsonian Institution Press.

Gunji, M. (1970) *Buyo: The Classical Dance.* (trans. D. Kenny). New York: Walker/Wetherhill.

Hall, E.T. (1959) *The Silent Language.* New York: Doubleday.

Hall, E.T. (1966) *The Hidden Dimension.* New York: Doubleday.

Hall, E.T. (1976) *Beyond Culture.* New York: Doubleday.

Hall, E.T. (1983) *The Dance of Life.* New York: Doubleday.

Hall, E.L. and Cokey, V.E. (1974) 'The world of crystallized movement.' *Main Currents in Modern Thought,* 31, 1.

Hallpike, C. (1972) *Bloodshed and Vengeance in the Papuan Mountains.* Oxford: Oxford University Press.

Halprin, A. (1995) *Moving Toward Life.* Hanover and London: Wesleyan University Press.

Halprin, L. (1966) 'Motation.' *Impulse* 26–33 (originally published in *Progressive Architecture* July 1965).

Hanna, J.L. (1965) 'African dance as education.' *Impulse* 48–56.

Hanna, J.L. (1979) *To Dance Is Human.* Austin: University of Texas Press.

Hanna, J.L. (1979a) 'Toward semantic analysis of movement behaviour.' *Semiotica* 25, 1–2, 77–110.

Hanna, J.L. (1979b) 'Towards a cross-cultural conceptualization of dance and some correlate considerations.' In J. Blacking and J. Kealiinohomoku (eds) *The Performing Arts.* The Hague: Mouton.

Harper, P. (1970) 'The role of dance in the Gelede ceremonies of the village of Ijio.' *Odu* n.s. 1, 4, 67–94.

Harwood, B. (1982) *Horse Guards.* London: Headquarters Household Division.

Haskett, W.J. (1828) *Shakerism Unmasked.* Pittsfield.

Hastrup, K. (1995) *A Passage to Anthropology.* London: Routledge.

Hay, D. (1977–78) 'Dance talks.' *Dance Scope* Fall–Winter, 18–22.

Hay, D. and Rogers D.L. (1974) *Moving Through the Universe in Bare Feet: Ten Circle Dances for Everybody.* Island Pond, Vermont: Troll Press.

Hay, D. and Rogers D.L. (1977–1978) 'Dance talks.' *Dance Scope* 12 Fall–Winter, 19.

Healey, C. (1990) *Maring Hunters and Traders.* Berkeley and Los Angeles: University of California Press.

Herskovits, M.J. (1948) *Man and His Works.* New York: Alfred A. Knopf.

Hodson, M. (1996) *Nijinsky's Crime against Grace.* New York: Pendragon Press.

Holt, C. (1939) *Dance Quest in Celebes.* Paris: Les Archives Internationales de la Danse.

Holt, C. (1958) 'Two dance worlds: a contemplation.' *Impulse.* Reprinted in M. Van Tuyl (ed) *Anthology of Impulse.* San Francisco: Impulse Publications, 1969.

Holt, C. (1967) *Art in Indonesia: Continuities and Charge*. New York: Ithaca University Press.

Holt, C. (1971) 'Dances of Sumatra and Nias.' *Indonesia* 11, April, 1–20.

Holt, C. (1972) 'Dances of Minangkabau.' *Indonesia* 14, October, 72–88.

Hood, M. (1971) *The Ethnomusicologist*. New York: McGraw-Hill.

Houghton, N. (1936) *Moscow Rehearsals*. New York: Harcourt Brace.

Houghton, N. (1962) *Return Engagement*. London: Putnam.

Houghton, N. (1973) 'Russian theatre in the 20th century.' *Drama Review* 17, 1 (T-57), March.

Hua Ching Ni (1994) quoted in Tsui-Po *Healing Secrets of Ancient China*. Hill of Content Publishing Company.

Huang, C. Al. (1987) (orig. 1973) *Embrace Tiger, Return to Mountain*. Berkeley, CA: Celestial Arts

Huang, C. Al. (1989) *Tai Ji Beginner's Tai Ji Book*. Berkeley, CA: Celestial Arts.

Hughes, C.W. (1948) 'Rhythm and health.' *Music and Medicine* 158–189.

Humphrey, D. (1929) 'Interpreter or creator.' *Dance Magazine* January.

Humphrey, D. (1934) Unpublished ms M34. Dance Collections. New York Public Library.

Humphrey, D. (1959) *The Art of Making Dances*. New York: Grove Press.

Hunt, V. (1968) 'The biological organization of man to move.' *Impulse*, 51–62.

Hutchinson Guest, A. (1981) 'The Bournanville style.' *Dance Chronicle* 4, 2, 112–150.

Hutchinson Guest, A. (1984) *Dance Notation*. London: Dance Books.

Ivanov, V.J. (1973) 'The category of time in twentieth century art and culture.' *Semiotica* 8, 2–45.

Jablonko, A. (1968) 'Dance and daily activities among the Maring people of New Guinea: a cinematographic analysis of body movement style.' D.Phil. dissertation, Columbia University.

Jablonko, A. (1979) 'An analysis of dance and daily life: the Maring of New Guinea.' Symposium report. London: Laban Centre.

Johnston, T.F. (1974) 'A Tsonga initiation.' *African Arts* 4, 4, 60–62.

Johnston, T.F. (1990) 'Context, meaning and function in Inupiaq dance.' *Dance: Current Selected Research Vol.2*, 193–266. New York: AMS Press.

Johnston, T.F. (1992) 'The social role of Alaskan Athabascan Potlatch dancing.' *Dance: Current Selected Research Vol. 3*, 183–226. New York: AMS Press.

Jowitt, D. (1973) [Twyla Tharp] *The Village Voice*, 3 November.

Jowitt, D. (1988) *Time and the Dancing Image*. New York: William Morrow and Co.

Kaeppler, A. (1972) 'Method and theory in analysing dance structure with an analysis of Tongan dance.' *Ethnomusiciology* 14, 2, 173–217.

Kaeppler, A. (1985) 'Structured movement systems in Tonga.' In P. Spencer (ed) *Dance in Society*. Cambridge: Cambridge University Press.

Kafka, J.S. (1957) 'A method for studying the organization of time experience.' *American Journal of Psychiatry* 114, 546–553.

Kagan, E. (1978) 'Towards the analysis of a score: a comparative study of *Three epitaphs* by Paul Taylor and *Water study* by Doris Humphrey.' *Dance Research Annual* 9, 75–92.

Kane, S. (1974) 'Ritual possession in a southern Appalachian religious sect.' *Journal of American Folklore* 87, 293–330.

Kapferer, B. (1973) 'Humour, healing and ritual.' Paper for staff seminar, Department of Social Anthropology, University of Manchester, February.

Karkoschka, E. (1966) *Das Schniftsbild der Neuen Music*. Cele: Moeck.

Kauffman, R. (1980) 'African rhythm: a reassessment.' *Ethnomusicology* 24, 3, 393–415.

Kealiinohomoku, J. (1967) 'Hopi and Polynesian dance: a study in cross-cultural comparisons.' *Ethnomusicology* 11, 343–358.

Kealiinohomoku, J. (1970) An anthropologist looks at ballet as a form of ethnic dance. *Impulse*, 24–33.

Kealiinohomoku, J. (1972) 'Folk dance.' In R.M. Dorson (ed) *Folklore and Folklife: an Introduction.* Chicago: University of Chicago Press.

Kealiinohomoku, J. (1976a) 'Theory and methods for an anthropological study of dance.' Ph.D. dissertation, Indiana University.

Kealiinohomoku, J. (1976b) 'A comparative study of dance as a constellation of motor behaviors among African and United States Negroes.' *Dance Research Annual* 7, 1–187 (masters thesis, 1965).

Kealiinohomoku, J. (1981) 'Dance as a rite of transformation' (ms. for *Tribute to Alan Meriam*).

Keil, C. (1967) 'Tiv dance: a first assessment.' *African Notes.* 4, 2, 32–35.

Kendall, E. (1979) *Where She Danced.* New York: Alfred A. Knopf.

Kendon, A. (1972) 'Some relationships between body motion and speech: an analysis of an example.' In A.W. Siegman and B. Pope (eds) *Studies in Dyadic Communication.* Oxford: Pergamon.

Kendon, A. (1989) 'Current issues in the study of gesture.' *Journal of the Anthropological Study of Human Movement.* 5, 3, 101–134.

Kendon, A. and Ferber, A. (1971) 'A description of some human greetings.' In R.P. Michael and J.H. Crook (eds) *Comparative Ecology and Behaviour of Primates.* London: Academic.

Kennedy, J. (1988) 'Giants, pygmies and a paradox on pointe.' *The Guardian*, 24 August.

Kestenberg, J.S. (1977) *The Role of Movement Patterns in Development.* New York: Dance Notation Bureau Press (first published in *Psychoanalytic Quarterly*, 1967).

Kightly, C. (1986) *The Customs and Ceremonies of Britain.* London: Thames and Hudson.

Kirstein, L. (1935) *Dance: A Short History of Classic Theatrical Dancing.* New York: Putnam (republished *Dance Horizons*, 1969).

Kirstein, L. (1942) *The Book of the Dance.* New York: Garden City Publishing Co.

Knox, C. (1992) 'Embodied knowledge: the cultural patterning of movement and meaning.' (unpub. D. Phil., Union Institute, California).

Koetting, J. (1970) 'Analysis and notation of West African drum ensemble music.' *Selected Reports UCLA Ethnomusicology* 1, 3, 115–146.

Koning, J. (1980) 'Fieldworker as performer.' *Ethnomusicology* 24, 3, 417–430.

Kramer, S. (1978) 'On Kabuki.' ILEA *Contact 6*, 26, 25–29.

Kubik, G. (1977) 'Patterns of body movement in the music of boys initiation in south east Angola.' In J. Blacking (ed) *The Anthropology of the Body.* London: Academic.

Kurath, G.P. (1951) 'Local diversity in music and dance. W.N. Fenton (ed) Symposium on Local Diversity in Iroquois Culture.' *Bureau of American Ethnology Bulletin 149*, 113–136.

Kurath, G.P. (1952) 'A choreographic questionnaire.' *Mid-West Folklore* 11, 1, 53–55.

Kurath, G.P. (1953) 'Native choreographic areas of North America.' *American Anthropologist* 55, 153–163.

Kurath, G.P. (1964) 'Iroquois music and dance: ceremonial arts of two Seneca longhouses.' *Bureau of American Ethnology Bulletin 149*.

Kurath, G.P. (1974) 'Research methods and background of Gertrude Kurath. New dimensions of dance research.' Proceedings of the Third Conference on Research in Dance. *CORD Research Annual 6*, 34–43.

Kurath, G.P. (1986) *Half a Century of Dance Research*. Flagstaff, Arizona: Cross Cultural Dance Resources.

Laban, R. von (1920) *Die Welt des Tanzers*. Stuttgart: Siefert.

Laban, R. von (1926) *Choreographie*. Jena: Diedricks.

Laban, R. von (1928) *Schrifttanz*. Vienna, Leipzig: Universal Editions.

Laban, R. von (1948) *Modern Educational Dance*. London: Macdonald & Evans.

Laban, R. von (1950) *The Mastery of Movement on the Stage*. London: Macdonald & Evans.

Laban, R. von (1956) *Principles of Dance and Movement Notation*. London: Macdonald & Evans.

Laban, R. von (1959) 'Notes on dance.' *New Era*. May.

Laban, R. von (1966) *Choreutics* (annotated and edited by Lisa Ullman). London: Macdonald & Evans.

Laban, R. von and Lawrence, F.C. (1945) 'Industrial rhythm.' (unpublished paper, Ullman collection).

La Barre, W. (1969) *They Shall Take Up Serpents*. New York: Schocken Books.

Ladzekpo, S.K. and Pantaleoni, H. (1970) 'Takada drumming.' *African Music Society Journal* 4, 4, 6–31.

Lamb, W. (1965) *Posture and Gesture: an Introduction to the Study of Physical Behaviour*. London: Gerald Duckworth.

Langdon-Davies, J. (1929) *Dancing Catalans*. London: Jonathan Cape.

Lange, R. (1975) *The Nature of Dance: an Anthropological Perspective*. London: Macdonald & Evans.

Lange, R. (1977) Some notes on the anthropology of dance. In J. Blacking (ed) *The Anthropology of the Body*. London: Academic.

Lange, R. (1996) 'Traditional dance in Poland and its changes in time.' *Dance Studies Vol. 20*. Jersey CI: Centre for Dance Studies.

Langer, S. (1953) *Feeling and Form*. London: Routledge and Kegan Paul.

Langley, A. (1981) Trooping of the Colour notes. London District Office.

Lasher, M.D. (1978) 'The pause in the moving structure of dance.' *Semiotica* 22, 107–26.

Lashley, K. (1951) 'The problem of serial order in behaviour.' In L.A. Jeffries (ed) *Cerebral Mechanisms in Behaviour*. New York: Wiley.

Lauterer, A. (1969) *Anthropology of Impulse* (ed M. Van Tuyl) (transcript of 1955 lecture demonstration). New York: Dance Horizons.

Laver, J. (1951) (orig. 1929) *Drama: its Costume and Decor*. London: The Studio.

Leach, E. (1954) 'Aesthetics'. In E.E. Evans-Pritchard (ed) *The Institutions of Primitive Society*. Oxford: Clarendon.

Leach, E. (1961) *Rethinking Anthropology*. London: Athlone Press.

Leach, E. (1966) 'A discussion on ritualization of behaviour in animals and man.' *Philosophical Transactions of the Royal Society of London*, Series B, No. 772, Vol. 251.

Leach, R. (1989) *Vsevolod Meyerhold*. Cambridge University Press.

Lee, D. (1960) 'Lineal and non-lineal codifications of reality.' In E. Carpenter and M. McLuhan (eds) *Explorations in Communication*. Boston: Beacon.

Legge-Bourke, Major Sir H. (1965) *The Queen's Guards*. MacDonald: London.

Leonard, G. (1981) *The Silent Pulse*. New York: Bantam Books.

Lévi-Strauss, C. (1966) *The Savage Mind*. London: Weidenfeld & Nicolson.

Lewis, I.M. (1971) *Ecstatic Religion*. Harmondsworth: Penguin.

Lex, B. (1975) 'Physiological aspects of ritual trance.' *Journal of Altered States of Consciousness* 2, 2.

Lex, B. (1979) 'Neurobiology of ritual trance.' In E. d'Aquili *et al.* (eds) *The Spectrum of Ritual* 117–151. New York: Columbia University Press.

Linderman, F.B. (1930) *American: The Life Story of a Great Indian.* New York: Doubleday.

Litvinoff, V. (1972) *The Use of Stanislavski within Modern Dance.* New York: American Dance Guild.

Lomax, A. (1968) *Folk Song Style and Culture.* Washington, DC, American Association for the Advancement of Science.

Lomax, A. (1971) 'Choreometrics and ethnographic film-making.' *Film-makers Newsletter* 4, 22–30.

Lomax, A., Bartenieff, I. and Paulay, F. (1974) 'Choreometrics: a method for the study of cross-cultural pattern in film.' *Dance Research Annual 6,* 193–212 (originally published 1969).

London Drug Policy Forum (1996) *Dance Till Dawn Safely.* London: LDPF.

Loring, E. and Canna, D.J. (1955) *Kineseography.* Los Angeles: Academy Press.

Lossing, B.J. (1848) *Two Years' Experience among the Shakers.* West Boylston.

Lowe, B. (1977) *The Beauty of Sport: a Cross-disciplinary Enquiry.* Englewood Cliffs, New Jersey: Prentice Hall.

Lowitt, D. (1977) 'Merce Cunningham.' *The Village Voice,* New York, 17 January.

Luce, C.G. (1972) *Body Time: The Natural Rhythms of the Body.* London: Paladin.

Mair, M. and Kirkland, J. (1977) 'Mirth measurement: a new technique.' In A. Chapman and H. Foot (eds) *It's a Funny Thing, Humour.* Oxford: Pergamon.

Maletic, V. (1983) 'Dynamics of phrasing in movement and dance.' *Proceedings XIIIth Biennial Conference.* International Council of Kinetography Laban.

Maletic, V. and Maxwell, C. (1995) 'Toward computer-assisted score analysis. Proceedings: a pilot project.' *Proceedings of the XVIIIthe Biennial Conference,* 84–119. International Council of Kinetography Laban.

Malinowski, B. (1948) 'The problem of meaning in primitive languages.' In C.K. Ogden and L.A. Richards (eds) *The Meaning of Meaning.* New York: Harcourt Brace.

Malm, W. (1960) 'Japanese Noh patterns.' *Ethnomusicology* 6, 2, 75–78.

Marshall, L. (1962) '!Kung Bushman religious beliefs.' *Africa* 32, 3, 221–252.

Martin, G. and Pesovár, E. (1961) 'A structural analysis of the Hungarian folk dance.' *Acta Ethnographica* 10, 1–40.

Martin, J.J. (1965a) (orig. 1939) *Introduction to the Dance.* New York: Dance Horizons.

Martin, J.J. (1965b) (orig. 1933) *The Modern Dance.* New York: Dance Horizons.

Martin, J.J. (1968) (orig. 1936) *American Dancing: The Background and Personalities of the Modern Dance.* New York: Dance Horizons.

Mason, B.S. (1944) *Dances and Stories of the American Indian.* New York: Ronald Press.

McKenna, P. (1996) *Nightshift.* Dunoon: ST Publishing.

McNeil, W. (1995) *Keeping Together in Time.* Cambridge, Mass.: Harvard University Press.

McPhee, C. (1948) 'Dance in Bali.' *Dance Index* 7, 7, 8.

Meerloo, J.A.M. (1962) *Dance Craze and Sacred Dance.* New York: International Universities Press.

Middleton, J. (1985) 'The dance among the Lugbara of Uganda.' In P. Spencer (ed) *Society and the Dance.* Cambridge: Cambridge University Press.

Millar, J. and Schwarz, M. (eds) (1998) *Speed – Visions of an Accelerated Age.* London: The Photographer's Gallery and the Trustees of the Whitechapel Art Gallery.

Moore, S. (1966) *The Stanislavski System.* London: Gollanz.

Moore, T. (1996) *The Re-enchantment of Everyday Life.* London: Harper Collins.

Morgan, L.H. (1850) *The League of the Iroquois.* New York.

Munn, N.D. (1973) *Walbiri Iconography.* Ithaca, New York: Cornell University Press.

Munro, T. (1951) *The Arts and their Interrelations.* New York: Liberal Arts Press.

Munro, T. (1970) *Form and Style in the Arts: An Introduction to Aesthetic Morphology.* Cleveland: Case Western Reserve University Press.

Murdock, G.P. (1967) *Ethnographic Atlas.* Pittsburgh: University of Pittsburgh Press.

Naehto, J.L. (1993) quoted in Molina, F. *Yoeme Paths of Life. American Indians of the South West.* Tuscon: Arizona State Museum.

Nakamura, Y. (1971) *Noh: The Classic Theatre.* New York: Walker/Weatherhill.

Nelson, E.W. (1899) 'The Eskimo about Bering Strait.' *Bureau of American Ethnology Annual Report* 18, 1, 19–526.

Neuhaus, H. (1973) *The Art of Piano Playing* (trans. K.A. Leibovitch). London: Barrie & Jenkins.

Newtson, D. (1971) 'The objective basis of behavior units.' *Journal of Personality and Social Psychology* 35, 847–862.

Ni, M. (1996) 'Cultivating the garden of life.' *The Empty Vessel* 3, 3, 28.

Nicholls, R.W. (1984) 'Igede funeral masquerades.' *African Arts* 17,3, 70–76.

Nicholls, R.W. (1992) 'Timing in West African dance performance.', Dance: Current Selected Research vol. 3. New York: AMS Press.

Nketia, J.H. (1975) *The Music of Africa.* London: Gollanz.

Noguchi, I. (1967) *A Sculptor's World.* London: Thames & Hudson.

North, M. (1972) *Personality Assessment Through Movement.* London: Macdonald & Evans.

O'Hanlon, M. (1983) 'Handsome is as handsome does: display and betrayal in the Walhgi.' *Oceania* 43, 4, 317–333.

O'Hanlon, M. (1989) *Reading the Skin.* London: British Museum Publications.

O'Hanlon, M. (1993) *Paradise.* London: British Museum Publications.

Olivier, L. (1986) *On Acting.* London: Weidenfeld & Nicolson.

Olson, S.A. (trans) (1994) Lun Chin. *The Intrinsic Energies of T'ai Chi Ch'uan.* Vol. 2. Saint Paul, Minnesota: Drogan Door Publications.

Ortiz, A. (1969) *The Tewa World: Space, Time and Being in a Pueblo Society.* Chicago: University of Chicago Press.

Painter, M.T. (1971) *A Yaqui Easter.* Tucson: University of Arizona Press.

Painter, M.T. (1986) *With Good Heart.* Tucson: University of Arizona Press.

Pantaleoni, H. (1972) 'The principles of timing in Anlo dance drumming.' *African Music* 5, 2, 50–63.

Parry, R. (1997) *The Tai Chi Manual.* London: Piatkus.

Pesovár, E. (1976) 'Three round verbunks.' *Dance Studies* 1, 47–52.

Pforsich, J. (1978) 'Labanalysis and dance style research.' *Dance Research Annual* 9, 59–74.

Pitcairn, T. and Schleidt, M. (1975) 'Dance and decision, an analysis of a courtship dance of the Medlpa.' *New Guinea Behaviour* 58, 298–315.

Plato (1934) (trans.) Taylor, A.E. *Laws.* London.

Plumer, W. (1782) 'The original Shaker communities in New England.' Letter printed in *New England Magazine*, Boston, May 1900, 305–306.

Pradier, J.M. (1989) 'Elements d'une physiologie de la seduction.' *L'oeil l'oreille, le cerveau.* Paris.

Preston-Dunlop, V. (1963) *Motif Writing*. London: Macdonald & Evans.

Preston-Dunlop, V. (1981) 'The nature of the embodiment of choreutic units in contemporary choreography.' Ph.D. thesis, University of London.

Prebble, J. (1967) *Culloden*. London: Pelican.

Proca-Ciorta, V. (1971) 'On rhythm in Rumanian folk dance.' *Yearbook of the International Folk Music Council* 1, 176–199.

Radcliffe-Brown, A.R. (1922) *The Andaman Islanders*. Cambridge: Cambridge University Press.

Radlov, S. (1975) 'On the pure elements of th actor's art.' *Drama Review 4*, 117–123.

Rainer, Y. (1965) 'Some retrospective notes.' *Tulane Drama Review* 10 (T-30 Winter).

Rainer, Y. (1974) *Work 1961–73*. New York: New York University Press.

Rameau, P. (1725) *The Dancing Master, or the Art of Dancing Explained* (trans. C.W. Beaumont reprinted 1970) . New York: Dance Horizons.

Rappaport, R.A. (1968) (1984 enlarged edition) *Pigs for the Ancestors*. New Haven: Yale University Press.

Rathbun, V. (1782) *Some Brief Hints of a Religious Scheme*. Norwich, 1781 (reprinted Salem 1782).

Rawson, P. (1997) *Sculpture*. Philadelphia: University of Pennsylvania.

Ray, D.J. (1967) *Eskimo Masks: Art and Ceremony*. Toronto: McClelland & Stewart.

Reyman, J.E. (1978) 'Evidence of annual and circadian rhythms in south western Pueblo ceremonial behaviour.' New York: *Congress on Research in Dance Annual XI*.

Reynolds, W.C. (1974) 'Foundations for the analysis of the structure and form of folk dance: a syllabus.' *Yearbook of the International Folk Music Council* 6, 115–135.

Reza, Y. (1996) *Art* (trans. C. Hampton). London: Faber & Faber.

Richardson, H. (1993) *Ceremonies of the Lhasa Year*. London: Serindia Publications.

Riddle, G.E. (1907) 'A theist's impressions of Judaism.' *The Jewish Quarterly Review* 19.

Riemann (1844) *Musikalische Dynamik und Agogik*. Hamburg: Rahter.

Roose-Evans, J. (1984) (orig. 1970) *Experimental theatre*. London: Studio Vista (revised edition).

Roose-Evans, J. (1994) *Passages of the Soul*. Shaftesbury: Element.

Royce, A.P. (1977) *The Anthropology of Dance*. Bloomington, Indiana: Indiana University Press.

Royce, A.P. (1981) 'Formal aspects of movement and meaning dance and mime' (unpublished paper).

Rudmitsky, K. (1981) *Meyerhold the Director*. Ann Arbor: Ardis.

Ryan, D.A. (1959) 'Clan formation in the Mendi Valley.' *Oceania* 29.

Ryman, R.S. and Rannie, D.S. (1978) 'A kinematic analysis of selected grand allegro jumps.' *Essays in Dance Research. Dance Research Annual No. 9*, 231–254. New York: Congress on Research in Dance.

St. Denis, R. (1939) *An Unfinished Life*. New York: Harper & Brothers.

Sachs, C. (1937) *World History of the Dance*. New York: Norton.

Salmond, A. (1974) 'Rituals of encounter among the Maori: sociolinguistic study of a scene.' In R. Bauman and J. Sherzer (eds) *Explorations in the Ethnography of Speaking*. Cambridge: Cambridge University Press.

Schechner, R. (ed) (1977) *Essays in Performance Theory*. New York: Drama Book Specialists.

Schechner, R. (ed) (1985) *Between Theatre and Anthropology*. Pittsburgh: University of Pennsylvania Press.

Scheflen, A.E. (1965) 'Stream and structure of communicational behavior.' *Behavioral Studies Monograph 1*. Philadelphia: Eastern Pennsylvania Psychiatric Institute.

Scheflen, A.E. (1973) *Communicational Structure: Analysis of a Psychotherapy Transaction.* Bloomington: Indiana University Press.

Schieffelin, E.L. (1998) 'Problematizing performance.' In F. Hughes-Freeland (ed) *Ritual Performance, Media.* London and New York: Routledge.

Schipper, K. (1993) *Taoist Body* (trans. K.C. Duval). Berkeley, Cal.: University of California Press.

Schlundt, C. (1962) *The Professional Appearances of Ruth St. Denis and Ted Shawn.* New York: New York Public Library.

Schmidt, P. (ed) (1980) *Meyerhold at Work.* Austin: University of Texas.

Schwartz, E. (ed) (1982) *Tracking, Tracing, Marking, Pacing.* New York: Pratt Institute.

Shanson, L. (1978) 'Life in a Mexican village' (unpublished ms).

Shawn, T. (1954) *Every Little Movement.* New York: Dance Horizons (reprinted 1963).

Siegel, E.V. and Blau, B. (1978) 'Breathing together.' *American Journal of Dance Therapy Vol.11*

Siegel, M. (1968) *At the Vanishing Point.* New York: Saturday Review Press.

Siegel, M. (1974) [Twyla Tharp] *Hudson Review* Spring.

Siegel, M. (1979) *The Shapes of Change.* New York: Houghton Mifflin.

Siegel, M. (1991) *The Tail of the Dragon.* Durham and London: Duke University Press.

Silvester, V. (1950) *Modern Ballroom Dancing.* London: Herbert Jenkins.

Singer, A. (1974) 'The metrical structure of Macedonian dance.' *Ethnomusicology* 118, 379–404.

Slade, P. (1954) *Child Drama.* London: University of London Press.

Snyder, A.F. (1978) 'Levels of event pattern: an attempt to place dance in a wholistic context.' Paper for American Dance Guild/Congress on Research in Dance conference, Hawaii, August.

Snyder, A.F. and Wynne, S. (1977) *Baroque Dance 1675–1725.* Berkeley, Cal.: University of California.

Sommer, S.R. (1975) 'Loïe Fuller.' *The Drama Review* 19, T-65 March.

Sorell, W. (1967) *The Dance Through the Ages.* New York: Grosset & Dunlop.

Souriau, E. (1961) 'Time in the plastic arts.' In S.K. Langer (ed) *Reflections on Art* Oxford: Oxford University Press, (originally published 1949, *Journal of Aesthetics and Art Criticism*).

Spencer, P. (1985) *Society and the Dance.* Cambridge: Cambridge University Press.

Spicer, E.H. (1943) 'Linguistic aspects of Yaqui acculturation.' *American Anthropologist* 45, 3, 410–426.

Spicer, E.H. (1954) 'Potam: a Yaqui Village in Sonora.' *Memoirs of the American Anthropologist (South West Issue)* 56, 4, 663–84.

Spicer, E.H. (1974) 'Context of the Yaqui Easter Ceremony.' *New Dimensions in Dance Research,* 309–346. Congress on Research in Dance.

Spicer, E.H. (1980) *The Yaquis.* Tucson: University of Arizona Press.

Spicer, E.H. (1984) *Pascua: A Yaqui Village in Arizona.* Tucson: University of Arizona Press.

Spicer, R.B. (1939) 'The Easter Fiesta of the Yaqui Indians of Pascua, Arizona.' Master's thesis, Department of Anthropology, University of Chicago.

Stanislavski, C. (1950) *Building a Character* (trans. E.R. Hapgood). London: Reinhardt & Evans (originally published 1936).

Stanislavski, C. (1958) *Stanislavski's Legacy.* (ed. E.R. Hapgood). London: Methuen.

Steinman, L. (1986) *The Knowing Body.* Boston and London: Shambhala.

Stern, D. (1973) 'On kinesic analysis' [interview]. *The Drama Review* 17, 3, 114–126.

Stone, R. (1981) 'Time, moment and movement in Kpelle music making' (unpublished ms).

Stone, R. (1984) 'In search of time in African music' (unpublished ms).

Strasberg, L. (1965) *Lee Strasberg at the Actor's Studio*. New York: Viking.

Strasberg, L. (1973) 'Russian notebook.' *The Drama Review* 17, 1 (T-57) March.

Strathern, A. and Strathern, M. (1971) *Self-decoration in Mount Hagen*. London: Duckworth.

Sweet, J. (1978) 'Space, time and festival.' Congress on Research in Dance. Dance Research Annual IX. *Essays in Dance Research,* 169–181.

Ta-chun, H. (1959). 'The expression of sound in singing.' *Collected Treatises on Chinese Classical Drama*. Vol. 7. Peking.

Tharp, T. (1977) 'Twyla Tharp.' *Chicago Tribune,* 17 July.

Thomas, E.L. (1978) 'Music and dance in Boccaccio's time, part II: reconstruction of *danze* and *balli.*' *Dance Research Journal* 10, 2, 23–42.

Thompson, R.F. (1974) *African Art in Motion*. Berkeley, Cal.: University of California Press.

Turner, V. (1969) *The Ritual Process*. Chicago: Aldine.

Turner, V. (1977) *Theories of Contemporary Culture* Vol. 1. (ed. M. Benamou and C. Caramelto). Madison, Wisconsin: Coda Press (Centre for 20th Century Studies).

Turner, V. (1981a) 'The anthropology of experience' (unpublished paper).

Turner, V.(1981b) (orig. 1968) *The Drums of Affliction*. Ithaca, New York: Cornell University Press.

Turner, V. (ed) (1982) *Celebration: Studies in Festivity and Ritual*. Washington D.C.: Smithsonian Institution Press.

Turner, V. and Turner, E. (1982) 'Performing ethnography.' *Drama Review* 26, 2, 33–50.

Ucko, P. and Rosenfeld, A. (1967) *Paleolithic Cave Art*. London: Wiedenfeld & Nicolson.

Ullmann, L. (1956) *The Art of Movement*. Leaflet published by Laban Guild, London.

Vakhtangov, E. (1947) 'Preparing for the role.' In T. Cole (ed) *Acting, a Handbook of the Stanislavski Method*. New York: Crown.

van Zile, J. (1977) 'Energy use: an important stylistic element.' *Dance Research Annual* 8, 85–96.

van Zile, J. (1979) 'Alarippu: a choreographic analysis.' Paper presented at the Laban Symposium, Laban Centre, London.

Verger, P. (1963) 'Trance states in Orisha worship.' *A Journal of Yoruba Edo and Related Studies* 9, 13–20.

Wallbott, A. (1982) 'Audio-visual recording.' In K. Scherer and F. Ekman (eds) *Handbook of Methods in Non-Verbal Behaviour Research*. Cambridge: Cambridge University Press.

Wardle, I. (1982) 'Spike Milligan and friends.' *The Times,* 4 December.

Watts, A. (1957) *The Way of Zen*. New York: Pantheon Books.

Weaver, J. (1706) *Orchesography, or the Art of Dancing*. London (trans. from Feuillet).

Wells, S.Y. and Green, C. (1823) *A Summary View of the Millennial Church or United Society of Believers*. Albany.

Wildeblood, J. and Brinson, P. (1965) *The Polite World*. London: Oxford University Press.

Williams, D. (1968) 'The dance of the Bedu moon.' *African Arts* 2, 1, 18–21.

Williams, D. (1972a) 'Signs, symptoms and symbols.' *Journal of the Anthropological Society of Oxford* 3, 1, 24–32.

Williams, D. (1972b) 'Social anthropology and dance.' B. Litt. dissertation, University of Oxford.

Williams, D. (1975) 'The brides of Christ.' In S. Ardener (ed) *Perceiving Women*. London: Milaby Press.

Williams, D. (1996) *Autism – An Inside-Out Approach.* London: Jessica Kingsley Publishers.

Wilson, M. (1957) *Rituals of Kinship among the Nyakyusa.* Oxford: Oxford University Press.

Wolcott, H.F. (1995) *The Art of Fieldwork.* San Francisco: Altamira Press.

Wolz, C. (1971) *Bugaku Japanese Court Dance.* Providence, Rhode Island: Asian Music Publications.

Wolz, C. (1977) 'The spirit of Zen in Nóh Dance.' *Dance Research Annual* 8, 55–64.

Woodard, S. (1976) 'Evidence for a grammatical structure in Javanese dance.' *Dance Research Journal* 12, 2, 10–19.

Young, M. (1974) 'Performance in Polish villages.' *The Drama Review* 18, 4 (T-64) December 5–21.

Youngerman, S. (1978) 'The translation of a culture into choreography: a study of Doris Humphrey's *The Shakers* based on Labanalysis.' *Dance Research Annual* 9, 93–110.

Recordings

Humphrey, D. (1950) Class (recording) Dance Collections. New York Public Library.

Humphrey, D. (1951) Lecture (recording). New York Public Library.

Whitelaw, B. (1982) 13 December. Interview on Beckett. BBC Radio 2.

Films

Connolly, B. and Anderson, R. (directors) (1987) *First Contact.* Ronin Films.

Jablonko, M. (director) (1969) *Maring in Motion; A Kaiko Entertainment; Planting Stakes at Gai; Clan Gathering.* (Maring research films).

Sherborne, V. (1982) *In Touch.* Concord Films.

Resources

Concord Video and Film Council Ltd, film and video hire, 201 Felixstowe Road, Ipswich, Suffolk IP3 9BJ.

Films/videos of ceremonies: see Video and Film Catalogue, Education Service (video and film department), c/o British Museum, London WC1

CD-ROM information: Department of Dance, The Ohio State University, 1813 North High Street, Columbus, Ohio 43210-1707, USA.

Traditional British Customs in Education: see English Folk Dance and Song Society publications such as:

Rowe, D. and C. Robson (1993) *May: an educational resource pack for the summer term on British traditions.* EFDS.

Rowe, D. and C. Robson (1994) *Mid winter: an educational resource pack for the winter term on British traditions.* EFDS.

Rowe, D. and C. Robson (1995) *Plough Monday to Hocktide: an educational resource pack for the spring term on British traditions.* EFDS.

Teachers Resource Guide (1990) 4th edition. London: RAI (Royal Anthropological Institute).

Subject Index